AFRICAN WOMEN IN TOWNS

African women in towns

AN ASPECT OF AFRICA'S SOCIAL REVOLUTION

KENNETH LITTLE
Professor of African Urban Studies
University of Edinburgh

CAMBRIDGE UNIVERSITY PRESS

CAMBRIDGE
LONDON · NEW YORK · MELBOURNE

Published by the Syndics of the Cambridge University Press
The Pitt Building, Trumpington Street, Cambridge CB2 1RP
Bentley House, 200 Euston Road, London NW1 2DB
32 East 57th Street, New York, NY 10022, USA
296 Beaconsfield Parade, Middle Park, Melbourne 3206, Australia

© Cambridge University Press 1973

Library of Congress catalogue card number: 73-77175

hard covers ISBN: 0 521 20237 X
paperback ISBN: 0 521 09819 X

First published 1973
Reprinted 1975

First printed in Great Britain at Eastern Press Limited
Reprinted in Great Britain
at the University Printing House, Cambridge
(Euan Phillips, University Printer)

Contents

'In a revolutionary Africa we women must become aware of our responsibilities both with the family and socially. For this, we ask the evaluation of our position and our participation in the life and progress of our people in a free united and happy Africa.'
Senegalese delegate at the First Congress of West African Women held in 1959

'For a long time, men have advocated equality; they loathed discrimination in any form in human society. But when it comes to practising what they profess, because of their own self-centred motives, they contradict themselves . . . But time and again many of our leaders have expressed favour for the women – although when it comes to give [sic] a woman something they have always dialled O . . . I am aware of the difficulties which men face when they consider the possibilities of women gaining positions of influence. They harbour the inevitable fear that men being superior to women, if women reached the same level, they would fall from the exalted stature they have exploited for so long.'
Mrs Ruth Habwe, Executive Secretary of 'Maendeleo ya Wanawake' – 'Women's Progress' – in Kenya; quoted by Audrey Wipper (1971b, p. 463).

'Women want to become true partners in marriage; they hope for more equal companionship with their husbands; they hope to share in making plans for the family.'
A member of The Uganda Council of Women

Acknowledgements

The literature available for this book is very rich in certain aspects of African women's urban position; but it would have been difficult to provide much of the necessary perspective without the aid of several studies which are as yet unpublished. For this reason I am particularly grateful to numerous colleagues for their very kind permission to use material which is not at this moment of writing in print. My debt is especially great, in the case of unpublished monographs, to Mrs Elizabeth Mandeville, Dr Christine Oppong, and Dr Barbara Harrell-Bond. It so happened that both the latter colleagues worked in association with the Department of Social Anthropology, Edinburgh University, on parallel investigations in Accra, Ghana, and in Freetown, Sierra Leone; and Dr Oppong's report is, happily, to be published as *Marriage among a Matrilineal Elite* by the Cambridge University Press. Also, Dr Harrell-Bond has, I understand, plans for publishing her material which will make an equally important and original contribution to the understanding of the modern marital problems of African women.

Dr Helmuth Heisler of the Lancaster Polytechnic has also been most generous in allowing me to draw on his forthcoming book; and Dr Margaret Peil of the Centre of West African Studies, Birmingham University, and Mrs Eugenia Date-Bah, too, have kindly permitted me to quote from papers they originally presented at the Second Interdisciplinary Family Research Seminar, Institute of African Studies, University of Ghana. In respect of the latter conference, I am also in debt to Dr. Oppong again for the opportunity of citing some data from a paper that she presented.

As indicated in the text, my approach to the legal side of African women's position is cautious and I might indeed have gone badly astray there had I not been forewarned and provided with some invaluable and down-to-earth advice by Mr J. S. Read of the School of Oriental and African Languages, University of

London. I should like therefore to say how very much I appreciated his painstaking and scholarly comments on preliminary drafts that he was kind enough to read.

Further, in addition to those colleagues whose personal communications are mentioned in the text, I have also to thank Dr Malcolm Ruel of Clare College, Cambridge, for giving me access to an unpublished study of his own, as well as for some useful comments. For similar helpful advice and also encouragement I am also in debt to Professor Meyer Fortes and Dr Audrey Richards.

It goes without saying that I have been assisted above all by the ideas, opinions and experience of numerous African friends and informants. Naturally, therefore, I wish to thank them, too. On the other hand, since my book deliberately raises some controversial issues the mention of particular persons might in some instances misleadingly convey the impression that the people named have communicated views that they do not, in fact, hold. In other words, although it has been much influenced by what I heard and observed, the substantive argument of this book is my responsibility alone.

This matter entirely apart, gratitude is specifically due to Madam Ella Koblo Gulama, Paramount Chief of Kaiyamba Chiefdom, Sierra Leone. Her kind permission has enabled this book's jacket to be graced by a picture which fittingly portrays both African womanhood and the dynamic personality of those who, as described herein, have pioneered the women's cause.

Last, but not least, I have to thank most sincerely as well the Trustees of the Noel Buxton Trust and the Trustees of the Carnegie Trust for the Universities of Scotland. The financial assistance they most kindly contributed helped substantially with the necessary research and preparation of this work.

K. L. L.

Edinburgh, December 1972

The author and publisher are grateful to the following for granting permission to reproduce copyright material: Cyprian Ekwensi and Hutchinson for extracts from *Jagua Nana* (Hutchinson, 1961); Valdo Pons and the International African Institute for the extract from *Stanleyville* (O.U.P., 1969).

Introduction

Those authors and editors who so diligently list the hundreds of 'personalities' and 'leaders of emergent Africa' rarely include as many as a handful of women (see Segal, 1961, and *Africa South of the Sahara*, 1971–2), and so we must not be surprised that African women's contemporary role has largely escaped systematic treatment by social anthropologists and sociologists. It is true that a few relatively comprehensive works do exist, including *Women of Tropical Africa*, edited by Denise Paulme (1963), and the authoritative *Survey of African Marriage and Family Life*, edited by Arthur Phillips (1953). The former work, however, is mainly concerned with women's traditional position, and in the latter volume Lucy Mair's important contribution was reprinted in 1969 (see References Cited). This reports Godfrey Wilson's (1941–2) pioneering study of Broken Hill in what was then Northern Rhodesia, and it also includes data concerning women in South African townships and urban locations. For much the greater part, however, it deals with the rural context and has little to say about women's urban situation.

Another anthropologist, Peter Gutkind, has several lengthy articles, but these centre more on the urban family as such than on women's position. The same author has collaborated, in addition, with Aidan Southall in a valuable work entitled *Townsmen in the Making* (1957) which includes a good deal of information about townswomen as well, but in terms of Kampala–Mulago alone. The scope of Laura Longmore's illuminating *The Dispossessed* (1959), is also limited to a single city, and much the same is true of most of the literature which bears directly or indirectly upon the urban position of women in the Francophone countries. Among the most important contributions in the latter context are those by Hennin, Balandier, Bernard, Mercier, Comhaire-Sylvain, Meillassoux and Rivière. Two stimulating articles by Audrey Wipper on the political activities of women in Kenya

1

deserve special notice; more generally, the pioneering studies of Clyde Mitchell, Gluckman, and Mayer provide a general background that no student of urbanization can ignore, while the Hannas (1972) have provided an invaluable source book. Very recently, the *Canadian Journal of African Studies* has brought out, under Wipper's editorship (1972), a special number of useful articles concerned solely with women.

The purpose of this present work is to pick up these numerous and varied threads and to weave them into a comprehensive pattern. The basic reason prompting this ambitious task was the observation on the part of this author and of others that African women's relationships with men are gradually undergoing radical alteration. Structural change of such great significance has implications for African social change in general, and so I decided to examine women's adaptation to the 'modern' city because, as will be explained later (Chapter 1), these particular urban populations possess certain social, economic and demographic characteristics in common. This limits the number of variables to be taken into account and so provides a specific sociological context for the general study of women's position.

This procedure, I submit, overcomes part of the objection which can otherwise be justifiably levelled against an investigation which seemingly takes for its canvas virtually the whole of sub-Saharan Africa. Not only does it mean that in methodological terms (see Chapter 1) this book's scope is relatively narrow, but that analysis is confined as far as possible to the bare essentials of women's social relationships. In other words, since this work is not in any sense encyclopaedic, the reader will find no record of customs associated with women unless they are relevant to women's contemporary role in the towns.

But that a book of this kind suffers from certain unavoidable drawbacks is equally plain. For example, I found the greatest difficulty in summing up for sociological purposes the legal situation in a general way. Even in colonial times the law regarding 'modern' matrimonial cases, for instance, varied a good deal and was often by no means clear. Since Independence seems to have made such legislation even more diversified I decided, discretion being the better part of valour, not to go into details over matters that in the circumstances involve legal expertise. A further admission is my dependence upon a large number of other students' work. The main reason for this and for my wide quotations of their writings, is that it is naturally impossible for a single fieldworker to cover in depth more than a very limited number of urban situations. True, with the exception of South Africa and

Zaire, I have visited and spent varying periods of time in most of the towns and urban centres named in the text. This includes some participation in the life and activities of both 'down-town' streets and compounds and residential suburbs, as well as helping farming families to harvest rice. But this experience has been gained over the years, and it clearly does not add to a full-length study on my own of every facet of African urban women's position. Secondly, it is binding on anthropologists to preserve their informants' anonymity if, and when, there is a likelihood of embarrassment being caused. Since, therefore, at the present stage of African urban development the source of particular incidents and categories of information can readily be traced, I have omitted certain case-studies of my own and have quoted in their place the equally relevant material of other authors, especially novelists. The appendix contains a good deal of illustrative material.

A further important difficulty in writing this kind of book is that such is the dynamism of the African situation that one's general frame of reference tends very quickly to get out of date. There are, for example, the results of frequent coups and counter-coups to contend with, and differences in time often make it difficult to assess the actual comparability of seemingly similar phenomena. For this reason, and because of the scarcity in some African regions of compact documentation, I have been obliged to 'telescope' a good deal of material. In consequence, some generalizations are offered for which continuous evidence is lacking, and some of my suggestions owe as much to speculation as to social fact.

My excuse – if there is any for such abuses of scientific method – is a desire to open up the question of African women's position for general discussion. Anthropological readers will be aware already of the difficulties of explaining this matter to the layman, and so for him I have pointed tentatively to some analogies with the American racial problem and with Victorian womanhood. It might have been useful to elaborate on the latter, but as present space does not permit this, I propose to deal with it in a later publication.

Finally, in respect of the data it will be obvious that whereas there is much rich and relevant material for the western side of the continent, the picture presented on the eastern and central parts is more rudimentary. For the latter, the available material is with important exceptions less promising, and its relative scarcity reflects, I believe, these regions' slower rate of change. On the other hand, although more data are available for southern Africa than my list of references suggests, I made no attempt to use them because apartheid's existence raised problems which, in my view, would have necessitated an additional chapter.

My wide employment of writings by African novelists may also be noticed. The reason is not simply that the portions cited describe relevant social situations more vividly and more graphically than my own pen could. It is also because the work of writers like Achebe, Aluko and Ekwensi often provides first-class source material which, as 'case-studies', is just as valuable as the anthropologist's own notes. I am not competent to comment on the literary value of these novelists' writings, but I can vouch for their sociological validity. Indeed, in that regard, some passages – as in Ekwensi's *Jagua Nana* [1] – are superlative stuff and fully confirm Leonard Plotnicov's observation (1967) to the effect that satisfactory study of the modern African city requires 'the research skills of the social scientist and the sensitivity of a good novelist'. Plotnicov's remark is true because there is an ebullience and vitality which the ordinary academic monograph generally fails to convey to all. Whether it be experienced in the steamy heat of the mid-day sun, within the daylight-clear rays of the dry-season moon, amidst the multifarious odours of the market place, in the bustle of a 'down-town' street through whose doors calypso, high life, and jive pour from a dozen radiograms in competition with drums from an adjacent compound, or even on the carefully clipped lawns of an élite couple's bungalow, there is a special urban 'atmosphere' to capture. Among 'serious' writers only Leslie, whose social survey of Dar es Salaam is accompanied by a 'scenario', has attempted this feat.

Finally, since it is part of my thesis that differences in the possession of formal education and of Western ideas and habits are sociologically significant for social change, my references to various categories of person are intended to carry the following fairly specific connotations:

Educated person: one who has completed a course of study at a secondary school, or its equivalent.

---

[1] A proposal to make a film out of *Jagua Nana* raised a storm in the Nigerian Federal House of Assembly. Those who objected to the idea argued that to portray a woman of 'Jagua's' type would denigrate Nigerian womanhood in the eyes of the outside world. Such fears were probably justified because the producers of films must necessarily employ stereotypes familiar to cinema-goers who, in the case of the Euro-North American public, would find it difficult to comprehend the subtleties of 'Jagua's' personality without reading Ekwensi's whole book. (See Chapter 6 in this connection.)

Literate person: one who has attended school for a number of years but without completing his education at a secondary school, or its equivalent. (It excludes, for present purposes, a person who is literate only in Arabic.)

Civilized woman: one who possesses 'Western' aspirations and follows certain customs of a 'Euro-North American' kind which have usually been acquired at school.

Semi-literate person: one who has very little or no formal education but can understand or make himself understood in English or French.

Illiterate person: one who has no formal education and who cannot understand or make himself understood in English or French.

African élite (except where more specifically defined): persons in the senior ranks of the administration, including ministers, party leaders, and top civil servants; persons in professional occupations, such as doctors, lawyers, university teachers, heads of important secondary schools and of training colleges; holders of important traditional titles; top-ranking Christian clergy.[2]

I also attach a specific meaning to the following two expressions:

Tribal group: a group of people who identify with each other, principally on the basis of a common language or dialect and set of traditional customs somewhat different from those of their neighbours.

Ethnic group: usually a relatively large population, sometimes comprising a number of individual tribal groups, but possessing a belief in its common origin which, despite differences in dialect and custom, is strong enough to produce feelings of nationality among the total population concerned.

---

[2] This categorization corresponds broadly with the Smythes' definition of the 'top-level' élite in Nigeria (1960, p. 92).

1 The urban situation

In a book of this kind the need to generalize may have an irritating effect upon the reader because what kind of creature, after all, is 'the African woman'? She lives under a wide variety of conditions – 'pagan', Christian, and Moslem – and exhibits outwardly, at least, an appearance ranging from meek submissiveness to complete self-assurance and confidence in manner. Moreover, although some institutions of African life, such as chieftainship, are close enough to European systems to be understood in similar terms, things are different in the case of women. Criteria relevant and valid in the latter culture may have little or no significance in the former.

The position of African women, consequently, has often to be subjectively assessed. Nevertheless, certain aspects can be objectively compared and we can say without much fear of contradiction that in African traditional society the greater part of woman's role is ascribed rather than achieved. Further, we can assume that her status is affected by rules of residence as well as kinship, though broadly speaking she is regarded legally as a 'minor' for the greater part of her life. Sometimes, she is a person of rank and, like the Queen Mother in Asante, has special prerogatives and duties of great importance to society at large. Also, older women, in particular, are usually held in esteem, and are selected, sometimes, as heads of extended families and other kinship groupings. In ordinary everyday life, however, there is generally a good deal of social distance between men and women, including the relationships of spouses. This separation is symbolized as well as reinforced by the sexual division of labour which, none the less, is essentially a form of co-operation. Consequently, it is tempting and fairly accurate to describe the role of women as complementary rather than subordinate to that of men, even though women are, as a rule, under the control of males. This is generally so, both before and after marriage, and is usually the

6

case in matrilineal as well as patrilineal systems because in matriliny a woman comes under the authority of her mother's brother or her own brother. (See Evans-Pritchard, 1965, for a thoughtful discussion of the general nature of the problem.)

The fact that in the above terms the position of African women is bound up inextricably with such fundamental institutions as marriage and kinship, renders it particularly sensitive to fresh developments. It makes the status of women one of the best indices available for judging and predicting social change, especially in terms of their adaptation to the ' modern ' city. I say ' modern ' in order to distinguish between the old-established, slowly-growing towns whose social structure is basically traditional, and those which are, in the main, of European creation. In making this distinction I follow broadly Aidan Southall's classification (1961, pp. 5–13), which involves two categories of town which he calls respectively types A and B. According to him, in Tanzania and Uganda, and in the former territories of French Equatorial and British and French Africa, most towns belong to A which are, in the main, old established. Type B comprises new populations of ' mushroom growth ' and is mostly found in industrialized territories which also have the largest white populations. Southall also draws attention to overlapping, because among those of type B it is some of the Congo (now Zaire) towns which stand nearest to type A, and among those of type A some Tanzanian centres stand nearest to type B. In fact, as Bascom (see his works in References Cited) and other authors have shown, local concentrations of population which fulfil Wirth's well-known minimal definition of the city as ' a relatively large, dense and permanent settlement ', though indigenously rare in sub-Saharan Africa, are not a unique phenomenon. In addition to numerous historical cities in the western Sudan, there were, in particular, the many and populous towns of the Yoruba. These urban settlements being based largely on agriculture, the inhabitants themselves were mainly farmers, and kinship was the principal factor in, and primary determinant of, behaviour in every aspect of community life. Indeed, since farming itself depended largely on family and kinship, these institutions set the pattern of life in both city and countryside (Bascom, 1955, pp. 446–54 and 1963–4, *passim*).

A number of such Yoruba towns continue to retain strong links with agriculture and the subsistence economy of the rural areas but in contrast to the traditional ' countrified ' urban situation is the ' modern ' African city referred to. This was brought into being by European colonialism and capitalist interest requiring administrative headquarters and urban facilities which previously had barely existed. For example, Nairobi is now the largest city in East Africa but it began as a construction camp on the Uganda railway which was being built up from the coast at Mombasa in 1899. Kampala, the present capital of Uganda itself, was founded by Lugard on a hill where there had been no previous settlement of any importance; and Dar es Salaam was chosen by the Germans as their colonial capital in place of Bagamoyo (Southall, 1966, pp. 463–93). On the other side of Africa, port towns inhabited by Europeans and partly Westernized Africans had been established at Accra, Freetown, Dakar and Lagos, and these were developed as entrepôts. Later, Enugu grew in response to nearby coal fields, and Port Harcourt was established in turn as a terminus for a railway bringing coal from Enugu to the coast. Also, some up-country towns, which, like Kumasi, had been the capitals of ancient states and chiefdoms, developed into modern urban centres for communications and collecting points for locally-produced commodities such as cocoa, groundnuts and palm kernels. In many other places, the extraction of minerals, including gold, diamonds, iron-ore and tin, was extensively undertaken, and gave rise to urban centres and agglomerations of varying size and significance (Little, 1973b).

Physically, urban settlements of this 'modern' kind are characterized, too, by the presence of banks, office buildings, schools, churches, mosques, factories, industrial plants, and so on. In other words, locally established there are many of the state's principal resources, and it is precisely this local concentration of relatively up-to-date economic, technical, educational and cultural facilities which distinguishes the 'modern' city. True, outside the capital or 'primate'[1] city itself the stock of buildings and con-structions is usually smaller, but most such 'modern' urban populations have a number of common characteristics, including large proportions of immigrants. Thus, according to the 1970 Population Census of Ghana, Volume II, Statistics of Localities and Enumeration Areas, only 37·3 per cent of the population of Sekondi–Takoradi, some 42·9 per cent of the population of Kumasi, and some 46 per cent of the population of Greater Accra are of local origin. In the Ivory Coast a 1965 estimate is that only 29 per cent of the total population of Abidjan and only some 7 per cent of persons over the age of 20 years had been born in that city.[2] In

[1] See Breese (1966, p. 48) and Little (1973a), among others, for a definition and illustration of the 'primate city'.
[2] Similarly, in Lagos five in every six householders were born outside that city; but Lagos is largely a Yoruba town and some 50 per cent of its immigrant population are from the nearby Western Region – the Yoruba homeland – (Ejiogu, 1968, pp. 320–30).

fact, in fifteen West and Middle African towns the percentage of the population born there was on the average about 42 per cent (Hance, 1970, p. 269), while in Kampala it has been estimated that those who have lived continuously in town for five years or more accounted for less than 20 per cent (Gutkind, 1962–3). Further, the Kenya Censuses show a similar movement and how recent an experience urban life is for many Kenyans. Thus, although in 1962 the aggregate population of the ten main towns amounted to no more than some 377,000 people, by 1969 the population of Nairobi alone was 509,286 of whom only 123,013 were born in that city. Also in towns of 10,000–99,999 inhabitants only 53,658 were born in the same district as enumerated against 112,600 born elsewhere (cf. 1962 Census, Vol. III (1964) and 1969 Census, Vol. II (1971)).

Demographic situations of this kind being due mainly to rural–urban migration, a not unexpected corollary is that the 'modern' town's population is highly heterogeneous. Thus, Accra contains representatives of 80 different ethnic groups and tribes in addition to the 'indigenous' Ga-Adangme people (1960 Census, Special Report 'E'); while the populations of Nairobi and Mombasa appear to be no less diversified (1969 Kenya Census). Dar es Salaam, again, has about 100 different peoples, the most numerous being the Ruhji, the Luguai and the Ndengerko (Leslie, 1963).

Consequently, unlike the inhabitants of villages, a large pro-portion of such urban populations are both culturally and personally strangers to each other. The latter point, moreover, is enhanced by the fact that, as explained in the next chapter, much of the immigration upon which the urban population is based is seasonal and 'circular'. In other words, a large proportion of the city's inhabitants only reside there for a limited period of time. They tend to come and go and do not necessarily return each time to the same town. For example, in a study made of this phenomenon in Ougadogou in Upper Volta, 73 per cent of the migrants had moved at least once; 47 per cent had moved at least twice; 31 per cent three times (Gregory, 1971). It was also found that, given a person had moved once, the probability of further moves was quite high, and that the largest single group of migrants spent a moderate length of time at each destination before moving on. A specific example of this kind of situation is provided by Nairobi where only 11 per cent of African employees were found to have had five years' service or more with their current employers (Colony and Protectorate of Kenya, 1954). In respect of South Africa, Houghton tells of a man aged 56 who over the past 40 years has made no fewer than 14 separate trips

9

to labour centres (1960, pp. 170–90); and according to estimations made in South Africa there are some 2 million workers who circulate in this way. (See also: Hance, 1970, pp. 128–208; Van der Horst, 1964; Warmington, 1956, pp. 16–22; and Wells and Warmington, 1962.) In short, there is a good deal of evidence to support Elkan's conclusion (1960) that

> African towns are to be compared with Army Barracks accommodating successive waves of National Service men, and perhaps in addition some also who have 'signed on' for five years, seven or even twenty-one, but sooner or later everybody leaves. So also in these terms permanence is exceptional.

A further feature of the 'modern' urban population is a tendency for young people to preponderate numerically over old.[3] This is because most of the migrants are young men and many of the older men retire to their rural towns and villages when their working days are over. What, moreover, is of particular relevance for this study is the tendency for adult men to outnumber adult women. Thus, there were in Accra, in 1960, 111·6 males per 100 females;[4] while on the other side of the sub-continent Kenyan towns had, in 1962, only 47 women to 100 men; and those in Tanzania had 69 and those in Uganda 54.[5] According to the 1969 Census, women constituted only some 32 per cent and 38 per cent respectively of the total adult populations of Nairobi and Mombasa. Overall, the disproportion of males to females varies from relatively small differences of about 100 males to 80–90 females in Middle Africa to 100 males to 55–75 females in East Africa, and even lower ratios in some large centres of South Africa.[6]

Further, in such urban centres, quite a large number of town-

[3] It is estimated that in Accra (Capital District–C.D.), Tema, Sekondi–Takoradi and Kumasi, the percentage of the population aged 56 and over was respectively 4, 2, 3 and 3.
[4] In Accra the disproportion of males to females is clearly the largest among people who migrate from the north, and the sex ratios of some of these northern tribes, in terms of men to women, were respectively: Lobi, 187·5: Zabrama, 441·47: Songhai, 522·5: and Fulani, 256·7 (1960 Census).
[5] Taking individual examples, in Dar es Salaam men and women comprised respectively 40·7 per cent and 27·7 per cent of the town's population; and in Kampala the proportions were respectively 42·4 and 22·5 per cent (Gugler, 1969).
[6] One of the few large cities where immigration has *not* resulted in a disproportion of male to female adults is Tananarive, Madagascar (see Southall, 1968).

dwellers engage in irregular or casual forms of employment which probably are not entered in official returns. Nevertheless, a feature of the modern town as we have characterized it is not only the small part played by agriculture in its economy, but the relatively large proportion of its inhabitants who, in contrast to the rural town or village, are dependent upon the sale of goods, services or labour for a livelihood. Though specific figures are difficult to obtain, the extent of salary and wage employment presumably varies with the extent of industrialization. This is greatest in South Africa, but among the most industrialized countries governed by Africans is Ghana; and in 1961, a sample survey in the largest towns showed that 47·4 per cent of heads of households had wage incomes. This figure may be compared with 16·6 per cent in the rural areas. In Accra (C.D.), the proportion was 53 per cent (Golding, 1962, pp. 11–33), and in more general terms, the 1970 Census, Vol. II, shows that of males over 15 years of age the following proportions were employed: Accra, 74 per cent: Kumasi, 73 per cent: and Sekondi–Takoradi, 75 per cent. In Zambia, which is more industrialized than Ghana, it has been estimated that in 1962 some 48 per cent of Africans working on the Copperbelt were wage employees (Hance, 1970, p. 156; see also, in this connection, Mitchell, 1954 and 1956).

These figures reflect the fact that under the 'modern' urban conditions housing, food and clothes have to be paid for. But not only do a relatively large section of the town's inhabitants now have to earn money; many of them are confronted with a market economy for the first time. These are people who in their country areas were organized in village communities, clans and tribes. Residence in the town puts them in contact with fresh work-mates and, sometimes, new friends; and so depending upon circum-stances and to a varying extent, they group themselves in different ways, align themselves differently and form different alliances.

The result, therefore, of this interplay of economic and cultural factors is that it is in the towns and industrialized areas that the new forms of life and labour crystallize and take shape. Nor does this role of the urban centre stop at its own boundaries. On the contrary, there is a constant coming and going of traders; and, as well as the movement of migrants, townspeople frequently visit or are visited by rural relatives. This happens because migrants frequently return home for ceremonies or to find a wife; others send their daughters to the bush to be educated rather than allow them to grow up in the 'corrupting' influence of the town. Ties are thus maintained with those left at home, and even during their stay in town the migrants send back part of their savings. If married they contribute to the support of their wives and children: if bachelors, they send remittances to their immediate kin (see among others Balandier, 1955, pp. 203–8, and 1956; Lombard, 1954, pp. 364–7; Rouch, 1954, p. 136; Van Velsen, 1961).

All this promotes the spread of 'urban' ideas and ways to the countryside; and also playing an important part in this diffusion are ethnic associations of migrants (see Chapter 4) whose aim, as among Nigerian 'Improvement' Unions, is to transport modern 'civilization' from the city to their home villages (Little, 1965, pp. 33–5). In consequence, a far-stretching network of social and other ties connects the town with its hinterland, and through it is transmitted to the countryside a new set of social needs. Instead of being confined to the town, their influence is felt over a much wider area. The result, as Southall has aptly pointed out, is that the town is the 'pace-maker' for the wider society: 'It is there that change proceeds furthest and fastest and economic and class considerations most successfully supersede those of tribal origin' (1961, pp. 191–2; see also Little, 1973a).

It is for these reasons that the 'modern' town is the place *par excellence* for studying changes in women's status. It is the more significant for this purpose because city growth in Africa seems now to be proceeding more rapidly than in most other regions of the world and exceeds even that of developed countries during their own period of fastest urban growth (Davis, 1968, pp. 38–42). For example, of the original port towns on the west coast Lagos had a population of 126,000 in 1930 and had more than doubled to 364,000 by 1960. (A recent estimate – Mabogunje, 1968, p. 19 – puts the population of Greater Lagos in 1963 at 1·2 millions.) Accra had only 40,000 inhabitants in 1930, had doubled in population by 1950, and had a population approaching a half million by 1960. Similarly, in the Francophone countries, there was an increase of 100 per cent in the populations of the principal towns of Senegal between 1942 and 1952, while those of the Ivory Coast grew by 109 per cent during the same decade, and those in the Cameroons by 250 per cent between 1936 and 1952. In what is now Zaire, Kinshasa (formerly Leopoldville) was a large country town of 34,000 in 1930, but in 20 years it had a population of 402,000. On the other side of Africa, Nairobi doubled in size during the 1940–50 decade and rose from 119,000 inhabitants in 1948 to about half a million in 1969 (Hance, 1970, p. 241), while Dar es Salaam grew from 69,200 in 1948 to 128,700 in 1957, and to 272,500 in 1967 (cf. Tanzania Census, 1968). Also, not only have existing towns swelled in size, but· in some cases entirely new urban centres and agglomerations have come into being. For example, Enugu, now one of the largest cities of eastern Nigeria was founded in 1914 on an empty site, had a population of some 10,000 by 1921, which rose to 138,457 by 1963; while the population of Port Harcourt – another 'new' town – grew to 208,237 by 1969.[7]

As well as natural increase some of this urban population growth is due, of course, to an improvement in health conditions, especially among young children; but the overall statistics leave no doubt that the principal reason is townward migration. Consequently, although there are, as a rule, fewer female migrants than men, the movement of rural women to the towns is nevertheless not inconsiderable. Moreover, not only is the latter probably increasing in proportion,[8] but the fact that at present only about 10 per cent of Africa's population lives in cities of 100,000 or more means that if city growth continues to be rapid the further effect of urbanization upon women is likely to be correspondingly extensive. Some of the implications of this point will be considered later; but in summarization, then, let us make clear that for heuristic purposes we are employing an arbitrarily-defined urban model. This is confined to settlements whose populations are characterized, on the whole, by the following features: they consist quite largely of rural immigrants, and are ethnically and tribally heterogeneous and relatively transient; contain a numerical preponderance of adult males over adult females and of young people over old; and have a relatively large number of people who depend for their livelihood upon the sale of goods, labour, or services. We choose these particular demographic and economic criteria because the nature of African urbanization [9] is such that these particular factors may be sociologically of more significance than actual population size (for discussion of this point, see Little, 1973a and b). For example, the population of Ikeja, a township near Lagos airport, is only about 7,000; but it is relatively heterogeneous and there is an imbalance in sex and age groups, etc. (Ruel, n.d.). We have also to take care at the same time of situations and problems ordinarily associated with urban life which arise in areas usually thought of as rural. For example, the plantation popula-

[7] For comprehensive figures of urban growth, see Little, 1972a, pp. 4 and 5.

[8] For example, according to Heisler (1973), it is quite likely that in the case of Zambia there were, by 1960, more girls than boys in the teenage category of immigrants to the towns and during the 1960s the immigration of all females exceeded that of all males.

[9] Our use of the concept 'urbanization' is briefly defined in the next chapter.

tions in the Victoria Division of the Cameroons contain a larger proportion of immigrants than local inhabitants and the proportion of males is of the order of 70 per cent of the population (cf. Ardener, 1961).

In short, for reasons also considered by other writers as well (see Ardener, 1961; Krapf-Askari, 1969; Miner, 1967) we follow a somewhat different approach from Louis Wirth's classical guide to the city (1938). This is primarily because our subsequent analysis of women's position does not depend upon the notion of urbanism as a way of life but is made in terms of the sociology of urban growth. We will be concerning ourselves, in other words, not only with urban patterns of social behaviour, but with the dynamic factors which underlie and give rise to them.

2 Women as migrants

We have suggested that the most useful locale for the study of
women's contemporary position is the town and that from it
'urban' ideas and practices spread out to the countryside. As a
result, it is in the rural village itself that numbers of prospective
female migrants are initially stimulated to move. They gain there,
like the men, an interest in the material and non-material elements
of culture, behavioural patterns and ideas that originate in or
are distinctive of the city. But urbanization amounts to more
than the acquisition of a certain type of outlook and behaviour.
It means that social relationships are formed in conjunction with
the taking on of cultural practices, and so the woman who subsequently becomes 'urbanized' selects new companions and
friends as well as new habits.[1] In other words, since we are here
concerned essentially with movement and change, urbanization is
to be regarded as a social process. This is different from the type
of definition which holds that urbanization is a process of population concentration in which the ratio of urban people to the total
population increases. Obviously, too, our use of the term involves
a great deal more than a simple reference to living in towns as
against living in rural settlements.[2]

However, before considering the implications for women of
urbanization in these terms we have first to understand their role
as migrants. This is necessary because, broadly speaking, movement from the countryside first took the form of male labour
migration. As the market economy introduced by colonialism
spread, workers were needed for the various economic enterprises

[1] This point is widely illustrated by Mayer's book (1961). For discussion
bearing on the subject in the African context see, among others,
Bascom (1963–4), Gugler (1969), Krapf-Askari (1969), and Mitchell
(1966).
[2] As an example of simple quantitative indices of urbanization conceived of as urban population size, the 1960 Census of Ghana defined
localities having more than 5,000 residents as urban.

set in motion and, especially in places like the Rand in South Africa and in Rhodesia and the Congo, the African male population was regarded as a labour reservoir. In what is now Zambia the system that developed involved villagers contracting to labour for a strange employer – often many hundreds of miles away – in return for guaranteed employment and subsidiary benefits. Others who were not motivated to work for wages were inducted by means of 'recruitment' into the money economy. Most contracts were of six to nine months' duration, and quite often a returned recruit's report of his experiences abroad induced others who had never worked for wages to move, in turn, to industrial centres. As a result, in addition to the recruited workers the migrant stream was increased by numbers of men seeking casual employment on their own, and this movement to the employment centres to earn money was further encouraged by tax liabilities payable only in cash. However, since these men worked for highly specific purposes and only for short periods of time their behaviour remained that of tribesmen impressed into the service of industry. Their attachment was to their rural villages and was expressed in terms of remittances sent back to their families and kinsmen. They did not bring their womenfolk to the labour camp which were largely male reserves (Heisler, 1971, pp. 425–35; Skinner, 1965; see also, among others, Van Velsen, 1961).

At first, therefore, the main rural input into the industrial-urban system was unwilling men who in time returned to their tribal birth place (Skinner, 1965). Later, when migrant labour became more and more institutionalized as the rural areas' principal mode of involvement in the money economy, interaction between village and town correspondingly increased and migrants stayed for even longer periods in the industrial centres. The result was that by 1951 two-fifths of the men on the Copperbelt, for example, had lived ten years or more in urban areas and about the same proportion had wives living with them. Hitherto, the nature of the migratory system had inhibited women's movement to the towns, and the Government considered that they were best kept in the rural areas. Not only did the Tribal Authorities share this view, but they enacted orders prohibiting female migration and applied them with even greater stringency than the Government itself intended. For example, the Cewa (Eastern Province) insisted on women passengers on lorries, unaccompanied by their husbands, producing marriage certificates before passing westward out of the province.[3] The mining companies, too, began in 1945 to

---

[3] Even greater efforts were made to confine the movement of women in Sierra Leone. For example, it was resolved at a chiefs' conference

require documentary proof of marriage before they would allocate housing to a man and woman in the townships. However, having recognized by the 1950s the need for institutions appropriate to the urban situation, the Government itself introduced reforms. These facilitated the migration of women to towns where they could marry whom they pleased. Then, with the collapse of the Federation of The Rhodesias and Nyasaland, the money economy boomed. This and the policy of 'Africanization' following Independence in 1964, enabled a notable advance in the employment of women. It took place in both urban and rural areas, and by 1969 the majority of rural women married to men resident in the town had joined their husbands (Heisler, 1971).

Urban growth and urbanization in Zambia, therefore, appear to have been essentially a function of industrialization.[4] In terms of money values urban incomes were 2½ times as large as estimated per capita peasant incomes in 1954, 3½ times greater in 1964, but 7 times greater in 1960 (Heisler, 1971). This apparently gave rise to a process whereby, broadly speaking, the men followed the money and the women followed the men. Thus, there came into being an autonomous urban system capable of generating its own population, and this developed because, in addition to target workers concerned with circular migration, an increasing number of men set out on one-way journeys to avoid rural poverty and maximize their family incomes. This stabilization seemingly went on despite the unaccustomed cost in monetary terms of urban living and despite the fact that according to some authorities impoverishment was widespread among migrants with families (cf. Garbett and Kapferer, 1970).[5]

during the early 1940s that women strangers in a town should be 'signed for' by their landlords. They were to stay with their host until called for by the husband or his representative (Little, 1951, p. 69 fn.).

[4] It is Heisler's thesis that once there were two nations in Zambia and that this disjunction between the tribal systems and the industrial system was originally so large that it was only by stretch of the imagination that the country could then be considered a society. 'Labour recruitment was the indispensable means by which a tribesman was prised out of his preliterate and technically primitive past and introduced to the culture and organization of the occident; casual labour was the way by which a tribal identity was discarded and either that of a peasant or proletarian was voluntarily assumed at different points in the life of every male' (1971, p. 433).

[5] But against this argument it may be contended that (a) the poverty datum line was decided according to certain measures determined in Western countries and not necessarily valid in Africa; (b) even if urban incomes were low they were higher than rural incomes; and (c) urban money incomes were only one element in the family

In West Africa, there is often less difference, sociologically speaking, between towns and countryside. Many of the people who come to reside in the urban centres are already acquainted with town ways, and they move into communities that are similar in some respects to the social environment they have left behind (Banton, 1965, pp. 131–6). For this reason examples from Central Africa are not necessarily typical of the entire sub-Saharan scene.[6] What, however, does apply to the picture as a whole is the increasing importance that social as well as economic factors have assumed. Thus, we can say fairly generally that though the movement of men was unpopular at first, it gradually became condoned and was even encouraged to the extent of male labour migration becoming a 'normal' part of the local culture (see Skinner, 1965; Van Velsen, 1961). This kind of outlook developed out of the rural countryside's gradual absorption into the industrial urban system which made the possession of money increasingly essential for local needs. The result was a circular process because there was a demand for consumption goods which, in turn, could only be met, as a rule, by earning money abroad. This withdrawal of male labour disturbed, in turn, the rural subsistence economy making the village more and more dependent upon the remittances as well as the goods and cash brought back by returning migrants. Reluctant, therefore, as the older people might be to see the young men depart, their temporary absence abroad became regarded as a necessary evil. For the migrant himself there was the prospect of earning cash for his own use, including bridewealth for a wife as well as personal equipment, new clothes and other necessities.[7]

But, not surprisingly, attitudes towards women migrating were different. A measure of tribal stability could only be preserved if adult women in their prime were kept at home, and it was also realized that if their womenfolk left the peasant systems the men would not return or make further remittances (Thomson, 1933, p. 79, cited by Heisler, 1973). In effect, therefore, the aim, conscious or unconscious, of regulations controlling women's movement was to bind them to the villages as hostages for the

---

income because there were cases where a man's wife looked after his family from the proceeds of subsistence (Dr Heisler in a personal communication).

[6] Nor, it hardly needs to be added, do these few cursory paragraphs do anything like full justice to the subject of migration itself. For the considerable literature involved the reader needs to consult the Newburys' *Bibliography* (1969).

[7] There is, of course, a great deal of literature on this subject as a whole which can be consulted through the Newburys (1969). Little (1973a) elaborates on the specific points raised here.

return of the absent men. Later, wives were allowed to join their husbands in the towns. This paved the way for a wider exodus of women which reflected, in turn, the direction of structural changes that the urban-industrial economy had set in motion. Position in the latter being based largely on such qualifications as education and technical know-how, it was the younger men who led the way and so achieved a degree of status and prestige unavailable in the traditional system to persons of their juniority.[8] Naturally, nationalism, too, was a particularly potent factor in this process, and although its earlier proponents were mostly elderly or middle-aged men it was the younger generations who eventually took over and provided the shock troops. This duly meant that when 'Africanization' got under way and Independence was gained it was members of the latter age groups who mainly filled the positions of influence and power. For example, in the Nigerian Houses of Assembly and the Central House of Representatives during the period 1951–7, the median age of the members concerned varied between the high thirties and low forties. There were very few over sixty. Among the regions, the Eastern Region had elected the most youthful legislature, with the median age between thirty-five and thirty-nine (Coleman, 1958, p. 378).

The factors which underlie this significant advance in the social status of the younger men are largely repeated in the migration of women and their reasons for moving to towns. True, since it is their duty, there are numbers of wives who accompany their husbands; but they go all the more readily because they expect to find urban opportunities of earning money for themselves. There are other groups of women, too, whose attitude is even more economic and who follow the familiar pattern of labour migration to the extent of moving periodically for work which, in their case, consists of prostitution. (See specifically Chapter 6.) Yet again, are other women and girls, some of whom – there being now fewer young men at home – have not succeeded in getting married, and so they leave their families and go to mining camps, recruiting centres, or housing developments, in order to find their husbands (*African Women*, 1962, p. 88).[9] And there are also women and girls who are divorced or have deserted their husbands: or who want

---

[8] For an elaboration of the above points, including the part played by the younger men's voluntary associations, see Little (1965, pp. 103–17, and 1973a) as well as the Newburys (*Ibid.*).

[9] Another motive is to avoid the dire sanctions applied by custom against unmarried mothers. These girls leave their families, have their babies far away, and then try to find a husband (*African Women, ibid.*).

an easier life than is a woman's lot in a farming community; or who have been lured by the town's reputation as an exciting place to be in.

But underlying or directly associated with these various motives is the fact that the women, too, perceive an opportunity of improving their status. Like the younger men before them, the women are increasingly impatient with their traditionally ascribed position and there is only one difference in attitude. Whereas the young men tended to rationalize their ambitions in terms of the benefits of 'progress', the women construe their apparent social inferiority in more personal language. They speak of their desire for 'freedom' and 'emancipation', and many of them see the town as a place where this can be achieved. There, as a Xhosa informant pointed out, 'A woman . . . is independent. You are free to do as you please. There are no homestead people watching you' (Mayer, 1961, pp. 249–50).

In fact, this whole situation is illustrated very clearly by Mayer's study of Xhosa women who 'seem to use East London as a semi-permanent escape' from their rural subjection to men and to other women. 'Most agree that East London is a place "to be free", "to be independent, to get away from the rule of the people at home"'. 'In different terminology', remarks Mayer, 'women have reason to like this new environment where status depends less on ascription and more on achievement' (*ibid.*).

That women and girls can keep their own economic and social footing, not by virtue of their relations with men, but in their own right – this is one of the great novelties of town life as compared with the Xhosa countryside. Mayer has described the two different groups of Xhosa; the 'Red'[10] whose men are, on the whole, typically pagan and illiterate and adamant in their refusal to internalize white values; and the 'School' who have been brought up in mission schools and have acquired a taste for Western civilization. However, for Red and School women alike, residence in the country means belonging to a domestic unit that is defined patriarchally, and where their right to live in a homestead at all depends upon their relationship to some man, alive or dead. The definition of a woman's household duties also depends indirectly on this, in so far as this determines her seniority relative to the other females of the homestead. Moving to town frees her from both the men and the senior women, and means that, although age and sex distinctions continue to be relevant in interpersonal relations, they lie more lightly as a whole. At least, money may

[10] Known as 'Red' through their custom of wearing a red blanket.

be earned, and lodgings hired and property acquired regardless of sex, seniority, or marital status. In the country, property rights hardly apply to women. Though women may retain the use of their deceased husband's fields, women cannot inherit land, and the transfer of land to unmarried women is frowned upon by the authorities. Town, in fact, is the only place where women can acquire real property. In addition, a woman can earn money, which, though it could not buy her a homestead, can buy her a location house or shack (*ibid.* especially p. 234).

Both the Red and the School Xhosa are wary of their daughters going to town and Red parents, in particular, attempt to regulate their movements. Nevertheless, Mayer found girls who had run away apparently in defiance of their families and who generally gave their desire for freedom as the motive. This might amount to an intention of breaking away from 'Red' life altogether, as in the case of one girl who wanted to continue her education and become a nurse. She was the only member of the family who had been to school and she was in rebellion against her family's attempt to marry her off quickly and so make her 'Red' again. At the same time, she was still governed by the 'Red' sexual code and insisted that she would not allow herself any lovers in town. Since it is apparently quite a common practice for parents privately to arrange matters so that their daughters are virtually abducted and married 'by capture', some Red girls run away in anticipation of this happening and take refuge in the town, sometimes eloping with a sweetheart or joining him there.

In the case of the School category, however, it is no longer a question of an occasional abscondment but of hordes of young girls, from the age of about seventeen onwards, coming into town deliberately, with or without their parents' consent. Their attitude is also more positive because these girls are usually running towards something they like, and not only away from something they dislike. In addition, while among Red people money is mainly of interest to men and to the mature economically responsible women, it is the idea of earning and spending one's own money that holds a particular charm for School girls. They are keen on clothes to an extent which a rural family can ill afford and so a School girl's stereotyped explanation is that she came to town 'to dress herself'. Also, having received some education them-selves, School girls particularly object to having an uneducated husband chosen for them. But the most general complaint is that the countryside is too 'dull' and 'old fashioned'. A picture of town life has been gleaned from school books, from newspapers and illustrated magazines, and above all from the tempting accounts of age-mates who have been to town themselves. All this is in striking and alluring contrast to the local morality because the School home pays at least lip service to the importance of ' Christian standards', including temperance and chastity and the sinfulness (in the case of girls) of lapses from a prudish sexual code (Mayer, 1961, pp. 240–1).

The position of more mature Xhosa women is somewhat different because the Xhosa peasant economy depends on wage-earnings as a necessary supplement to agriculture. Since, therefore, the loss of the husband's earnings may cripple a widow economically her only course may be to become a wage-earner herself. Moreover, although the widow is able to go back to her parents' home, her presence there may soon become an irritant, similar to that of a mature unmarried daughter, with status rivalries *vis-à-vis* the ' wives of the kraal'. Also, since in the case of School families the Christian expectation is that a widow remains chaste (short of remarriage), to take lovers in the country involves a special burden of shame and secrecy. A divorced wife, too, suffers from similar disabilities. She can also go back to her parental home where she may be allowed love affairs with men; but for both her and the widow going to town offers more hopeful prospects for independence (Mayer, 1961, p. 242). Finally, in the rural areas, pregnancy outside wedlock brings such shame and disgrace among the Red people that, as one such unmarried mother explained, she stayed at home only until the child was weaned. She told Mayer, ' My chances of getting married were very small indeed, as I was now *inkazana*.[11] I could no longer mix with the girls of my own age, which made me very unhappy. All these thoughts pushed me away from home. I felt I must go to town.' Among School unmarried mothers, on the other hand, such strong arguments of disgrace were rarely heard, because, on the whole, the School girl can live down the shame at home. There are occasions on which she may feel ill at ease in her age-mates' company, but the local community normally includes several other girls in the same position and they are all accepted in due course and readmitted to social gatherings. Hence it may not be so much the disgrace which drives a School unmarried mother to town, as the positive hope of making a new start, supporting her child, and perhaps finding a new lover (Mayer, 1961, p. 243).

[11] Meaning that she had now a wholly different status from her still marriageable age-mates. *Inkazana* is often translated by a term such as ' concubine' but another of its equally basic meanings is that of a woman who will not bear children out of her parental home. Being ineligible for marriage, she and her children (if any) will always

That these women's motives for migration to the town are not unique to the Xhosa, or indeed to southern Africa, is indicated even more graphically by West African novelists. The most interesting of these literary sources is Ekwensi's *Jagua Nana* because its heroine's career provides what is virtually a sociological case-study of the adventurous type of young woman who has migrated to the more cosmopolitan towns of the West Coast.

' Jagua ' was born in Eastern Nigeria and was an only daughter. Her father, a catechist, doted on her and wanted her to marry a serious man from the village. The husband he approved of said he worked in Enugu and he wanted to take her back with him as his wife. ' Jagua ' was in her early thirties in those days and she was already fond of changing her clothes and painting her face. She loved to swim about in the clear cool water of the local river. All the girls in her age-group had married and had had children, but ' Jagua ' was more ambitious. She held out always hoping for some eminent man to arrive who would marry her. She shocked the villagers by wearing jeans, riding her bicycle through the narrow village streets and laughing and talking loudly. She had been to bed with most of the local boys and looked down on them.

The man from Enugu persisted, paid £120 in bridewealth, and her father gave ' Jagua ' away in church with his blessing. She intended to settle down and be a good wife, but was bored. She was *Jagwa*,[12] but the man lacked style. All he thought about was his petrol filling station. He worked there early and late and soon acquired a chain of filling stations, but he never took ' Jagua ' to parties and he begrudged spending money on clothes for himself. This kind of life did not suit ' Jagua ' at all – the desire for adventure was still strong within her and even after three years there was no child. Her husband's family made a great fuss over this, and told him that ' Jagua ' was too old – he should take another wife. ' Jagua ' accepted the blame for sterility, but it pained her that her husband was obviously looking out for a younger girl.

So, one day on an impulse she enquired about trains for Lagos – the city with a magic name ' where the girls were glossy, worked in offices like the men, danced, smoked, wore high-heeled shoes and narrow slacks, and were " free " and

belong there, will never be transferred to another homestead or lineage (*ibid.* p. 235).

[12] For the meaning and implications of this term, see Chapter 7.

"fast" with their favours'. In Lagos, there were night-spots; there was something going on all night. Here, people went to bed at 8 p.m.; everywhere was shut down and the streets deserted. From that moment on, to 'Jagua', her husband was as good as dead. She continued to sleep with him but her thoughts were on the slim young men in the dark, bow ties and elegantly cut lounge suits. She cooked for her husband, but all the time 'she was dreaming of quiet elegant restaurants where the music was soft and the wine glasses clinked'. A serious quarrel with her husband was only a matter of time and after they had not spoken to each other for two days, 'Jagua' caught the train for Lagos. She knew no one there and so was glad when a young band-leader gave her shelter. He made up in style what he lacked in money, and after meeting his other girls, 'Jagua' realised how provincial she herself was.

Another of Ekwensi's heroines is equally typical of the would-be 'city girl' because she 'would be content to walk about a Mayfair-type of neon-lit shop all day, hang about the city hotels, the ice-cream bars with not a penny in her handbag, rather than marry a farmer with a thousand pounds a year for his income, and no spice of life than the prospect of security and raising children' (1954, p. 63).

The latter kind of attitude implies that what is sought, in particular, is a different relationship with the opposite sex, and in another novel (Dipoko, 1968) about fishermen and their wives, this point is made quite explicit. The scene takes place in the neighbourhood of Douala, Cameroun, and the heroine, 'Ewudu', has just become the mistress of 'Ekema', whose intentions are seemingly more serious than her own because he insists on taking her to see his mother. 'Ekema' has qualities that appeal strongly to 'Ewudu'. He is tall and 'proud' and he has a good job, but 'Ewudu' feels that she is being 'rushed'.

> 'She wanted to be free because she was still young and having lived with a free woman in Douala she wanted to go on playing with life, enjoying herself without being attached to any particular man. She wanted to love the most handsome and proud men and to be loved by them all.' [13]

In *Jagua Nana* we left off at the point where the heroine ensconced herself in Lagos. The story goes on to relate how, in

---

[13] According to the Dutch merchant, William Bosman (1705), this kind of attitude was also held by some of the girls in what is now Ghana as early as the seventeenth century.

order to compete for male attention, 'Jagua' sets out to acquire the 'urban' arts of coquetry, fashion and deportment. In the process, she also goes on to Accra and soon has a coterie of town friends of both sexes. Later, deserted by a lover, she returns to her own people up-country and enjoys, at first, the freshness of the air and the warmth and friendliness of her rural relatives. She is even courted and offered every material comfort by a wealthy though elderly admirer. But the city's hold over 'Jagua' being too strong, she knows instinctively that to remain in the countryside would be wrong. Better from her point of view, the squalor of a Lagos slum so long as there are sophisticated people around her, the bright lights of a night-spot, a high life band, and the chance of picking up a handsome and well-to-do patron.

'Jagua', in other words, became 'urbanized'. But the significance of Ekwensi's story is that 'Jagua's' adjustment to town ways was a deliberate choice on her part and so suggests that the female migrant's position is different from that of many of the men. This is because for the ordinary male as unschooled as 'Jagua', migration may be a mere interlude in his life-history; simply a means to an end conceived of in monetary terms and perhaps bringing some prestige on returning home. For his female counterpart, on the other hand, movement to the town may start as an adventure; but it is often made with the conscious or unconscious intention of severing existing ties and starting a new life. Not only have Mayer's empirical data pointed strongly to this motive, but there is confirmation of it, too, from East Africa. Thus, in a study by Elkan (1956) of women who had moved to factory work in Jinja the one strain that passed, apparently, through all their lives was disruption of normal marital relations. All but four of those interviewed had been married and had left their husbands before they came to Jinja. Among the reasons given were physical ill-treatment; the husband's impotence, or unwillingness to sleep with the wife; and the husband's introduction of other women. Also, the manager of the factory had been asked on several occasions either to provide houses for single women or to persuade the housing estate to let houses to them, and Elkan's impression was that these requests were inspired by a real desire for independence and emancipation from the control of men. He also mentions that a surprisingly large number of the women claimed either that they lived alone or that they lived with a sister. It is probable that at least some of those concerned were accommodated in houses rented for them by their lovers; but all but seven said that part of their wages went on rent, and this suggested that the number who lived independently might be even greater. Also relevant in this regard is that in addition to remittances to parents, some of the women were paying off bridewealth in monthly instalments.[14] Only two women lived with husbands and both were married in Jinja to men working in the town.

As explained, between the town and its neighbouring villages people frequently come and go for purposes of trade, ceremonies, and so on, and this applies to women as well as men. Indeed, the custom is well established in West Africa of country cousins staying in town as paying guests for a shorter or longer period.[15] In Zambia, too, established urban families now act largely as temporary hosts to relatives seeking either to settle in the urban area or merely to visit the town for some special reason or other (Bettison, 1959). This means that sometimes there is thus available to migrant women as well as men a ready means whereby they can find temporary shelter and support. In other words, provided she has urban relatives or a friend from the same village, a woman can plan to remove herself from the countryside and be fairly confident of security and protection until she is able to fend for herself.[16]

This is the case when the distance between town and village is relatively short and when travelling conditions are good; but it is another matter to journey to town from the more remote rural areas. As we have explained, unless it is to join their husbands, village women are discouraged from making such a trip at all and this opposition is, as a rule, particularly strong against the movement of young unmarried girls. For example, Caldwell found that while five-sixths of the Ghanaian male population he sampled

---

[14] Women have also found other ways of paying off their bridewealth. During the Second World War an allotment was made to the wives of African soldiers serving abroad with the British Forces. Some of the wives concerned who received it used the money for the above purpose, usually with the connivance of other soldiers with whom in the meantime they had formed liaisons (Little, 1951).

[15] In Sierra Leone, for example, workers move from the provinces into Freetown after the harvest has been gathered in early January and again in the rainy season when there is little farm work. These migrants remain only a month or two at a time, their aim being to earn a little money before it is time to return to their village. They mostly lodge with relatives, paying for their accommodation with presents brought from the rice harvest (Banton, 1957, pp. 60–1); Koroma and Proudfoot, 1960).

[16] In a recent study of Lusaka it was found that 41 per cent of the primary type households contained 'additional persons' who, broadly speaking, were new arrivals to the town. Under 1 per cent of these households contained unrelated males, all households were related to '*additional females*' (my italics) (Opadike, 1971).

approved of young men going to the town for a while in order to earn money, acquire skills and achieve some sophistication, only about half felt the same way about young women. The great majority of those who disapproved cited as their reason (not without grounds) the danger that the female migrants would become prostitutes (cf. Caldwell, 1969, pp. 106–7 and Birmingham, Neustadt and Amaboe, 1967, p. 140); and this feeling is so strong in some countries that for a girl to leave without parental consent is tantamount to burning her bridges. True, irrespective of what she has done she will still be accepted back, as a rule, by her own kinsfolk, but will have to comply with the very conditions from which she fled. Since these may mean not only humbling herself but accepting any husband chosen for her, the incentive is greater for the girl who has decamped to persevere and hold out to the point of destitution. A male migrant whose affairs in town go badly may be ashamed to return to his native village empty-handed; but this is his only problem and there is nothing to prevent his trying his luck in town again.

It would be quite wrong, however, to imagine that the migration of single or 'unattached' women implies automatically a loss of contact with the rural areas. On the contrary, many of them are just as assiduous as the men in sending gifts and remitting money to their kinsfolk at home. What the situation does amount to is, as Mayer found in East London, that while a few women migrants were forced to remain 'incapsulated' like the men in their own circle of fellow villagers, the temptation to develop important interests in town seemed less easy for them to resist. As a result, having become independent many such women 'emphasized that their participation in urban life had come to mean a great deal; here is their business, here alone is the possibility of maintaining themselves by their own efforts' (Mayer, 1961, p. 250). In other words, the more usual pattern was the doubly rooted one. The woman has not cut herself off from the countryside decisively, but she stays on in town and admits to enjoying life there more than in the rural areas (*ibid.* p. 235).

Finally, the marked presence in town of 'husbandless' women requires some comment because, as Southall has put it, 'women living singly or without legal husbands, and in economic independence is one of the most striking characteristics of Africans in towns in contrast to rural areas' (1961, p. 51). According to Gugler, it is marital instability which pushes these women into the city (1969, p. 139), the argument being that urbanization creates immigration of the men who are pushed to new jobs. This imposes a strain on the wives they have left behind and divorce follows; as a wife is dependent upon her husband their divorce leaves her destitute and to escape from her predicament she flees to a town and its surplus of men in search of relief.

There is, Heisler points out (1973), superficial support for some such hypothesis because, as noted above, it was the men who went first and the women who followed them into town. However, given the wider context we have endeavoured to describe, our own view of this matter is somewhat less specific. It hinges on the general idea that for women migration is to be seen as an end in itself as well as being, in the case of the categories of women concerned, an integral part of the urbanization process. We contend, moreover, in supporting this point that urbanization often starts not on the housing estate or in the urban slum, but in the rural compound or village street; indeed in any place where there is sufficient urban contact to fire the initial spark. Nor, although often associated expressly with girls who run away and wives who desert their husbands, is this desire to be 'free' *necessarily* a deviant attitude. On the contrary, instead of its being confined to any one category the wish to feel 'emancipated' is seemingly shared by many women, illiterate and literate alike. These women are not always clear about specific goals, but one aim appears to be held by many. They want to be able to decide their own destiny and, if they feel like it, to be independent of men altogether.

We shall return to this point in succeeding chapters.

3 Women in the urban economy

It was pointed out in the last chapter that the apparent aim of many women is to live independently of man. However, even among the educated class, girls who wish to remain spinsters are very much the exception and so a desire to be 'free' does not rule out marriage. Rather is it a generalized reaction [1] to a number of anomalies, such as the men's frequent insistence on their right to a double standard of sexual morality. Also, some women, educated and illiterate alike, experience a sense of unease. This springs from the paradoxical fact that while offering individual women a much wider scope, the urban economy does not provide women as a whole with the safeguards and security they traditionally enjoy in most rural systems. In the latter milieu, with all its drawbacks, women have groups of their own, including age sets, secret societies, initiation schools and other associations which, as well as playing their part in the general life of the village, engender an *esprit de corps* among its female members. Also, many wives are able to support themselves and their children through horticulture; and although in the rural system women depend for protection upon their families and husbands, both on the farm and in the home the women's co-operation is, in turn, essential to men.

In the city, by contrast, the economy is based not upon the sexual division of labour, but on workers who are mainly selected according to criteria appropriate to the operation performed.

---

[1] Naturally, there is also another side to the picture, and that women respond differently when treated with consideration is shown by empirical data quoted later and is indicated also in literary sources. For example, Ekwensi's character, 'Chief Mrs Jolimo', explains to the girls who work in her prosperous boutique how her husband won her over. 'Anyone who knew me as a girl would wonder that I ever settled down . . . And ever got a shop where I stay in one place. All because my husband just lets me get ahead with what I like to do, and he helps me, too' (1966a).

Physical strength and endurance may be what are needed and, for the better paid jobs, qualifications which among women are also relatively scarce. In other words, there is a considerable lag in female education. This is the case because in most countries the ratio of girls to boys in primary schools has ranged from a quarter to two-thirds, and according to figures provided in 1960 by UNESCO (pp. 1–23) the only places where girls constituted 50 per cent of the enrolled primary school population were Basutoland, Bechuanaland and Lagos. Other states and territories may be grouped as follows in terms of the number of girls enrolled as a percentage of the enrolled school population:

40–50 per cent: Malagasy Republic

30–40 per cent: Gabon, Ghana, Nigeria (Eastern Region and Western Region), Nyasaland, Northern Rhodesia, Sierra Leone, Tanganyika, Zanzibar and Pemba

20–30 per cent: Cameroons, Congo, Dahomey, Guinea, Ivory Coast, Kenya, Liberia, Niger, Northern Nigeria, Ruanda Urundi, Senegal, French Somaliland, Somaliland (Trust Territory), Republic of Togoland, Uganda, Upper Volta

10–20 per cent: British Cameroons, Central African Republic, Chad

Less than
10 per cent: British Somaliland.[2]

In respect of education at the secondary level, the ratio of girls to boys drops, of course, to an even lower figure. Thus, in the following countries where girls formed from 20 to 30 per cent of the primary school population, the proportion fell to the level of 10 to 20 per cent when it came to secondary education:

French Cameroons	17·6	Somaliland (Trust	
Guinea	11·1	Territory)	11·3
Ivory Coast	19·1	Togoland	18·1
Kenya	10·6	Uganda	11·2
Liberia	16·0	Upper Volta	15·9
Niger	11·5		

[2] Also, there was an even greater disparity between primary and secondary enrolment in some countries where the situation in primary schools was particularly favourable to girls. Thus, in the following countries where girls comprised between 30 and 40 per cent of the total enrolment at the primary level, the figures in brackets show the enrolment of girls in percentage terms at the secondary level, namely Gabon (16·3); Eastern Nigeria (12·7); Western Nigeria (19·8); Northern Nigeria (12·3); Tanganyika (8·9) (UNESCO, 1960).

As mentioned above, these statistics are for 1960 and so presumably they provide a rough estimation of the educational status today of the 20–40 age groups among the female populations concerned.[3] However, not even these relatively low figures convey the full story because attendance at primary schools in most areas has, in the past, been begun late, been irregular, and has been characterized both by a considerable amount of repetition of classes and by a tendency to leave school before completing a course. Opposition on the part of conservatively minded parents also comes into the matter and the consequence is many girls did not in fact finish more than two years of schooling. Further, there is also considerable wastage due to girls leaving the secondary school before the end of the course for much the same reasons. The incentives to remain in secondary school, such as gaining a diploma, may be stronger, but the expenses involved are often greater, particularly if the girls are boarders or living with relatives away from home. Moreover, at the secondary school level, marriages are more frequent. Other reasons may be found in the failure of some girls to make progress in studies for which they are ill-prepared; discouragement due to the lack of prospects, or inadequate vocational guidance which leads the girls to give up their studies at the first offer of employment. In some cases, where new employment possibilities are open to women, girls may abandon secondary school before completing their studies to take up training in a particular field (UNESCO, 1960).[4]

Though it is not the only factor, this relative lack of education and training naturally means that in competition for jobs women are at a considerable disadvantage.[5] True, in cities like Accra and Lagos individual women are to be found in a wide variety of occupations requiring skill. They include journalists, broadcasters, dress designers, hairdressers, hotel managers, charge hands in factories, telephonists, beauticians, radio announcers, and bank employees. But, overall, so small a proportion of women are engaged in wage employment at all that in 1961 it only rose to double figures in South Africa and Kenya (15 per cent), and

[3] For further statistics bearing on these age groups, see Junod, 1963.

[4] See also Chapter 5. Brokensha (1966), Foster (1965), Richards (1960), and Shrubsole (1965) among others, throw further light on this general situation.

[5] As, apparently, are women in England and Wales, too, *if* crude statistics tell the whole story. Of the nearly nine million women in full-time employment 65 per cent earn less than 30p. per hour compared with 2·6 per cent of men. Of 3,218 university (full) professors only 44 are women, and out of 36,000 members of the Institute of Directors only 962 are women (Collins, 1972).

Swaziland (16·5 per cent). In most other countries, including Ghana as well as Sierra Leone and Liberia, women employees did not exceed 3 per cent of the total industrial labour force (Boserup, 1970, p. 109),[6] although the situation is marked by one interesting and important feature. This is the relatively large proportion of women in the professions. There are numbers of doctors and lawyers [7]; but it is at the primary level in teaching that women are most strongly represented. In Dahomey, for example, 70 per cent of primary school teachers are women (Lefancheux, 1962), and in Ghana, South Africa and Kenya the percentage of women of all personnel in teaching was, respectively, 22, 50 and 23. In fact, two-thirds or more of all women professionally employed are in this occupation, while a large proportion of the remaining one-third are nurses or perform medical services. Thus, according to Boserup's figures, in Ghana and South Africa the percentage of women of all personnel in nursing was respectively 61 and 93; in other professions, 10 and 13; and in all professions, 20 and 42.[8]

In Africa, not only do nursing and teaching usually carry more prestige than in the Western world, but the position of nurses in relation to, say, skilled male workers is economically more favourable than is the position of nurses in industrialized countries. Especially is this so in South Africa where, according to Leo Kuper (1965, p. 230), nursing both brings high economic rewards and is the one career open to African women even after marriage and the birth of children. The bridewealth of nurses is as high 'as for the daughters of kings', and 'they are the princesses of the modern community'.[9]

In short, nursing, together with teaching, ranks as the most

[6] This is one of the most important differences between Africa's and Britain's 'industrial revolution' because in the latter case there were few industries from which women were excluded, and in a number of principal industries, like textiles and pottery, more women were employed than men.

[7] Mostly in certain West African countries. In Ghana, for example, more than 60 women have qualified as barristers-at-law since 1945 (communicated).

[8] So far as can be judged of individual cities, Lagos has perhaps the largest proportion of women in the professional category. In 1962 there were 1,376 women as against 7,404 men (Economic Commission for Africa – E.C.A. – 1962, p. 38).

[9] Among industrial workers in Cape Town covered by an investigation, 37 per cent wanted their daughters to become nurses or teachers. This desire was described as 'not entirely unrealistic' because most African nurses and teachers are in fact children of African workers and peasants, there being almost no African middle class from which recruitment for the professions could take place (E.C.A., 1962).

suitable occupation for respectable girls,[10] and the profession of nursing is rapidly changing over from male to female. Moreover, there is a demand for professional women even in countries with a tradition of seclusion for women and with few girls among the students.[11]

Commerce is carried on by women in both the traditional and the modern sectors of the economy and more will be said about this matter in the following pages. In addition, women have also been able to move latterly into certain posts left vacant by the men, setting their sights higher. This results from the expansion of the economy and it means that instead of regarding a job in an office or a factory as their goal men aim at something better and do not therefore oppose the employment of women in posts which were formerly considered an exclusively male province.[12]

Consequently, in addition to working as shop assistants, and in domestic service, women are gradually being allowed to take up kinds of employment traditionally denied them, such as weaving and sewing and using a sewing machine (Int. Lab. Off., 1961 and 1964). However, needless to say, these minor improvements barely alter the general position which amounts to the fact that, apart from trading and the professional activity referred to, the modern sector is in every country virtually a male preserve.[13] Since Ghana has a level of economic activity above the average, the following data abstracted from the 1960 Census (Special Report 'A') of Accra (Municipal Council) provide a convincing illustration of this and the other points mentioned. Incidentally, the proportion of women in employment as a whole reaches its peak only among those in their forties and fifties, and this also appears to be the

[10] It will be recalled that although nursing was carried on by nuns, this occupation was not regarded in Britain as suitable work for decent girls until Miss Florence Nightingale made it respectable.

[11] This is because custom requires that if a girl is to be educated she should be educated by female teachers. Similarly, it is thought that decency requires women to be taken care of by female health personnel, female social workers, etc. In other words, as Boserup points out, where women live in seclusion, 'the demand for professional women does not violate the rules of seclusion, but indeed is a necessary *result* of those rules' (Boserup, 1970, 125–6).

[12] There is an interesting analogy in this regard with the racial situation in the United States where, in recent years, blacks have moved into jobs vacated by white workers on their way up in the occupational hierarchy (Pettigrew, 1964).

[13] The only important exception is the employment of white and Cape Coloured women in South Africa. Even there, however, Bantu girls are not found in the modern sector, although their rate of literacy is higher than female literacy in most other African countries (Boserup, 1970, p. 190).

case in Dakar. A study of 200 market women revealed that 82 per cent of them were between the ages of 30 and 59 years and 55 per cent between the ages of 40 and 59 (Institut de Science Economique Appliquée, 1963).[14]

	Males	Females
Professional medical workers and medical technicians	623	60
Midwives and nurses	373	896
Teachers	1,463	990
Administrative, executive and managerial workers (Government)	1,561	105
Directors, managers and working proprietors	661	9
Clerical workers	12,581	1,824
Working proprietors (wholesale trade)	234	29
Working proprietors (retail trade, street venders and news venders (mainly petty traders)	5,751	31,187
Working proprietors (retail and wholesale trade combined) mainly fishmongers	128	4,213
Tailors, cutters, furriers, and related workers	3,306	4,157

Domination of the modern sector by men is closely linked with their leadership in government and means that in the quest for social prestige, wealth needed for purposes of conspicuous consumption is gained partly through political position. This tends to depend, in turn, not only upon education but a person's social network.[15] In other words, a position of authority and influence, once achieved, can often be used to gain additional emoluments, both legitimate and illegitimate. This is the path to fame as conceived by many of the ambitious men, and the women, too, perceive just as readily the central importance of money. Its possession connotes ' power '[16] and is in these terms the ' open

[14] In Dakar, domestic work is an important standby when there is a shortage of industrial employment (Le Cour Grandmaison, 1969, pp. 113–37).

[15] See the narrator's remark concerning the road to success in Achebe's characterization of an *arriviste* federal minister – ' After Independence . . . it didn't matter *what* you knew, but *who* you knew ' (1966, p. 19).

[16] Thus, a young Tanzanian girl in Dar es Salaam wrote about her desire to go to other places, and that if she should have *power* (my italics) she would have come to the United Kingdom.

sesame' to 'independence'[17] as well as to the acquisition of up-
to-date modern houses and fine clothes; and to the education of
one's children. These are the kind of values which urbanization
instils, and it is significant that such ambitions are apparently
typical even among very economically disadvantaged groups of
women (see later paragraphs).

What means do women in general have of realizing such
objectives, given that a large proportion are girls from the countryside? Some of the latter are literate,[18] but there are many others
whose immediate problem is to get accustomed to the urban
economy. This is the case because numbers of these females
migrants have hardly seen money before or have used it to such
an extent that they are able to calculate how long it will last
and to allocate it throughout a month or a fortnight (Leslie, 1963;
Mandeville, n.d.). Members of a cultivator, or a labourer family, are
used to producing their own food in the village and they soon
discover that nearly all their wages go in acquiring the products
with which their subsistence activities in the village had previously
provided for them.[19] Money wages for the types of jobs which
male immigrants are likely to obtain – in the construction industry,
in public works or in more traditional industries – are often less

[17] As Jellicoe has put it, basing her observation on illiterate women
in Sierra Leone, there is a 'desire for power in order to lead one's
own life and – as a necessary means to this end – the desire for
economic gain' . . . (1955b, p. 42). Of course, 'power' also connotes
'authority' – the ability to control other people's lives – and this is
the light in which many of the men see this matter. However,
although individual women want 'power' for these reasons and
employ, or seek to employ similar methods as the men to obtain it,
this is not the general aim. As indicated, what the women are after
more often is not political kudos or office, but the feeling of
'freedom'.

[18] The extent of literacy among migrant women appears to be a
debatable point. On the one hand, according to Caldwell, it is the
literate rather than the illiterate elements who migrate in Ghana
from the villages (Caldwell, 1968 and 1969); on the other hand,
according to Leslie's estimation in 1963 (p. 30), 82 per cent of Dar
es Salaam's women were entirely uneducated. Only 1 per cent were
educated to beyond Standard 4.

[19] Statistics of family budgets from urban areas in developing countries
are not necessarily comparable in this respect. Nevertheless, they
show that, on the average, the town family spends between one-half
and two-thirds and sometimes much more of their income in buying
food and fuel and in paying rent. Moreover, the family in town
may need to spend more on clothing and to pay for transport to
and from work, an item which may sometimes swallow as much as
10 per cent of the family income for urban workers (see Birmingham,
Neustadt and Amaboe, 1967; and Boserup, 1970, for discussion of this
point).

than twice the wages paid in villages and sometimes little higher than rural wages. Consequently, migrants who get such jobs may be worse off than in their home villages because they must pay for the goods which they or their wives provided for family use in the village (Boserup, 1970, pp. 170–2). There is also a good deal of unemployment with the result, according to some sample surveys, that quite a large proportion of the male population of most African towns are out of work (Gutkind, 1968).[20] One such place is the Federal Territory of Lagos where, in an estimated population of 600,000, some 65,000 persons, all males, were said in 1964 to be actively seeking employment (*ibid.*).

All this makes it necessary for women to contribute to the household's budget, but, as explained, relatively few women are in wage employment. One of the principal reasons is the lack of local industrialization, but there are also complaints that women do not adapt satisfactorily to industrial conditions. For example, the employment of women in a Léopoldville (now Kinshasa) hosiery factory was studied by Capelle and the purport of his report is as follows:

> One category of women works on a belt system of pro-
> duction, and another carries out ancillary work such as
> folding, ironing and packing. In the sewing operations per-
> formed by the first category the workers are almost exclusively
> young women who alone can adapt themselves to the high
> speed of the sewing machines. This work requires a dexterity
> and capacity of adaptation necessitating about three months
> training and even after this period women older than 30
> years of age are unable to keep up. The operators concerned
> displayed the same faults as young factory girls in Europe;
> thoughtlessness, the absence of dependants and therefore of
> real needs, changeable temperament and an almost total
> absence of a sense of discipline, made this labour force
> highly unstable. The problematical attendance rate and out-
> put varied without apparent reason by 30 to 40 per cent
> from one day to another, and with few exceptions the girls

[20] Gutkind puts the figure between 10 and 20 per cent. However, there is the question of whether the term 'unemployed' means in Africa what it does in Western economies, because there are situations in the former context when workers voluntarily or involuntarily engage in employment that takes up only a part of their work potential. In other words, although a man's work sheet will show, perhaps, only three or four days worked in the month he may have been 'gainfully' employed the remainder of the time in, say, petty trade (see Birmingham, Neustadt and Amaboe, pp. 148–9; and Leslie, 1963, pp. 124–5).

came to work for the sole purpose of obtaining enough money to buy a piece of cloth or satisfy some passing need. When they scored the target sum they left without scruple, although the whole period of their employment had been taken up by training. The most trivial event was a sufficient pretext for leaving, although the wage for women was made up on the same basis as a man's wage, i.e. wage, ration, housing and, if applicable, family allowances. They might also qualify for attendance bonuses and, in certain cases, production bonuses.

The lesson of those few years of experience was that there was certainly a real possibility of employing women in wholly mechanized workshops organized on modern lines. The difficulty was to find supervisory staff capable of controlling them and getting an output from them which made their employment worth while. Some women workers able to read and write were found, who exercised a real ascendancy over the others and did the work of forewomen-time keepers. But there was obvious need for supervision as close as that appropriate to highly complicated work entrusted to men, otherwise the advantage represented by a cheaper labour force would be lost. It was felt that only time and the progressive training of a force of women workers could give hope for a substantial improvement in the profitability of female labour

(see Capelle, quoted in *African Women*, March 1956; and 1959)

Also, in Elkan's study of a tobacco factory at Jinja, in Uganda, the main disadvantage was that the women appeared to be consistently slower than men at every task. The work performed included the packing of cigarettes into boxes and feeding tobacco leaves into a machine which removes their stems; but the women's output was always lower than that of men. Possibly the difference was due to differences in training because women's work on the farm requires strength and endurance and a job, such as hoeing, does not develop subtlety of touch. The women were also at a disadvantage over speed and efficiency because they have had less contact with Western gadgets or modes of thought and behaviour than men, and this difficulty was further increased by the fact that hardly any of them speak Swahili, let alone English. The gap between the speed at which men and women reached maximum efficiency was greatest where the job to be learned was most complicated; for example, in the training of machine operators as compared with the training for purely manual jobs like packing.

In other ways, however, there were fewer differences between the performance of men and women, and the latter found it easier, apparently, to spend long hours without a break in monotonous, repetitive work (Elkan, 1956 *passim*).

In these circumstances, it is not surprising that employment policy varies a good deal. Some employers are, for the technical reasons described, not always ready to receive women as a labour force or to pay them at the same rate as men. Others do not discriminate, and in a Kano factory, for example, in which both men and women were employed on sewing machines, payment was made entirely by the results. In other cases, as in Ghana, women are only used in clerical positions (Peil, 1972, p. 30), but a particular difficulty from the employer's point of view is that the habit of early marriage makes childbirth a more frequent event among women workers in Africa. In this regard, whereas Ghana makes provision for three months' pay for women in Government service during their maternity leave, in Malawi women civil servants are required to resign when they marry.

But an equally important factor in this whole matter is traditional opposition to the idea of wives working. In Jinja, for example, Elkan heard it argued that since women are exempt from poll tax opportunities of earning money ought to be reserved for men. This was said even when employers were finding it difficult to fill all their vacancies. Fears were also expressed that women who went out to work would not bear children, and this objection was particularly strong when the employment of wives involved being under the authority of a man who was not their husband. The men's objection [21] was not only to their own wives working for wages but extended to any employer who was prepared to employ women (Elkan, 1956, pp. 45–6). This was because, in the view of some men, for a wife to earn money not only constitutes a threat to a husband's authority and to his ability to control her but may enable her to abscond.[22] Nor are the men necessarily alone in this conservatism. Peil found that even in the relatively industrialized towns of Ghana employment in factories was mostly confined to the younger women, because the working of regular hours was regarded as incompatible with marriage and the rearing of children (1972, *passim*). Women also have their own

[21] The husbands' objection extends, sometimes, even to wives teaching, nursing and minding children. Indeed, male approval of wives taking employment is so far from being universal that there are occasions when a husband will do everything in his power to get his wife dismissed from her post (see also Chapter 9).

[22] That the latter fear is not always imaginary but may have some basis in fact has been indicated in Chapter 2.

ideas of what is suitable work and, despite their desire for economic prosperity, apparently prefer destitution, sometimes, to employment that they regard as derogatory.

Light has been thrown upon this paradoxical situation as well as upon the economic condition of the barely literate category of migrant women by a study made in Kampala by Elizabeth Mandeville. It was designed to enquire into the standard of living available to local households, and so two socio–economically and culturally distinct groups were studied whom Mandeville called respectively 'Drinkers' and 'Employees'. Nearly all 'Drinkers' live on one piece of ground and their houses face in towards a common central area. Some women members of this group sell beer or spirits, several men work locally as odd-jobbing builders or gardeners; and there are also dancers, traders and a prostitute. However, no women, and only three men, are regularly employed. These 'Drinkers' are distinctive in their nostalgia for the old days, their cynicism about power, and the chances of progress and in their choice of entertainment – principally getting drunk. Though landless, the 'Drinkers'' own image of themselves is of friendly and co-operative people; 'Employees', on the other hand, pride themselves on being respectable and particularly on not getting drunk. Being in employment they are not so poor as the 'Drinkers', and their most important characteristic is the desire to get on in the world. This they believe to be possible through patronage and they put less emphasis than do the 'Drinkers' on friends and neighbours. Also, unlike the 'Drinkers', they could probably move to various other parts of Kampala without having to alter their behaviour or attitudes very greatly. Although most of the 'Employees' are manual workers, they typically speak of each other as being clerical workers and they regard people as 'ignorant' and 'local' if they drink native beer (Mandeville, n.d.).[23]

Mandeville estimated the hypothetical needs of a family of two parents and two children in terms of four diets named respectively A, B, C and D. Diet A came first in terms of quantity, quality and cost of food and was followed in turn by diets B, C and D. Of 84 'Employee' households, Mandeville found that 40 per cent could afford diet A and have more than 20s. a month left over; 29 per cent could afford diets A, B or C with not more than 20s. over; 13 per cent could afford D; and 18 per cent could not afford even D. It was also discovered that all-male households had a higher

[23] As indicated in my Acknowledgements I am particularly indebted to Mrs Mandeville for permission to quote these extensive data from her unprinted monograph.

standard of living than households containing both men and women and that the latter were much better off than all-female households. In addition, just over a quarter of childless households, one-third of households with one or two children, and nearly half the households with three or more children could afford only diet *D*, or less. Of 27 'Drinker' households, 33 per cent could afford *A* with more than 20s. a month to spare 33 per cent could afford *A* with less, or *B* or *C*; 19 per cent. could afford *D* and 15 per cent could not afford even *D*. In this 'Drinkers' category most children lived in relatively well-off households. More than half of the 'Drinker' households pay no rent, and for most of those who do pay rents are low. The generally lower standard of living and the different distribution among households were due not to the presence of children or to payment of rents but to lower incomes. Thus, 18 per cent of 'Employees' and 15 per cent of 'Drinkers' could not afford to live at what seemed to be the lowest possible standard.

The incomes of many other people, too, were insufficient if, in addition to their minimum food needs, they required medicine, bus fares, extra clothes or anything beyond a little food, shelter and clothes. How, then, did people make up the deficit? Is the way they do it really a necessity or is it perhaps preferred to other ways of earning a living? These questions were particularly pertinent, because, in addition to the 20 households which could not manage even diet *D*, there were 11 households which had no income from work or rents. These households thus depended entirely on other methods of 'raising the wind', and this included taking irregular extra work; for women, obtaining money from men in exchange for sexual services; accumulating debts; and dependence on other people in exchange for deference: possibly theft also played some part. Irregular work, including weaving mats, cooking for other families and occasionally working as domestic servants, selling firewood and looking after children.

As will be explained later, one of the main ways in which some women subsist in town is by rendering sexual services. Having regard, therefore, to their economic position it is not surprising that a number of households in Mandeville's sample depended wholly or in part on money obtained from men as lovers. Earnings were supplemented in this way in 8 'Employee' households and in a further 7, 'Employee' households had no other known source of income.[24] Some of the women concerned

---

[24] La Fontaine (1970, p. 56) mentions a similar practice in Léopoldville (now Kinshasa) where an unmarried daughter may help her parents or other kin out of her earnings as a prostitute.

were considered prostitutes (*malaya*) while the others could be respectable women. (The distinction between prostitution and other extra-marital forms of sexual relationship will be considered in Chapter 6.) But it appeared from Mandeville's sample that only young women could depend on lovers and only 4 of the 28 involved were over 30 years of age. Only 4 households accumulated debts; that is, owed money over a long period of time without becoming dependent. Five households made themselves dependent on others and this meant that they built up debts of loans and unpaid rent, it being understood that repayment would not be required so long as they were respectful and made themselves useful.

The position of the sexes was quite different in respect of availability of work and attitudes towards it. Thus, 16 'Employee' women, who did no work at all, belonged to households with no income or an adequate income. This was accounted for partly in the fact that 8 of them had young children and so could only work profitably if they earned more than what it would have cost to have their children minded. The other 8 had no special domestic skills but could almost certainly have jobs as servants to Indian or African families. The fact that they did not implied their preference (if single) for getting money from lovers, for working irregularly, or for depending on someone else outside their household. In the case of those who were married, perhaps it was the husband who stopped his wife going out to work.

Of the 'Employee' women 40 work, and of these a small number had sufficient education to gain 'white collar' jobs. Many of the remainder had no education at all; although 2 'Employee' women worked in bars and 1 was a waitress, most of this group were in domestic service. Nineteen of them belonged to households which would be financially independent of others, and 8 came from households living beyond their normal means. Also, it seemed certain that the women in financially dependent households were in that position because of the poorly paid nature of their occupations; and only in 8 cases of women doing no work did it appear that their dependence on others was the result of preference rather than of necessity. But the fact that some women were forced to some form of dependence – usually on men as lovers – did not mean that all women with lovers had them of necessity. On the contrary, most women below the age of about 45 had lovers if they had no husband, whatever their income might be.

Like women in other towns and regions of Africa, the 'Employee' women often said that they wanted to be independent of marriage and, if possible, of men in any relationship. Their typical ambition, too, required a lot of money because what they wanted to achieve was independence through building houses and letting rooms. At the same time, while generally optimistic about the future, the many 'Employee' women depending on lovers' contributions knew that their attractions for the opposite sex could not last for ever.

It was also significant that unskilled and unqualified as most of the 'Employees' were, they themselves rule out certain jobs as quite unsuitable for women (see Xydias, 1956, p. 294). These include beer-selling, spirit-selling, trading in the market, selling from the home, dancing professionally and working in bars. Food-selling, for example, was represented as the work of old, 'local' women, smoking and shouting obscenities; it was by no means regarded as a 'civilized' thing to do. Trading by married women was also ruled out because it would bring them and their children into constant contact with strangers and undesirable company. For similar reasons, bar work, selling beer or spirits independently, and dancing were all rejected as unrespectable. In fact, beer brewers and dancers are in a position to make a lot of money, but 'Employee' women chose poverty and independence in preference to jobs that were looked upon as unsuitable and degrading. They chose, in other words, to be 'Employees' rather than independent, and even the prostitutes passed muster because in other respects their behaviour was proper. They had 'beautiful manners', did not drink, went to the mosque, and took good care of their children as well as being related to the 'old élite' of Kampala and to a very respectable 'Employee' household.

Among 'Drinkers', on the other hand, trading, alcohol-selling and dancing were not at all disapproved of, and some of the most respected women were in those occupations. Whether 'white collar' jobs were suitable did not arise because none of the women had any secondary education or could speak English or Swahili with any fluency. In addition to 3 mixed households which could not manage even diet D, there were 4 households which had no normal income and a number of the women were primarily or entirely dependent on lovers. In fact, the general evidence suggested that 'Drinkers' women voluntarily did not work. Instead, the aim of most of them seemed to be to get by until their children were old enough to support them; and it also appeared that the selling of alcohol – mostly by middle-aged or elderly women – was normally taken up after a period of changing husbands and lovers and bearing children. In other words, a woman did not normally set up in business until her charms had faded; but the 'Drinker' tendency to ask and to give help freely made the danger of pennilessness between one lover and the next less in their case.

Indeed, it appears that inadequate incomes and consequent dependence on others were largely involuntary among 'Employees' and voluntary among 'Drinkers', the requirements of respectability being a major factor among the former group. To 'Drinkers' of both sexes, on the other hand, an unregulated and undemanding working life came first, and although many 'Drinkers' came with the intention of going home prosperous, they later gave up the attempt to do so. Probably, the 'Drinkers' casual attitude towards work and their over-riding loyalty between neighbours were incompatible with the pursuit of a career or of money; and so the norm of friendliness and co-operation might be as much a constraint for 'Drinkers' as was respectability for 'Employees'. In other words, 'Drinkers' and 'Employees' alike were prevented by their respective norms from remedying their economic plight. Also, most people in these two categories were poor in some degree because only 40 per cent of 'Employee' and 30 per cent of 'Drinker' households had more than 20s. per month for minimal requirements; and to make matters more difficult, people normally expected to spend at once some of their weekly or monthly income before settling down again to austere living. For example, men and women went out for a drink, women had their hair done, and men, perhaps, looked out for temporary mistresses. In addition, there were essential items, such as medical expenses and powdered milk for babies whose mothers could not breast-feed them.

The case of one of the 'Employees' illustrates the above points. She was a young woman with three daughters who earned, on average 60s. a month and had, in addition, 150s. from her former husband to support the children. This enabled her to live at the level of Diet C, but a large part of her income disappeared at the beginning of the month: in rent, debts, having her hair done, an evening's entertainment, and in cakes, milk and meat for her daughters and a few shillings' gift to someone poorer than herself. By the middle of the month she had little left and there was rarely a lover willing, or able, to help her. Such relatives as she had in Kampala were also poor and if they, too, were unable to feed her children, she simply left them without food in the hope of neighbours taking pity on them. She regularly obtained credit at the market, but was on bad terms with her father and his wife because her husband had never paid bridewealth. Since, moreover, they lived thirty-five miles away she could not afford the time or the fares to seek help from them in person. And so what could she do? Well, in the last resort – if, for example, several months' rent were outstanding – she might resume sexual relations with her former husband for more money; sell furniture or clothes; obtain rent by sharing her room temporarily with homeless people; or, finally, risk both pregnancy and disease by sleeping casually with men for money. The last few days of the month she rarely eats at all but drinks sweet, milkless tea and sleeps a lot instead. She rejects beer-selling or trading as a solution and pins her hopes on other things – on being lucky enough to find work or on being made pregnant by a man rich enough to support her as a permanent ' outside wife ' [25] (Mandeville, n.d.).

These Kampala communities have been described not because they are typical of African urban women as a whole, but because of the wide difference in women's living standards as well as ambition. Thus, in striking contrast are business women in the larger West African towns who have shops and stores of their own. These women merchants are not nearly so numerous as male buyers of produce and retailers. Nevertheless, some of them conduct their business on an extensive scale and in Nigeria, for example, they trade chiefly in textiles bought wholesale from European firms, a thousand pounds' worth at a time, and sell retail, through their own employees in bush markets as well as in town. Others trade in fish or palm oil, own lorries, build themselves European-type houses, and have their sons educated overseas. Most of these ' merchant princesses ' are illiterate or semi-literate,[26] but Bauer's reference (1954, p. 31) to three Onitsha women who traded in partnership for 25 years and had an annual turnover of £100,000 indicates that at least, in individual cases, women are commercially much more successful than the great majority of their male counterparts.[27] Some Ghana women, too, are said to have credits of thousands of pounds sterling with overseas firms and to act as intermediaries to women retailers (Galleti, Baldwin and Dina, 1956). One such female entrepreneur, now the managing director of a tinned fruit company with an annual turnover of about £35,000, started business with 6s. capital (*West Africa*, 1969a).[28] But in Ghana, as in Nigeria, women

---

[25] This is a technical term whose usage is explained in Chapter 7.

[26] In the background of Ghanaian women traders, middle school education seems to have been a great help, although Garlick found no correlation between education and turnover among the traders he interviewed. Illiterate traders employed relatives, usually sons or nephews, to keep the accounts for them (1971, p. 32).

[27] For a short case-study on successful entrepreneurship on the part of a Nigerian woman, see the appendix, pp. 201–2.

[28] She began by selling a dozen pots of marmalade at 100 per cent profit in the Accra market!

seem to do best in textiles and, according to Addae, even market women dealing in these goods had incomes of several hundred pounds a year and some had incomes running into four figures (1954, p. 49).

However, the great majority of these West African market women and others in commerce are petty traders to an extent which in Ghana, for instance, amounts to 28 per cent of the women, compared with 6 per cent of the men, earning money in this sphere. For example, in Accra nearly 9 out of every 10 women gainfully employed were in trade [29] and this was also the case in Lagos, where women petty traders were approximately 15 times more numerous than those who sewed and made dresses – the next most popular occupation. In Dakar, too, the percentage of women traders is almost as large and so is the proportion in some of the smaller towns.[30] Also, in addition to market women are the numerous petty traders who are to be found at a crossroads, along the side of a busy street or on the verandah of a house. Although their stock does not amount to more than a tray of goods and their profit is usually very modest [31] it is a useful way of supplementing the household budget.

Women also dominate the markets in Zaire, and in Rhodesia, Zambia and Malawi there are more women than men among the sellers. Also, among the numerous Luo in Kenya, it is rare to find a woman who does not trade in some small way (Ominde, 1952), but in East African towns a large proportion of the shopkeepers are Indians and it is more customary for men than women to engage in commerce. On the other hand, despite some traditional prejudices of the kind described above, the situation varies and of the 1,664 venders counted in a study of Kampala markets, women formed 40.6 per cent of the total (Temple, 1968/9, pp. 155–65). On the whole, however, the sale of beer rather than trade is the women's main commercial occupation; and although the women of Kampala act as assistants in African-owned shops, none of these occupations can rival the attractions of beer-selling. It is

[29] In fact, according to Nypan (1960) 85 per cent of the *stall holders* (not of all traders) in Accra market are women.

[30] For example, in Koforidua, a Ghanaian town of between 25,000 and 30,000 inhabitants, McCall (1961, p. 92) found that 70 per cent of the female population was engaged in selling. McCall's article provides some interesting illustrations of the social implications of market trading. See next chapter.

[31] Nypan (1960), for example, estimates in a sample of Accra street traders, that one-half had turnovers of less than £2 per day. However, a higher than average profit may result from selling commodities in very small units (e.g. a few matches or a single cigarette) (Garlick, 1971, p. 50).

therefore mainly in West Africa where trading has the greatest economic importance for women,[32] and so it will suffice if we conclude this chapter by a brief reference to the functioning of some households studied in Monrovia.

In this investigation Fraenkel found that in the 'civilized', middle-class communities elementary families accounted for nearly half of the households in her sample and were twice as frequent as extended ones. At the other extreme (in New Krutown), households consisting only of one elementary family numbered 3 of the 50 in the sample, and there were eleven times as many extended families. The majority of these households drew their corporate income from a number of different sources, and 30 out of the 50 households concerned contained more than two income-earning adults, the number of such earners per household being greater in this community than in any other surveyed. One large house, with ten rooms, containing in all thirty-four interrelated members, had no less than twenty income earners, including stevedores, a carpenter, women market-sellers and fish-sellers (1964, pp. 126–9).

All these people ate together and made their budget as one unit, and this is the usual pattern in such circumstances. Cooking may be done in turn by the women, or one woman who is not engaged in market-selling may be assigned this task. Fraenkel explains that:

> Wages and trading profits are, theoretically at least, handed to the household head and re-allocated by him among the various members of the household. The man who brings in cash normally gets part of it back; the *sla bi* [house father] retains a part to cover household maintenance and repairs,

[32] This point is in its contemporary context correctly stressed. But as far back as pre-colonial times both urban and rural women had some experience in trading and were already accustomed to the idea of taking charge of their own property. Thus, in Yorubaland during the earliest tribal wars, the mutual need to hold markets seems normally to have been recognized sufficiently to allow transactions to be safely carried out on neutral territory: the women would go to the market, the opposing warriors remaining at a distance on either side. Possibly, too, the predominance of women in Yoruba markets dates back to times when it was unsafe for men to move away from their farms while women enjoyed relative immunity from attacks.

This prominence of women in markets was commented on by the earliest European travellers, and Lander, for instance, remarked that at Egga (Egua), 'the principal market-town in this part of Africa, women were the chief if not the only traders'. On the other hand some of the early observers also noted significant numbers of men in the markets (Lander and Lander, 1832, Vol. 1, pp. 179–80; quoted in Hodden and Ukwu, 1969).

purchase of land, and so on, and sometimes for his personal use; the remainder he hands to his wife, or his head wife if he has two. She in turn subdivides the amount into cash to be spent on food and cash used for the purchase of trade goods [i.e. goods for sale], and divides the latter sum between herself (if she is a trader) and other women traders in the household. Profits from the women's trading return to the *sla bi* through the head wife, a fairly clear distinction being made between capital and profits, the individual trader retaining the capital. This income is then re-allocated by the *sla bi* in the same manner as the wages of the men in the household. *(Ibid.* p. 131)

Fraenkel points out, however (p. 132), that the above is a somewhat idealized picture because individual members may often retain some of their earnings for various personal purposes, and there is also considerable variation in the balance of authority between household head and head wife. In addition, each married couple within the house may be given some autonomy in the management of its earnings.

Fraenkel's report thus brings out especially the importance of the women's trading activities to the household economy. In five detailed budgets compiled daily over three months, the proceeds of women's trading amounted in one case to 47 per cent of the household's total income and in another household the equivalent figure was 78 per cent. In all cases where the household contained women traders other than the head, the women worked as a group, the head wife sharing out cash for the purchase of trade goods, and the other women, in return, handing their profits to her. The former retain the *capital* to use as they wish – for spending, saving, or for the purchase of more trade goods, and in one such household the head wife gave the second wife $7.50 during the month for buying trade goods. The latter made a total profit of $29 which she handed to the head wife as it came in and retained the capital of $7.50. This second wife was investing money in a savings club and, in addition, was paying some of her savings over to a friend for safe keeping. Not all of the women traders are so successful, although one of Fraenkel's informants was so impressed by his former wife's trading abilities that he was moved to express as much affection for her as for his mother. He said:

I give her [the former wife] a pack of cigarettes, she twist small small, and come back in the evening with 5 cents profit. I give her a carton, and she bring me back 2 cartons. I love that woman, she is like my ma, my heart was broken when she left me. Some time man has no work, women must provide. (*Ibid.* pp. 145–6)

Indeed, the seasonal and intermittent nature of much male employment emphasizes the household's underlying dependence on the women. If they are out of work men go fishing sometimes, or paint houses, but these activities are only possible during the dry season. The women, on the other hand, are able to carry on their trading activities all the year round despite the heavy rains making it difficult, sometimes, for them to get to market. In fact, women traders are a relatively new phenomenon among the Kru, but the new authority and independence which these women traders in Monrovia have thus gained in financial matters has changed relationships between the sexes. This factor, plus the periodic absence of many of the men on trips down the coast, gives rise to a good deal of marital disharmony.

This species of problem, however, will be discussed in a later chapter.

4 Women's urbanization through voluntary associations

In the last chapter we pointed out the widespread role of women as venders. This occupation is popular because it can often be combined with domestic duties, including the minding of children, and is relatively pleasant in comparison with farming. Also, although market women work hard, there is a social atmosphere in the market: it is their club as well as their place of business. Women plait each other's hair while waiting for customers to buy their goods; they gossip or nurse their small children, or otherwise occupy themselves. The market has become virtually a woman's world (McCall, 1961, p. 291). This is particularly the case among Yoruba women for whom attending a market is part of their way of life. Petty trading in Yorubaland is more than a commercial activity, it is a pleasure and a necessity, as well as a skill, the 'essence of social life'. In the market not only are bargains to be made, but there is gossip and banter and a chance to make assignations. Indeed for these reasons many West African women do not regard trade as an occupation, and not all women in the market are interested in material gain to the same extent. Those who have a 'pin-money' trade,[1] for instance, do not think primarily in terms of making a profit, the point being rather that they have something there for sale (cf. Bauer, 1954, p. 11; Hodden and Ukwu, 1969, pp. 50–1; Mabogunje, 1959, pp. 5–12; Marris, 1961, p. 45; Marshall, 1962).

However, the fact also that in West Africa, at least, trading is the urban woman's main form of economic support can be explained by two main reasons. Firstly, it is quite often the custom for a husband to give his wife a small weekly stipend; or alternatively he may allot her a sum of money at the time of her

---

[1] This applies, also, to numbers of élite women among whom it is the 'done thing' to run a small business, such as a boutique or a poultry farm.

marriage and she is expected to maintain herself from that through trading for the rest of her life (cf. McCall, 1961).

Secondly, the women's trading is greatly assisted by the voluntary associations which, in many cases, they themselves set up. These organizations help their members to start a business or to enlarge the trade they are already doing by providing the necessary capital. They put the woman trader in touch with customers and they show migrant women and other women who are new to business methods how to save and how most effectively to re-invest their profits in further enterprises. What is equally important for women who are endeavouring to establish themselves is that these associations also regulate trading practices and prevent under-cutting. For example, in Lagos market there is a separate section for each commodity – fish, the different kinds of vegetables, cloth, etc. and the women sit according to the commodity in which they deal.[2] Each such section has its own such association, or *egbe*, which discourages competition between women trading in that particular article. Such is the sense of solidarity – the women gossip together, eat, drink, and spend the entire day in each other's company – that it is said to be unthinkable for a trader to disobey her market *egbe* in this matter. Any women under-cutting is ostracized by her fellows, who may even take a case against her, reporting it to the leader of the *egbe* and if necessary to the *Iyalode* (Queen of the Markets). It is said that this official is a recognized chief, taking second place only to the *Oba* (king) at official functions (E.C.A., 1962, p. 37). The *egbe* also sees to it that no male trader deals in certain commodities customarily regarded as the business of women (Baker, n.d.; Comhaire-Sylvain, 1950, pp. 183–4).[3]

Similarly, sometimes, there are also informal arrangements for regulating trading in places where independent women retailers dominate the street markets. For example, in a suburb of Kampala women selling *matoke*, or charcoal, referred to each other, according to age, as – 'daughter' and 'sister', and although there was no set obligation or rule of behaviour they endeavoured to prevent

---

[2] Herskovits provides a similar example from Dahomey, though at a rather earlier date (1938). For a detailed description of these women's associations in general, see Little, 1965, especially Chapter 7.

[3] Somewhat similarly, a Bread Sellers' Union was formed in Sekondi–Takoradi when supplies were very short, with the object of acquiring flour and sugar from the importing firms for distribution amongst the members, all of whom were licensed bakers. Other Sekondi traders, mostly women, tried to restrict the buying and selling of corn, rice, yams and other vegetables to the members of their own Foodstuffs Sellers' Union (Busia, 1950, pp. 25–6).

too many women selling *matoke* all within the same spot. Since they attempted to disperse sellers and to prevent too intensive competition there appeared to be a market-sharing system – a form of guild (Southall and Gutkind, 1957, pp. 138–9). Thus, on one occasion, a prostitute who had been driven by the police from another part of the town, settled at a place where there were many sellers of *matoke*. Not having ascertained first to whom and where she might sell her own *matoke*, she was asked by the local venders to leave. If she had refused, they would have asked a native doctor to remove her. This would have caused a lot of trouble and so she departed (*ibid.*).[4]

Sometimes, market *egbes* also attempt to buy in bulk for their members, thus obtaining produce from the farmers at a cheaper rate and saving the overheads of buyers. Other women's organizations take steps to ensure supplies of the commodity in which its members trade. For example, members of a fish-sellers' union in Takoradi clubbed together in fours and sixes to raise money to buy fishing nets, which were sold to the fishermen on agreed terms. A fisherman who received a net sold his catch during the fishing season to the creditor group, and the value of the fish was reckoned against the net. If a fisherman was able to pay for the net in one season, it became his own, but he continued to sell his fish to his fishermen creditors who now became his regular customers. In this way, the women were able to obtain the fish on which their livelihood depended (Busia, 1950, pp. 25–6).

In addition, women's associations have undertaken the production of goods for themselves in some cases. In southern Nigeria, for instance, their societies have run a bakery, a laundry, a calabash factory, and a 'gari' mill,[5] and one of the most interesting of these, the Egba Women's Union in Abeokuta, claimed a membership of 80,000 women paying subscriptions of 1s. a year. It operated as a weaving corporation, and it ran a maternity and child welfare clinic (Hodgkin, 1956, p. 90). The latter association also conducted classes for illiterate women, and this is a service that other women's groups provide since it enables the people concerned to acquire a rudimentary knowledge of English or French. This is useful for trading [6] because both the registration of goods and the necessity of dealing with wholesalers and customers speaking a different language are helped by literacy.

---

[4] Note how, as mentioned in Chapter 6, a dispute over 'territory' gave rise to physical combat between rival groups of prostitutes in Abidjan.

[5] 'Gari' is made from cassava.

[6] And also for social and political purposes. See later paragraph and Chapter 8.

A final example of the numerous organizations and schemes which provide women with benefits and helps them to save is 'Nanemei Akpee' (Society of Friends) in Ghana. The great majority of Nanemei Akpee's members being market women, its principal function is the regular provision of working capital, and this is done by holding meetings once every week at which a collection is taken. All the women present hand over as much money as they feel they can afford and their contributions are written in the book supplied to each member for this purpose and containing her number and name. The officials receiving this money also have a list of the society's members in order of seniority, depending upon the date on which they have joined. When the collection is finished, all the money is given to the member whose name has the first place on the list; the following week it is given to the second, then to the third, and so on. Eventually, all members will in this way receive a contribution, though the process as a whole naturally takes a very long time. However, the system is also fairly elastic, and if a member urgently needs cash, perhaps because of some business or domestic crisis, she may be allowed to jump the queue of weekly subscriptions, and so receive her collection before she is entitled to do so. This provides a very useful alternative to negotiating a private loan.

Nanemei Akpee has branches in several towns and it also provides its members with a donation each time they have a child. Substantial gifts of money or toys are also given at the 'outdooring' ceremony which takes place eight days after birth. There are sick benefits too, and on the death of a member, about £10 is given to the deceased's family and a contribution made to the funeral expenses.[7] The association also comes to the aid of a member whose property has been stolen, and on one occasion the society arranged for two of its well-to-do members to make an interest-free loan of £500 to another member in danger of being imprisoned for having embezzled this sum from a trading firm. The society's own funds depend upon an entrance fee of 5s. and weekly dues of 3d. per member, but it may appeal to its members for a special contribution in the event of financial difficulties of its own. The amount levied per head is fixed by the committee after discussion at a general meeting. Dances, jumble sales and bazaars are also organized as further methods of raising money (Bandoh, n.d., Carey, n.d.).[8]

[7] The society does not pay for a memorial service, however, in the case of a pagan's burial.

[8] Institutions of the above kind have been termed 'rotating credit

Women's urbanization through voluntary associations

These, then, are some of the ways in which women's adaptation to the economic life of the town is assisted by voluntary associations. In fact, women's participation in these organizations has even wider implications because, in addition to the various ethnic and tribal groups which tend to segment the urban social structure, there are wide differences in living standards which are, as a rule, spatially demarcated in the larger towns and cities. For example, in Ibadan there is the 'Core Area' or 'Old Ibadan' where a rough estimate of the average family income was between £50–£100 per person; the newer residential area between 'Old Ibadan' and the suburbs, where average annual incomes ranged approximately between £200 and £1,500 per annum; and the residential area around the periphery of the city, where average annual incomes ranged between £350 and £3,000 (Mabogunje, 1962, pp. 56–9). The result of this social and economic differentiation is an embryonic system of 'classes' whose members are broadly characterized by certain similarities in outlook which tend, at certain points, to over-ride ethnic affiliations. This means, in effect, that a degree of re-orientation in 'class' terms is part of the process of becoming 'urbanized' and that the individual involved needs to conform with the norms of the urban status aspired to. In other words, although in the latter wealth, education, political position and education tend to be the major criteria, associated canons of personal behaviour have also to be followed. These are consonant with local ideas of what constitutes proper 'civilized', Christian or Islamic conduct, and the individual displaying it enjoys social prestige and certain practical as well as social advantages.[9]

Caught up in this situation are women already resident in the town as well as migrants and so its implications affect even some of the leaders. These are women who already have authority and are influential, but they went to school twenty or twenty-five years ago when the significance of English was not foreseen and the headlong pace of political and social development unsuspected. They feel handicapped because their command of English is insufficient to express their thoughts and ideas to the wider public they wish to reach.[10] Consequently, when it was suggested by the politicians that Swahili should be adopted by Uganda as a *lingua*

associations' (Geertz, 1962). For a fuller description of these organizations among West African women, see Little, 1965, p. 47ff.

[9] It is important to appreciate that the illiterate woman is probably just as 'status-conscious' as any other category (see Jellicoe, 1955b, pp. 41–2).

[10] The significance of this point becomes evident if one studies some reports of parliamentary debates. From these it is obvious that English is not the politicians' first language.

franca in the cause of political unity, the women did not agree. They opted, instead, for English, pointing out that it is the language of government, business, commerce and industry, and of all kinds of education after the sixth grade. Furthermore, not only is it the means of communication between Africans of different language groups, between Africans and other racial groups, but English is the only key to vast quantities of printed material (Bell, 1962, p. 74).[11] Then, there are other semi-literate women of mature years who, having made their little 'pile' in trade, want to acquire some of the social graces as construed, perhaps, in terms of sewing and crochet work skills. Younger women of marriageable age, too, wish to 'keep in the swim'. As explained more fully in Chapter 8, having had but a few years at school themselves, they feel that the best chance of getting the kind of husband they are after is to imitate the ways and mannerisms of their more educated and sophisticated sisters.

There is thus a widespread urge to become 'townswomen' in a fuller sense, and since they cater for these social needs the function of voluntary associations is correspondingly extensive. As subsequent paragraphs will show, every level of society is affected, but the contrast between her rural environment and that of the more cosmopolitan city makes it illuminating to begin with the female migrant. She, it is true, may have relatives or village-mates to shelter her; but their own experience of town ways may be as limited as her own. Further, if such support is lacking, to whom can she turn for help, advice, and solicitude? She may need, in effect, a substitute for the accustomed warmth and companionship of family life at home, and it is precisely this that most voluntary associations are designed to supply. They invariably emphasize a fraternal spirit in terms of members being actively urged to regard each other as brothers and sisters, to sympathize with each other in times of difficulty, visiting each other when sick, or swelling the procession at a funeral. 'Family' feelings are further enhanced by emblems, mottoes and banners and by the custom of wearing a uniform style of dress. Above all, meetings themselves are sociable occasions; they include excursions and picnics; concerts, singing, dancing and drumming; religious talks and discussions, literary classes, debates, and cinema shows; first-aid services; initiation ceremonies for new members; and the laying of wreaths on graves of former members. All this

---

[11] In expressing a similar point of view, women in Rhodesia said that they wanted literacy in a vernacular language and in English for reason of status, for practical purposes, and because it is the language that their husbands and children learn.

helps to restore to the migrant woman the sense of identity she may have lost in moving so far from her own community. In addition, voluntary associations often offer a host of minor titles and offices, thereby giving even the most humble individual an opportunity to feel that she 'matters'. It also facilitates her making friends with women more sophisticated than herself (Little, 1965, pp. 85ff.).

To have such a reference group [12] is important because membership of a voluntary association imposes duties different from those of the rural village. Not only is a member expected to appear punctually at meetings, but she is encouraged to adopt up-to-date standards of dress and personal hygiene and take part in recreational activities with members of the opposite sex. This experience is valuable because life in town being more individualistic, a 'new girl' finds herself in sexual as well as social competition with other women. She needs, therefore, to know how to deal with men, young and old, on her own; and the requisite re-socialization in this and other sectors of urban life is provided very effectively by the kind of ethnic or clan union which abounds in West and East African towns. These regional associations, as they are alternatively called,[13] are referred to in this way to distinguish them from organizations that also practise mutual aid but whose members are united by other factors, such as age, occupation and education.[14]

Eight such associations entirely composed of Luo migrants (Parkin, 1969, pp. 151–2), exist in Kampala, for example, and it has been estimated that in Accra municipality more than 16,000 persons belong to such groups, the sex ratio being 1 female to 2·4 males (Little, 1965, p. 27). Since the primary aim of such organizations is to maintain a close attachment to the home town or village, membership keeps women immigrants from the same rural area in touch with each other. For example, social activities include periodical celebrations, the organization of dances on festival days, and some of these unions produce an annual maga-

[12] As explained later (Chapter 8), the importance of a reference group whose style of life, dress, deportment, etc., can be copied, is evident at higher social levels of society as well.

[13] The term applied to them in the French-speaking countries is *associa-tion d'originaire*.

[14] In fact, although members of a particular union speak of themselves in tribal terms, membership qualifications are relatively liberal. For example, membership of the Luo Union in Kampala 'is open to . . . all adult Luo men and women . . . any other adult person other than Luo who lives within the Luo community and agrees with Luo customs and traditions and with this constitution' (Parkin, 1969, pp. 151–2; see also Parkin, 1966, *passim*, for further relevant information).

zine, called an Almanac. In this their members' activities are recorded, and special efforts are made to look after and welcome persons newly arrived from the country. In these ways – through reception committees and by holding 'send off' parties – they maintain a means whereby the migrant women can maintain contact with their rural relatives and friends (cf. Little, 1965, p. 29). Tribal and ethnic unions also operate mutual benefit schemes which provide monetary assistance in the case of sickness and bereavement (*ibid.* p. 28).

Sometimes, the idea is to supply the members' own native village with up-to-date amenities – hospitals, schools, roads – equal to those of the place into which the migrants have moved. The fact, however, that these and other organizations frequently combine indigenous practices with modernity, introduces innovations within a familiar context and so makes them seem less strange. For example, in a Bamako association known as the *bara*, membership is confined to youngsters of both sexes, and traditional dances are performed. A *tabaski* (modern feast) is an occasion for special celebration, including friendly contacts between the various branches in town. It begins with a usual performance, but a dinner party in the European fashion is then put on. Thirty to forty tables are set in the street with plates and silverware,[15] the food being prepared by the female members. The dinner starts at 9 or 11 p.m. and goes on until 3 or 4 o'clock in the morning, while between courses the guests dance modern European dances. The next Sunday, the several *bara* in town invite each other to perform together, the host association offering drinks (Meillassoux, 1968, pp. 112–16).

The *bara*, in other words, provides a bridge between one social universe and another. Although its cultural background is traditional, the young unmarried people concerned have taken up the cultural inheritance of their elders, and have transformed the association into a dynamic and lively institution devoted not only to carrying on customs and folklore from an ancient social order, but to adapting to the urban milieu and to new social needs. If the entertainment is still founded on tradition, *bara* members, nevertheless, dance European jive and, once a year, adopt European manners and attitudes (*ibid.* p. 116). The girls, moreover, enjoy special privileges. They are a representative body, have the advantage of paying lower fees than the boys and, possess above all, the freedom to choose their own partners.

The way in which girls are encouraged to adapt to Western and

[15] Although it is still common in all social circles to eat with the hands (Meillassoux, 1968, p. 115).

urban styles of life is also shown in the organization of the *gūbe*, which is another Bamako association. For one thing, some of the names such as ' Jeunesse ', ' Esperance ' etc. are clearly an attempt to sound ' foreign ', and the girls as well as the boys are expected to behave in the European manner. Also, that new values, linked to modern economic life, are replacing the old ones, is indicated by the fact that a job and money incomes have become the most important qualifications for membership. In short, the trend being in the direction of a new form of social stratification, the young people and their associations are scaled according to socio-economic criteria. Looked at, therefore, from the point of view of women's changing position these Westernized young people's clubs represent a ' groping attempt ' not only to shape a new society and a new social order, but new sexual relationships as well (Meillassoux, 1968, pp. 120–42).

The latter development is symbolized in the *bara* dancing, in which every boy was supposed to have a girl friend. The choice of partner being made by the girls, new female members who join are given the opportunity of selecting their male companions.[16] Choice is restricted to those who were not already 'affianced ', since ' monogamy ' is the rule (*ibid*. pp. 112–16). The purpose of the *gūbe*, too, is to facilitate meetings between young people; and, as in the *bara*, girls are entitled to choose partners, but must renew their choice every three or four months. On this particularly agonizing day for the boys, each girl, in turn, throws her scarf on her *kamele*, the rule being that the boy selected must accept the girl as his *amante* or *to-suguru*.[17] He can repudiate her later, but at the cost of a heavy fine. Girls can also quit their *kamele* (lit. young men of the age to be married), even though it was they who chose him, but they pay a lower fine. Several girls can pick the same boy, who must ask the first *seguru's* permission to accept the new ones. These *gūbe* arrangements provide an opportunity of courtship, but they do not necessarily lead to matrimony. Nevertheless, they enable a girl as well as a young man to exert

---

[16] The girls were given a scarf to throw on the boy they selected. This appears to be a widely spread method of selecting a male partner because its use has been reported in a traditional type of *compin* organized by Fulbe migrants in Sierra Leone (Butcher, 1964). Also, as reported in Chapter 6, prostitutes sometimes follow a similar practice. In both these cases, the choice is made for sexual purposes; but girls dancing in the traditional manner sometimes throw their head-tie as a polite gesture to a distinguished male member of the audience. Needless to add, the recipient is expected to return the compliment with money.

[17] According to Meillassoux's glossary (p. 153), ' to-suguru ' means literally ' association-girl '.

charm and appeal within the safety of an institutional or limiting organization (Meillassoux, 1968, pp. 120–), and 'La Goumbé,' a recreational association in the Ivory Coast, is the example *par excellence* of such facilities. Membership is restricted virtually to young people, only girls of marriageable age being admitted; but the important thing is that under the auspices of La Goumbé marriages are contracted and celebrated and the society provides both wedding presents and maternity benefits (Holas, 1953, pp. 116–31).

Advantages of the above kind largely depend upon the rules which most associations with a mixed membership have in order to regulate relationships between persons of opposite sex. In particular, the societies which arrange entertainment take care to prevent unchaperoned women from being seduced. Thus, another Bamako dancing association – '*segu-ka-bara*' – punishes adultery by fining or expulsion (Meillassoux, 1968, pp. 103–6); a Freetown dancing *compin* (Krio for 'company') sternly decrees that no male member 'shall fall in love with any female members of the society'; and, in addition, there are certain less formal but salutary methods, of a traditional kind, for checking anti-social or improper conduct. Banton has described how some of the *compins'* songs can wield the weapon of ridicule and ensure conformity with the association's standards.

The shame of it, Ai Kamara, the shame of it!
Ai Kamara bore a child:
He had no sooner grown up than she made him her husband.
Ah, friends, let us come together
And consider if this is what is done in Temne-land?

(1957, p. 175)

Nor is this display of respectability a mere pretence. For married women the advantage is that they can go out at night, and the reputation of unmarried girls is safe-guarded because it is known that there is a woman official to supervise them. Voluntary associations also concern themselves quite often with the public behaviour of their members and have methods of disciplining those who jeopardise the group's good name in the town by rowdiness and quarrelsome behaviour. That these organizations are able to control personal conduct to such an extent is due to their members being taught to regard themselves as belonging to the same family.

These considerations are the more important for women anxious to live on good terms with their new neighbours because among the town's ethnically heterogeneous population there are few agreed patterns and social values are confused. Younger people could previously go to an elder of the kin group for advice; but, now, they have to make decisions on their own and to assume personal responsibilities for which they have not been groomed. Nor is the situation for adult people any clearer. According to which standard of behaviour, for example, is an illiterate mother to prepare a daughter at school for marriage? Tradition emphasizes its economic and procreative purposes, whereas it is to the 'Western' idea of a companionate relationship that the educated girl learns to aspire.[18] It is this kind of dilemma that makes the voluntary association's position so influential because in answer to ambiguity they have a definite policy of their own. They may, as in the separatist churches, compromise with traditional attitudes to the extent of condoning polygamy; but they all support marriage as an institution. They do their best to remove causes of marital friction and they endeavour to strengthen the relationship of man and wife in various ways. This is the case irrespective of whether the groups concerned are led by educated or illiterate women (Little, 1965, *passim*). For example, in Lagos as in other towns, there are church associations and the husbands of members are invited to meetings so that the difficulties of modern marriage can be discussed with them. Guidance is also given individually in some cases (Baker, n.d.), and in Bo, Sierra Leone, a Moslem women's society follows the same practice. It intervenes in domestic quarrels, and attempts to reconcile man and wife. Members who are constant troublemakers in the home risk expulsion from the association (Little, 1951).

Consequently, the exclusiveness and conventional behaviour which characterize élite associations of women (see Chapter 8) are not confined to the educated class. Many of the traditionally based associations gain their reputation in a similar way; and, to take a single example, the most highly regarded Sierra Leone *compins* are those with the strictest rules. Next come the other companies, and after them the benefit societies, which resemble them in limited respects. Tribal dancing societies come low down, and informal dancing groups are at the bottom. In Freetown, at any rate, it appears that prestige attaches to associations the more they copy certain European practices, the more Islamized they are and the more they call upon valued elements in the traditional culture of the tribe concerned (Banton, 1957, pp. 191–2).[19] Thus,

[18] See Chapters 8 and 9 for an elaboration of this important point.

[19] The Islamic element is important as representing the alternative to the magical basis of indigenous associations, for while the 'progressive' young people look down on the latter societies they seem to be a little afraid of their medicine (Banton, 1959).

by insisting on the desirability of certain practices, the societies concerned set standards of social achievement. Since this, in turn, marks out their members as persons worthy of respect (Little, 1965, pp. 155–67), it is something that the migrant woman can use to her advantage. It means, in other words, that by gaining admission into a particular association, she may raise quite considerably her rating in other people's eyes.

Young women who are less well-off are also helped to ' better ' themselves by clubs of business and professional women who have philanthropic interests. One organization of this kind was formed in 1962 at Enugu, Eastern Nigeria, and had twenty members by 1964. Members included teachers, nurses, a physiotherapist, a dietician and the country's first agricultural superintendent, the main aim being to bring more and more women into the professions and into trade by helping girls through secondary school. In its efforts to provide information on careers for schoolgirls, the club has started a ' careers project '. This involves a well-prepared meeting in a rented hall where a member gives a talk on her own profession; what qualifications were needed, how these can be obtained, what opportunities offer for employment, and so forth (*Women Today*, 1964).

Also, in addition to women's élite associations, such as the Red Cross, there are usually groups which are formed or led by schoolteachers and other educated women. Most of these organizations endeavour to provide instruction free of charge in such things as child and family welfare, domestic skills, literacy, and so on. Sometimes, these organizations have the wider aim of training women in better understanding of national and world affairs and the part that women could play in community leadership.

Finally, there are the almost countless associations connected directly or indirectly with Christian bodies and sometimes with Islamic institutions, mainly the mosque. Though primarily concerned, as a rule, with religious education and evangelical work, these associations also provide practical instruction in homecraft and in hobbies useful to women.[20] Quite often they have branches in several towns and there is a highly ramified system of ' Mother Fellowships ' centred on the association's headquarters in the capital. To the extent, therefore, that these groups also help their members to adapt to the life of the town they, too, play a part in the general urbanization of women.

[20] For a short description of this type of association in West Africa, see Little (1965, pp. 66ff.); also Parkin (1966).

5 Women in the political arena

In Chapter 2 it was explained that there are certain categories of
rural women who take refuge in the town and that for these
persons townward migration frequently has positive implications.
It represents a conscious or unconscious attempt to improve status.

In this regard, therefore, the women are motivated by the same
basic urge as that which, during colonial times, prompted the
younger men to organize themselves for political and other forms
of action. The women and the younger men may have started
from different positions but they have been equally eager to
promote social change. They have aspired to a better place in the
sun. This being the case, it is not surprising that both parties have
frequently joined forces, especially in the Christian churches and
in the new voluntary associations which have introduced innovations. Anang Ibibio women, for example, believed that being
Christian afforded more opportunity for religious expression, for in
the indigenous religion manipulation of the supernatural rests
largely in the hands of men. Women possess no shrines and are
seldom allowed to take part in rituals, although they may pray
and sacrifice at the female fertility and farm *idem* (shrines). In the
Christian mission churches, on the other hand, men and women
worship together and are equally capable of receiving God's grace.
Syncretist cults, which combine the indigenous and Islamic religious
elements with Christian doctrine, go even further; they favour
women evangelists over men and although the leading officials
are usually men, women members provide the major support and
have no difficulty in making their influence felt (Little, 1965, pp.
119–92 and pp. 35–46). It is also of significance that many of the
organizations set up by the younger men are not only anxious to
recruit women members but allocate to them responsible positions
in the running of the associations formed. Co-operation of this
kind between the sexes has been described in detail by Banton
in his study of the Freetown dancing *compin* (1957, pp. 162–74).

Compins are concerned with the performance of 'plays' and traditional music and dancing, as well as with the raising of money for mutual benefit. The music is provided mainly by native drums and calabash rattles, and is accompanied by singing. A 'play' is generally given in connection with some important event and in the *compin's* quite elaborate organization women hold offices appropriate to their sex. For example, there is a Mammy Queen, who is the counterpart of the male head of the organization; a Sister, who is in charge of the Nurses, young girls who bring round refreshments at dances, and there may be a woman Doctor to assist the male Doctor with members who are invalids. In the *compin*, most of the initiative is taken by men. But, as explained in the previous chapter, not only do women themselves set up many associations in connection with their business or trade but there is a tendency for women to predominate in and to control many such organizations. In other cases, where membership is mixed, the men and women members have an equal share in the mutual benefit schemes and savings groups concerned.

But what, perhaps, has most significance for women's position in general is the part that they have increasingly played in political affairs, sometimes on their own. For example, during the 1920s Ibo and Ibibio women rose *en masse* when it was rumoured that the Government proposed to tax them.[1] Following the sending round of palm leaves – a sign of distress – the women gathered together from all over Owerri Province; and, in addition to demonstrating against taxation, they demanded that an unpopular 'warrant chief' be handed over to them (Gailey, 1970). There were riots, and at Aba only firm action dispersed a mob estimated at

[1] The whole trouble had its origin in the political structure that the British imposed on south-eastern Nigeria. Indigenously, the principal peoples concerned – the Ibo and the Ibibio – had a very decentralized type of society, but the British created a native-court area with a chief to whom they gave the warrant to rule. Not only were these 'white cap' or 'warrant chiefs' completely alien to the traditional system, but many of them proved to be so corrupt as well as incompetent that in the period after pacification village affairs were largely conducted by the elders. Even so, the Ibo and the Ibibio might have remained docile had the central Government not decided in 1928 to extend the taxation system which existed in northern Nigeria to the East. Unlike the North, the Eastern Region had no political hierarchy enabling commands, instructions and information to flow smoothly from the higher to the lower levels of authority, and so considerable suspicion was aroused by the initial counting of heads carried out to ascertain each district's economic wealth. To make matters worse, some of the 'warrant chiefs' themselves spread rumours to the effect that in addition to the men, women were to be taxed (Gailey, 1970).

10,000 women. Within a short time dozens of towns were in open defiance and in one place a platoon of soldiers were obliged to form a square with bayonets drawn in order to extricate themselves. A District Officer tried to parley, but the women ran berserk and in the ensuing fighting, rifle fire killed twenty-six of them.[2]

The local men themselves were very surprised by the women's actions because as one of the 'warrant chiefs' remarked: 'Women never banded before in that way. If they had grievances they came to the head of the house with the complaint.' That, indeed, is usually the indigenous procedure, but these Nigerian women worked so effectively together that the Administration was brought to a standstill. They displayed a degree of militancy associated traditionally with male rather than female behaviour, and this was also the case in Zambia, where, when African nationalist organizations began to emerge as alternatives to indigenous and colonial power, the women's brigades also played, sometimes, a violent part (Heisler, 1973). In Kenya, too, the women fought vigorously for Independence, even going into the forests with the Mau Mau bands (see Rosberg and Nottingham, 1966), while in the Ivory Coast there was a general mobilization of African women against the French regime. This action kept the nationalist cause alive during the imprisonment of its male leaders, and prompted the well-known politician, Modiko Keita (later president of Mali), to point out that 'in all the [French] territories women have taken part in militant action with more enthusiasm than men. While the latter are less liable to discouragement, the women on the other hand are less responsive to offers of place and office, and thus less open to corruption' (quoted by Hodgkin, 1961, pp. 120–1).

Nor have women in the Moslem areas of West Africa held aloof. In northern Nigeria, for example, Government party leaders believed that women for religious reasons could not take part in politics, but were bluntly told that they were only trying to bamboozle the women. 'Some of us', women leaders from the south declared, 'have been to other Moslem countries and have seen what is happening there.' Following this 'persuasion', there emerged two women's organizations in the north, one of them the women's wing of the Northern People's Congress, and the other the women's wing of the Northern Elements Progressive Union. The latter, like other women's groups, drew inspiration from Mrs

[2] Naturally, it was only a matter of time before the Government regained control; but these 'Aba Riots' produced constitutional reforms which included a more flexible framework for the functioning of local government and a more diversified and decentralized type of Native Authority (Gailey, 1970).

Ransome-Kuti, who at the time was President General of the Nigerian Federation of Women's Organizations. A conference was held for the first time under the federation's auspices at Jos, where the women's leaders of the north expressed what they themselves thought about the franchise for their members.[3] Previously, it was the southern women who had repeatedly petitioned the authorities on behalf of their northern sisters (*African Women*, 1958).

The fact that the women and the younger men were united basically by common interests was clearly recognized on both sides, especially by the more radical type of male politician. This applied not only to Kwame Nkrumah, but to Sékou Touré, whose policy in Guinea was as realistic as it was pragmatic. He said, it is reported:

> I would never stop showing respect for the action of women for the good reason that in public opinion I qualify as a lady's man. If Youth, as is said commonly, is the future of a country, we think that woman is the future of the country before Youth and as a consequence of this, we favour the social, intellectual and moral advancement of the people. In the revolutionary type of action which we have conducted in order to substitute our regime for the colonial regime – that of liberty – we were only able to base our efforts on the most disinherited levels of society – those who had everything to gain by a revolution. As so there are, above all, the women practically untouched by the colonial regime, and not associated with the economic or administrative organisation of that regime who form the essential prop of our actions. It is from them that we receive the most dynamic force because in them lies the total hope for progress [4] (Rivière, 1968, p. 409).

[3] The conference appointed delegates to meet the Premier of the North and the Prime Minister of the Nigerian Federation on the issue of women's suffrage. They based their argument on the fact that the North was allowed 179 members in the new Federal Legislature and there was no doubt that they (the women) were counted during the franchise (Gailey, 1970).

[4] In fact, an important reason for wooing the Guinean women was that the tendency to ethnic division, particularly between the Fulani and the rest, remained a serious problem to Sékou Touré's party, the P.D.G. (Parti Démocratique de Guinée). To overcome regionalism a variety of symbols were used, including P.D.G. banners and colours; clothes such as head-scarves and the grey Moslem hat. The women wore dresses cut out of identical cloth; there were party songs, poems, dances and slogans, and women were again singled out for special mention. This was because, along with the children, the women cut across clan, ethnic and regional divisions (Rivière, 1968; see, also, Hodgkin, 1961, *passim*).

Indeed, spokesmen of the P.D.G. claim that for fifteen years 'woman' and 'party' were complementary expressions. The idea was that the women would support the party and the party emancipate the women, because – the argument ran – to build the nation required women having the same status as men. From 1953, it is said, a kind of political euphoria filled the country; the women, in particular, rallied to cries of 'Freedom', and their participation in party affairs became an obligation. Then, in a famous speech delivered just before Independence, Sékou Touré made the women of Guinea both his election agents and a means of political pressure by exhorting them to deny sexual intercourse to their husbands unless they joined the party. In short, the women were extolled, and striking imagery was used to eulogize them.

> My mother carried me. She carried me for twenty years and five months before my birth. My age is her age. The women are the fire of the R.D.A. When we want to make a knife we need iron, water and fire. The knife is African. We are the blacksmiths. We must use fire to make our knife. Our knife is our women. Our women mould us, and carry us.
> (Quoted in Morgenthau, 1956, p. 238)

It was further declared that 'through their loyalty, endurance, and militant activities [the women] have not only earned for themselves a revolutionary role, but the right to a full share of the professional, technical, economic opportunities in the new form of Guinean society'. They were saluted as the 'indispensable elements in life', and to them was entrusted 'the life of the Guinean revolution' (Rivière, 1968).[5]

That moment came when many people in Guinea refused to accept the official results of the 1954 election which, it was alleged, was rigged by the French administration. Sékou Touré's opponent had to be given police protection in Conakry, while larger crowds acclaimed Sékou Touré as the 'real chief', the 'real deputy'. Sang the women:

> You are a new chief.
> You are chosen as chief,
> The people is with you.
> You are a new chief;
> Lift up your head,
> Look at the sea of faces
> That answers when you call.
> (Morgenthau, 1964, p. 241)

[5] Sékou Touré's recruitment of women as a potential revolutionary force echoes rather curiously somewhat similar appeals made in

Though women themselves seem to have been attracted by Sékou Touré's personality, their own outlook was pragmatic rather than ideological. In other words, they associated themselves enthusiastically with the P.D.G., but regarded it mainly as an instrument of social liberation with whose co-operation a number of important successes had been achieved. These included matrimonial legislation; the education of women; certain measures protecting women; the participation of women in the national economy; and their places in political life (Rivière, 1968, pp. 406–25).[6]

Also, despite the popular desire to keep girls at home in order to help in the house, the reported proportion of girls of school age at school rose from 9·5 per cent at Independence to 45 per cent by 1966. As a result, the ratio of educated women to men increased from one educated woman to every four men in 1959 to one educated woman to every two men in 1966, there being some 70,000 educated girls and women to 140,000 boys and men by that time.[7] In fact, the first six years of Independence showed a

recent periods of European history to women in the mass. An interesting exposition of the latter is provided by Beard (1962, pp. 18–24).

[6] Taking these measures briefly in turn; marriage legislation made it compulsory to register a marriage before the performance of religious rites, illegal for girls to marry before the age of seventeen, and stipulated that a valid marriage required the consent of both parties. Also, the amount of bridewealth was restricted and it had to be paid in front of an official to the woman whose exclusive property it became and also remained in the event of divorce; a wife could oppose her husband taking a second wife if it were proved that he lacked the means adequately to support two; women were entitled to dispose of their personal property as they wished. It was also decreed that applications for divorce were to be heard by a tribunal empowered to grant damages to the spouse in whose favour an application for divorce was decided. In addition, while further legislation made the widow the heiress of her deceased husband, it also contained various provisions in favour of the children.

In regard to polygamy, Sékou Touré himself has pointed out that no law can effectively put an end to it so long as polygamy is motivated by economic reasons. ' Youth of Guinea ', he announced in a speech, 'polygamy is in your hands, you can perpetuate it or make it come to an end according to how firm in your will you are to building a new Africa forever free from the inferiority and oppression of women ' (Rivière, 1968).

[7] Naturally, as is shown by the comparison of Conakry, the capital, with an up-country area growing profitable crops, there are differences between town and country. Thus, whereas in 1964 there were in Conakry primary schools some 5,270 girls to some 7,160 boys, in up-country areas – where girls are heavily employed in agriculture – the ratio of girls to boys was as one to 3·5.

remarkable increase in both primary and secondary education; 215 per cent in the case of the boys and 397 per cent in the case of the girls. However, as in other African countries, the number of girls at the more advanced levels of education tapers off more sharply than that of the boys, and in Guinea in the three highest classes before the baccalaureate the ratio is approximately one girl to nine boys.[8] This means, not only that there are only relatively few girls at secondary schools, but the educational significance of those actually there must be regarded with caution.[9] So far as university education is concerned, only a Faculty of Letters and Social Sciences exists at Conakry, and in 1967, 17 per cent of its students were girls. Some 250 girls are at a school of health education for midwives, and about 130 girls are being trained as secretaries (Rivière, 1968).

It is also reported that in Conakry, where some 92 per cent of 'active' women are classified as housewives, a species of domestic science training has been started, somewhat on the lines of adult education. The attempt to reach women in this way has been made through the ranks of the J.R.D.A. ('Youth of the African Democratic Revolution'), there being daily broadcasts in the vernacular from Radio Conakry which give advice to mothers on hygiene and child care. It is claimed that even in the villages these programmes are followed by numerous listeners, and each Sunday there is a programme, 'For you, Madame', which, within a context of local music, provides information about household matters, women's fashions, etc. A number of towns as well as Conakry have social centres for the education of adult women, including practical courses in nutritional hygiene and child care as well as in 'culture'.[10] Also, child and mother protection services exist in each medical district under the direction of the National Centre of Conakry. A midwife, and two or three male and female nurses

[8] Factors responsible for this 'tapering' off in Guinea are similar to those reported in more general terms in Chapter 3. In other words, they include marriage, lack of interest in study, and the opposition of parents to their daughters' 'emancipation', especially when it means their residing at 'mixed' boarding schools. Indeed, the mass of the people appear to have a profound hostility to any extended education for girls.

[9] This is because the Government attempts to solve the educational problem in a way that, as Rivière remarks, is rather curious. For example, a girl who has failed her examination may be advised by her teachers to repeat that year, but the Government orders her to be passed on to a higher class.

[10] At the village level, the militia are in charge of fumigation and of seeing that the women dispose of all the household refuse, etc.

occupy the centre which is linked in the small villages with the dispensary.[11]

It is claimed that thanks to these various actions taken by the Party (i.e. the P.D.G.) the Guinean woman now feels 'liberated' from her husband. In addition to the spread of education, urbanization and industrialization have favoured her position, and Government policy has paved the way for her to earn money in the professions as well as through commerce. Thus, two years after Independence, a pay scale was set up and President Sékou Touré ordered that women should be trained for and admitted into occupations and professional positions, including that of doctors, in which men had previously had a monopoly. The result, it is claimed, is that women now have responsible positions in the administration of hospitals and businesses and have great prestige as teachers. Occupations, in which women now work, until recently reserved for men, include a tobacco and match factory and a canning company in each of which women hold 30 per cent of the jobs. A larger proportion of these women than of the male workers are married and this may be because it is difficult for single girls to get their parent's consent to work in a factory.[12]

Though a limited number of women are attracted by the public

[11] The rationale of all these measures and propaganda is that upon the proper education of women depends the welfare of society at large; hence, it is necessary for a woman's health to be fully protected while pregnant and after she has given birth. Women, accordingly, are eligible for prenatal, maternity and family allowances, and they are also entitled to half-pay up to six weeks before and up to eight weeks after the delivery of a child. Maternity allowances are fixed according to salary, and medical consultations, attentions and hospitalization for pregnancy are free. The table below illustrates the development of social services, principally in relation to women:

	1958	1965
Midwives	49	114
Nurses	1	90
A.T.S.	3	209
Social helpers	2	8
Social workers	–	49
Consultations	2,000,000	5,000,000
Hospitalizations	30,000	41,000
Births in maternity homes	14,000	35,000
Hospitals	2	21
Dispensaries and infirmaries	46	271
Maternity and infant welfare clinics	4	38
Maternity hospitals	29	35

[12] There is an apparent contrast here with Ghana where there are more young unmarried girls than married women in industry. Possibly this difference reflects the well-known greater economic independence of Ghanaian women.

sector's improved salaries, many of them work in handicraft industries near the urban centres. Indigo dyers are organized in co-operatives of which the most important are Kindia – 2,000 women; Conakry – 600 women; and Lobe, where there are 120 women dyers and about 30 knitters.

Finally, what is not least in importance is the fact that Guinean women have their say in government through the medium of their own organizations and through committees of the Party which include female members. Special committees of women existed for a while but were discontinued because they appeared to cause dissension between the sexes. However, the women themselves forced President Sékou Touré to re-establish these groups so that there would be 'militant' women beside the men at every level of the Party. Their functions include making Party policy known among the women, offering advice on women's education, keeping under review the actual implementation of Party decisions as they affected women, the organization of various social activities, and the general mobilization of women with the men for communal and co-operative activities.

Much of the earlier enthusiasm of Independence has worn off, although 'Women's' Day' – a holiday throughout the Republic – is celebrated and there are eloquent speeches to the effect that 'Man is the anvil, children the iron and women the fire'. Addressing the first Congress of Guinean Women on 27 January 1968 in this fashion, the President reported the extent of the women's political contribution, and claimed that in the P.D.G. there were, at ward and village level, some 8,000 special committees consisting exclusively of women. Annually, each of these committees elects 13 women to executive positions, and in the pyramidical structure of the Party there are at every level women representatives. Consequently, some 3,040 elected women take a leading part in the P.D.G.'s affairs, and in all, some 150,000 women out of a total of more than two million women of all ages were to the fore, Sékou Touré said, in revolutionary activity. In fact, he claimed, one out of every 15 women had a job of public responsibility. He also pointed out that of 75 national delegates chosen by universal suffrage, 20 were women and that out of 870 regional delegates the women took 140 seats. In all, women occupied 27 per cent of the seats in the National Assembly and 16 per cent of the Regional Assemblies' seats. In addition, hundreds of militant workers were elected to positions in the trade unions and thousands of women were in charge of co-operatives and of associations of artisans and food-sellers. Last, but not least, were the women who held important posts in the Government itself.

Undoubtedly, if regarded numerically in terms of parliamentary representation and membership of 'militant' committees the advance of Guinean women is impressive. But does the presence of large numbers of women in responsible positions do more than reflect official policy? How far is the impression given of women's progress borne out in actual performance? Are, for example, the women employed in the public sector reliable; are the women cashiers in the banks and commercial firms persons of integrity; and are the girls employed as secretaries competent? Such questions are not easy to answer, but what certainly does stand out is the urban women's readiness to keep a watchful eye on the Government itself. For example, when, between 1959 and 1964, there was a gradual and sometimes total disappearance from the market of such essential commodities as rice, sugar, oil and cloth, it was the women who, in particular, dared show dissatisfaction. Also, in both September 1964 and January 1967, they complained in forthright language about the inadequacy of promised educational reforms. It has also been claimed that it was the women who, at the end of 1966, forced President Sékou Touré to withdraw Dr Kwame Nkrumah's title as Co-President of Guinea (Rivière, 1968, p. 424).

The political organization of Guinean women has been described in some detail because it exemplifies a significant way in which women have gained an important voice in public affairs. Their distinctive place in Ghanaian politics, too, involved a tie between the women's section and the Party structure with horizontal links at the branch or constituency level. Thus, as explicitly laid down by the Convention People's Party's (C.P.P.) constitution:

> Each Party Branch shall have a Women's Section to cater for the special interest of women, but the Women's Section shall be part and parcel of the Branch. There shall be only one Executive Committee for each Branch, including the Women's Section. The same applies to the Ward and Constituencies.
>
> (Hodgkin, 1961, p. 120)

This was after the very active part played by Ghanaian women's organizations in the nationalist cause, when they helped financially, organized boycotts of trade, and so on. Later, all voluntary associations – including women's groups – were 'politicized' by Nkrumah; and, in 1966, the National Council of Ghana Women, for example, was established as an integral part of the C.P.P. It helped to select candidates for the ten regional parliamentary seats reserved for women.

Nor is the P.D.G. in Guinea unique in its claim that women have the same rights as men within the Party, because most African mass parties emphasize sexual equality. They create a distinct and parallel form of organization for women, which is considered to be consonant with the traditional social pattern rather than a deliberate segregation of the sexes. This division provides a convenient basis for the organization of specific Party functions, which may include the holding of rallies, dances and picnics. These are also run sometimes by associations and clubs which, although not a component of the Party itself, are affiliated to it. For example, one such club in Bamako, known as ' Association des Artists du Mali, l'Ambiance', is connected with ' Union Soudainaise–Rassemblément Démocratique Africain ' (U.S.–R.D.A.) in Mali. L'Ambiance organizes dances to mark and honour meetings of the Party's convention (Meillassoux, 1968, pp. 108–12),[13] and another Malian association of young women has similar connections. Its ostensible aim is to participate in parades, and to help at weddings, baptisms, or circumcisions within the members' families [14]; but nearly all its members are the wives of relatively well-to-do people, including civil servants and small businessmen, who belong to the U.S.–R.D.A. The result was that although not an official section of the Party, this *muso-mise-to* (young women's association) received an invitation to send two representatives to the U.S.–R.D.A. ward committee (Meillassoux, 1968).

Thus, many of the women's activities involve a mixture of social

[13] Actually – politics apart – l'Ambiance is in Bamako the marriage society *par excellence* and during the dry season it celebrates the weddings of members' relatives. Congratulations are offered to the bride and groom and their families and many of the speeches made are ' political ' as well as witty (Meillassoux, 1968).

At the same time, l'Ambiance provides the U.S.–R.D.A. with a thorny problem. Overtly, the association has completely rallied to the Party's position and when it organizes an outstanding celebration the President of the Republic or some of his representatives are always invited. However, although propagating very effectively Government policy, l'Ambiance keeps alive at the same time a picturesque and valuable piece of tradition and folklore which closely binds the artistic background of the association to the permanency of castes. In effect, therefore, l'Ambiance leaders, instead of working towards dissolution of the caste system, emphasize its usefulness and value and assign to it special functions in a modern society.

For a description of l'Ambiance's traditional activities see Meillassoux, 1968.

[14] The degree of kinship was limited to first cousins on both sides of the family, and the composition of this association's committee was typical in that the posts of treasurer and secretary were filled by literate persons (*ibid.*).

and political objectives, but this does not mean that those who belong to the mass parties are – as Hodgkin has put it – solely 'preoccupied with organising picnics and tam-tams'. True, the outlook of rural women is likely to be parochial;[15] but in the towns women think much more about their economic interests, and the latter author has pertinently quoted the case of the Ghana market woman who was asked what she was going to vote. She replied, '*mebeko vote apatre*' ('I am going to vote fish') – as a Lancashire woman might 'vote cotton' (Hodgkin, 1961). This is important because, as explained, in some regions women control most petty trade and much of the large-scale commerce, too. Such crowds of market women are, in Ekwensi's words, 'astute, sure of themselves and completely independent' (1961, p. 109). Since, moreover, they are in the habit of voting *en bloc*, politicians have found that their demands cannot be ignored (Comhaire-Sylvain, 1951, p. 183),[16] while it is also the case that liaisons between aspiring Party leaders and influential market women's leaders can be mutually advantageous and satisfying in practical as well as emotional terms.[17] The effect of this is that, in addition to successfully urging improved amenities at local markets, women's groups, acting on their own, have frequently achieved the provision of social services, such as schools, maternity homes, ambulance services, and the employment of larger numbers of female nurses. Both in the Western and Eastern Regions of Nigeria they showed themselves capable of opposing Government plans and policies which they regarded as inimical. Inspired by Mrs Ransome-Kuti, the Egba women's union, for example, was chiefly responsible for the agitation that, in 1948, led to the abdication of the Alake of Abeokuta[18]; while in Uganda, the Y.W.C.A. called for the return of the exiled Kabaka of Buganda.

It is significant, too, that numbers of women's associations have

[15] For example, in Kassena–Nankanni North, a Ghanaian rural area, out of the 13,755 people who registered in 1954, nearly 5,000 were women. However, it is asserted even by the women that generally speaking they vote the way the compound or villages vote, the decision being left to the compound head and elders, the *tendaana*, the locally acclaimed leaders of the young men and other male sections of society (Austin, 1961).

[16] For a brilliant exposition of the technique requisite to electioneering among this category of women voters, see Ekwensi, 1961, pp. 109–11.

[17] Aluko's (1970) reference to the latter point must suffice for present purposes: 'Some said that hers was the hand that rocked the Throne of Government' (p. 139).

[18] 'Henceforth', *West Africa* commented, 'the ruler interested in his throne must count on the support of his feminine subjects and the politician must accept that the old order has changed, that "kitchen is not just the place for the woman"' (1953c, p. 917).

banded themselves together in national organizations which, in addition to exploring some of the practical problems confronting women in a changing society, also hold conferences and act indirectly as a pressure group in the interests of women's rights and 'emancipation'. For example, the Uganda Council of Women [19] has taken up questions of marriage and divorce and in order to influence public opinion it drew up a booklet describing in simple English the nature of the existing law and raising matters for discussion. For instance, should marriages under native customary law remain unregistered? If so, how can there be any law regulating them? Further subjects included bridewealth and property and inheritance; and women's associations all over Uganda – development clubs, the Y.W.C.A. and so on – were invited to a conference based on the booklet. This was held in March 1960, and on the basis of delegates' reports and discussion a number of resolutions were adopted. Among these were that the return of the customary payment of bridewealth should be abolished in respect of all marriages which may be dissolved in the future; that after due provision for the widow, a just division of a man's property would be for a major share to go to the heir if he is a son of the deceased; if there was not a son, a token share should go to the named heir and the remainder be shared among the remaining children. The education of people in the making of written wills was also urged. These resolutions were forwarded to the Uganda Government, but the most significant effect, perhaps, was on male opinion as a whole. Many men, including Government officers, were made aware of the strength of women's views on the subject of marriage and their own position as wives (*African Women*, 1960, p. 204).

A further meeting – this time in West Africa – took as its theme 'The African Woman Designs her Future', and was held under the auspices of the International Alliance of Women. It was attended by some 60 women, including numbers from the former French colonies as well as from the Anglophone countries. They were leading townspeople, rural women, market women, and politically active women drawn from Government departments of education, church organizations, private industry, co-operatives and women's organizations. These women wanted to preserve

[19] As explained in Chapter 6, the grouping together and affiliation of women's associations as a national federation have become a familiar and important feature of the women's 'emancipation' movement. For example, the Ghana movement referred to above was formed in 1953, including over 40 affiliated women's groups. It attained a total strength of over 2,300 members by 1957, and it has looked into specific problems affecting women, such as registration of native customary marriage.

what was good in African culture, including the indigenous religious tradition. They also argued that technical advance must not be the monopoly of the men and that women must keep up with the men as living conditions improved. In other words, not only must girls have equal opportunities with boys in academic and technical schools, but as careers and opportunities opened up to African men, so they should open up to African women as well. Also discussed were the conditions leading to a high death rate among infants and older children; and, in addition, a sound adoption law safeguarding the interests of both the child and the adopting parents was advocated. Child neglect was thought to be more a matter of ignorance than lack of affection. Finally, it was generally considered that although polygamy and 'matriarchy' served traditional society well enough, they did not make for stable home life in the new situation. Nevertheless, it would be a great mistake to attack these institutions frontally until something better had been built to replace them (*ibid.*). A Council of West African Women was formed on the basis of these discussions to promote solidarity and co-operation among members in the tasks lying ahead.

Finally, a natural corollary of these developments is the growing number of women who have politically come to the fore, sometimes as election candidates, but more often as organizers of associations and inspirers of and spokesmen for women's aspirations. In addition to Mrs Ransome-Kuti, among the more prominent and influential of these leaders are, or have been, Miss Mabel Dove in Ghana, Madame Ouezzin Coulibaly in Upper Volta, Miss Margaret Kenyatta in Kenya, and Madam Ella Koblo Gulama, Madam Honoria Bailor-Caulker and Mrs Nancy Steele in Sierra Leone (see appendix).

In Kenya – about which more will be said later – although 'progressive' rural women provide the broad basis of such movements, leadership is solidly in the hands of a core of urban women. They form a small interlocking group because they have mostly been to the same schools, known each other for years, and are related through birth or marriage to the political and professional élite. A typical leader will have attended mission-run primary and secondary schools and this means that she knows the Bible and is probably a Christian convert. She has had between eight and ten years of schooling, during which she was introduced to the Girl Guides and the Y.W.C.A.: later, she was a member of the executive of one or other of these organizations, the Girl Guides being an especially important training ground. From secondary school the typical leader will have gone on to a teacher-training course or to the former Jeanes School, which was designed to give training in leadership, social work, and the technical specialities, and played an important part in training Kenya's social and technical workers. Ages range from the mid-twenties to the late forties, and most such women are mothers of large families even though many are employed full time. Some of the most militant women, however, have been unaided by family position and have, nevertheless, achieved an education on their own through hard work and determination. These women tend not to be related to the political and professional élite but are employed professionally, either by women's organizations or in some other full-time job (Wipper, 1971a).

As indicated, also, in the appendix, the dedication of some of these women leaders is very great. One of them in Kenya, a full-time social worker and former president of the principal women's organization, had, when she required leave of absence from her work, to take it unpaid, and was obliged, in addition, to use her own holiday time in order to visit her association's branches (Celinas, 1965, p. 56). More, however, will be said about the problems of women's leadership in the final chapter.

6 'Walk-about women'

In the previous chapters we have described some aspects of women's involvement in urbanization explaining that in the 'modern' town's economy many women are educationally at a disadvantage. However, women's formation of and participation in voluntary associations, their co-operation with men in politics, and their trading activities are all ways of off-setting this particular drawback.

The data given above also show that the personal situation of some migrant women and girls is economically very precarious. Yet, having savoured the atmosphere of the town, such a person is unwilling, or unable, for the reasons cited earlier, to return home. Lacking any pronounced motivation in a vocational sense, she is apparently content to accept whatever comes along; and certain inter-related circumstances do, in fact, reinforce this Micawber-like attitude. Firstly, it is plain to her notice that other African women and girls, equally unlettered, have apparently done quite nicely for themselves. They are to be seen around the hotels, dance halls and bars, wearing fine fashionable clothes, driving or being driven about – their eyes shielded by dark spectacles – in cars of the 'long' American type. Secondly, although the town's indigenous population may contain as many, and sometimes more, adult women as men, the number of men in some migrant groups may be six or seven times greater than the number of women.

The general effect of this demographic imbalance is to place a special premium on women's domestic and sexual services, and the fact that a proportion of the migrant 'bachelors' are relatively well-to-do Europeans and Asians as well as Africans enhances this. It creates the kind of economic opportunity for which the qualifications needed are not university degrees, but physical attraction and the capacity to flirt, charm, captivate and seduce. True, feeling against inter-tribal marriage is frequently strong, but less notice is taken when the relationships between persons of different tribes are extra-marital. Usually, attitudes towards the latter kind of affair are tolerant and the general 'atmosphere' of the city, as conveyed by African novelists' descriptions (see, among others, Achebe, 1966 and Ekwensi, 1954), is as 'sexually permissive' as in Euro-North American cosmopolitan centres.[1] The main difference is that in the latter most extra-marital sexual behaviour goes on 'underground' and involves call-girls, whereas in African urban society it is more overt. Also, as indicated in succeeding paragraphs and the next chapter, prostitution as such plays a much smaller part.

Thus, even among professing Christians, reasons are usually found to condone adultery when committed by husbands, and although traditional norms continue to deny a similar licence to wives, in the relative anonymity of the cosmopolitan city such rules are difficult to enforce.[2] The main sanction, so far as most illiterate women are concerned, is the fear of discovery and of being severely flogged by the husband. Wives, too, will physically attack an unfaithful spouse, sometimes while admitting at the same time that his behaviour is 'natural'.[3] Also, although the matter gives rise to a great deal of ribaldry, it is acknowledged that women, too, have sexual appetites. In general, therefore, attitudes towards the sexual act are, by contrast with the West, simple and straightforward. In Euro-North American society, not only has 'sex' become the hub of an enormous advertising, as well as pornographic industry, but there are numerous religious, ethical and psychiatric vested interests which treat the matter with tremendous solemnity. In the African 'modern' town similar delicacy is not uncommon among families with a long tradition of Western contact and, to some extent, among church-men and those members of their congregations whom Christian evangelism has made sexually self-conscious. As yet, however, 'sex' has not become for the generality of urban inhabitants a matter for either moral or scientific speculation. As a later chapter

---

[1] Hunt (1969) provides perspective for the above statement and in-cludes a useful bibliography, mainly with reference to the United States.

[2] That, however, the situation is different in 'up-country' towns is illustrated by one of Ekwensi's short stories (1966b).

[3] Psychiatrists have suggested that for spouses physically to attack each other, especially for the husband to beat up the wife, is a way of displaying interest and even affection. A wife, it has been claimed, will be deeply disturbed if her husband fails to treat her regularly in this way. If this argument holds good for marital relationships in some sections of Euro-North American society it is likely to be just as true of the relationship of man and wife in some sections of African society.

will seek to show, sexual intercourse is a subject of considerable social and personal interest, but the basic implication is that it fulfils a natural function. In other words, the sexual appetite is akin to hunger and thirst, with the difference that in the former case a man's gratification requires a woman's co-operation. As reported by McHardy in *Présence Africaine* (1968, pp. 55–60), a Ghanaian woman's view of 'love in Africa' seems to express this, but in more idealistic terms:

> The man is indebted for his wife's sexual companionship. He has to deserve it. By acquitting himself of his duty, by showing affection for her, by performing services for the children . . . only in this way can he win their love and retain an influence . . . our concept of love . . . is the privilege of a mature personality, socially and emotionally. If neither partner is an object for the other there is much more honesty.

Another West African young woman similarly spelled out the importance of reciprocity. Describing her particular idea of male–female relationships she wrote

> Generally, one would hope that the affection given to a man will be returned. When this attention includes sincerity and love one would hope and expect these from the man. Depending on how far this relationship has developed and towards what goals it is geared, it is generally symbolized by love-making. (Communicated)

This informant makes the further interesting point that although *basically* the attitude of educated girls is not very different from that of illiterate ones, the formers' greater sophistication and knowledge of Western 'styles' may affect their response. She considers – and it is this writer's impression, too – that the illiterate girl's attitude to a man will be the same irrespective of social category. That of an educated one, on the other hand, will vary according to whether the man is educated or illiterate, a student as opposed to a civil servant, and so on.

The result, at any rate, is that being less trammelled by traditional norms sexual relationships are, by contrast with rural society, felt to be a relatively individual matter. In the latter milieu they are of wide concern and affect other people because of the importance that procreation has for the group as a whole. But in the modern town there is less need of children and so sexual services, having less significance, tend to be regarded as something which, like a commodity, is obtainable by favour or by bargaining. This, needless to add, is very far from saying that all 'urban' women are promiscuous or that every sexual contact is commercial. On the contrary, as succeeding chapters will seek to show, there is a growing tendency for women to choose for themselves the men they will favour. What it does mean is that sexual contacts are often casual and fleeting, and that the woman's agreement may be looked upon by both parties as no more than reciprocity for a 'good turn', rendered to her in cash or in some other way. It will also be explained later that this kind of *affaire* may go on for some time without arousing strong emotions. Considerations of personal prestige may enter the matter, but the attitude of both parties remains relatively impersonal; and it may even be mutually understood that pecuniary or other interests may, in an expediency, take precedence over the relationship itself. Sometimes, however, jealousy does gain the upper hand; and, in consequence, the game's rules are broken.

These points are illustrated by a scene in *Jagua Nana* (p. 11) in which 'Jagua' and her young lover 'Freddie' are at a night club, the 'Tropicana'. 'Freddie' leaves 'Jagua' for a few minutes and while he is away a Syrian [4] comes over and loads 'Jagua's' table with drinks. 'Jagua' wonders what he is up to. Since the Syrian was said to have a lot of money and to be lavish with it, she would not mind taking him home. 'Freddie' returns and realizes what is afoot. He tries to take 'Jagua' away; but, instead, she accepts a cigarette from the Syrian. This, she tells herself, is her bread and butter. She pictures herself in the fine dress she saw in a window display and the Syrian's money will buy it for her. She loves 'Freddie' well, but his whole salary could not purchase that garment. He must understand that taking money from the Syrian does not mean that she loves 'Freddie' less. And so,

> 'Jagua' turned a smiling face at the Syrian. Out of the corner of her eye she saw 'Freddie's' fist tighten. Then, raving mad, he turned and walked out of the Tropicana. At that instant 'Jagua' forced back a small cry of pity for her loved one. He should know by now that in the Tropicana money always claimed the first loyalty.

'Freddie's' reaction can readily be understood in terms of a Western or highly Westernized culture, but in the opportunistic atmosphere of the African cosmopolitan city, 'romantic love' has a different function. As will be explained in Chapter 8, among 'civilized' young people this kind of notion serves increasingly to characterize socially mobile groups, but for women in 'Jagua's'

---

[4] Although popularly referred to as 'Syrians', most of these people come in fact, from Lebanon.

position most relationships with the opposite sex have a pecuniary goal. Romantic love is a luxury that women in her circumstances can rarely afford. Their point of view is that although Providence has not endowed them with riches, He has provided them with the next best thing – sexual attraction for men. It is almost God's Will that they should use what He has given them.

We do not suggest that this is the women's way of rationalizing their role in a situation wherein relatively small numbers of women are surrounded by relatively large numbers of sex-hungry unattached males. Nevertheless, it amounts to a significant factor if, to the proposition of men requiring women, is added the equally important fact that, in the urban situation described earlier, women need men.[5] Consequently, ' sex ' often provides in itself, the primary basis for mutually convenient arrangements between individual women and men. There are complementary reasons for this being the case. Thus, whereas an older woman with experience of town life can perhaps look after herself and support children, a younger and less experienced woman or girl may require not only economic opportunities but physical protection [6]; and both categories of women need somewhere to live. Owing to the housing shortage this is also a problem for the male migrant who, in addition, may be seeking the domestic as well as the sexual services a woman can provide. Other men whose marriages have broken up may also find themselves with a handful of children. If such a person cannot make arrangements to live with his parents' family he, too, must find a woman to look after and keep house for him. Since, in these circumstances the women and the men concerned have, though for somewhat different reasons, similar needs, there is a natural inducement to join forces. Perhaps the woman has relatives within reach or call : otherwise, living in a world that is dominated almost entirely by men she is initially at some disadvantage. On the other hand, when the numerical preponderance of males is a constant factor, there

[5] In reference to ' men's towns ' Southall remarks on the ' tremendous demand ' for the sexual services of the scarce women in town. ' Irresistible pressure carried the latter into irregular liaisons, brewing and petty trade, which seem at first to offer even to the poorest woman emancipation from the male-dominated tribal social system '. The result is said to be ' general lack of respect for urban women as a whole, preference for marrying country girls, and so a perpetuation of the whole cycle ' (Southall, 1961, p. 56).

[6] In reference to life in Johannesburg, Longmore points out that ' Any woman living in an urban African township needs male protection and she seeks any available man, whether free or not, and whether belonging to her tribe or not ' (1959, p. 265). For an account of these conditions as observed through the eyes, seemingly, of some of the participants in them see Lytton (1960) and Boetie and Barney (1969).

is a relative scarcity of female services and so a woman on her own is, to that extent, strategically better placed than her male counterpart. She may need this extra bargaining power if she enters into a relationship which proves to be unsatisfactory.

Consequently, although a common pattern consists of a woman and a man setting up house together in order to co-operate economically as well as for sexual purposes, there are variations upon it. For example, since there is money to be made through prostituting herself, the woman may prefer this less exclusive kind of arrangement, taking a room and sharing it with a more or less permanent lover who acts as her protector. Alternatively, she may operate from the house of an older woman who, in return for the accommodation and other services provided, is paid a share of the girl's earnings. In the former type of arrangement, the bare essentials are that the woman cooks for and sleeps with the man; he, in return, pays the rent. The advantage from the woman's point of view is that she has some security and a base from which to carry on such 'legitimate' activities as petty trade or as a seamstress. Also, having at least the use of a room provides opportunities for manoeuvre. She can choose between the former occupations and prostitution; or, indeed, surreptitiously augment her income by judiciously combining both.

This was the situation in Kampala as described in Chapter 3, most of the women concerned being members of low-income households. But similar patterns of sexual behaviour and domesticity are not confined wholly to the economically poorer classes. Also, although in such relationships the man tends to be financially better off than the woman, this is not invariably the case because there are also women who are economically in a position to pick and choose. Nor does a woman who is in financial difficulties necessarily accept the first man who comes along; and, as will be explained later, there are various types of marriage itself. In other words, relationships between men and women in the urban environment being often highly complex makes it essential to approach such matters warily and to be clear, in particular, about certain terms. Caution is needed because most attitudes in Africa towards the sexual act have a quite different basis from those in Euro-North America, and situations involving it are not necessarily construed in the same kind of way. Above all, we have to remember that the urban population includes 'animists' as well as Christians and Moslems, and that each of these groups has its own system of values. In short, the analyst seeking a common factor has a variety of problems to explore.

The first of these arises when money is paid because, to the European, it is this that fixes the divide between unvirtuous living and prostitution. Indeed, Southall and Gutkind define prostitution as ' an *ad hoc* commercial transaction between strangers, and love affairs, in which the parties do not establish a common menage but simply visit one another, the woman receiving gifts and even some sort of maintenance allowance from her lover '. This is a definition which could extend to ' kept women ', but some African peoples go even further. They tend to regard all extra-marital intercourse as prostitution,[7] and in Swahili the same word – *malaya* – is often used to describe both vagrant and prostitute. The Mende of Sierra Leone use a somewhat similar expression, *letay nyahanga*, which means ' walk-about women '– women who move about on their own, especially at night time. Thus, in introducing the Yɔmeh, a traditional type of ballad, a Mende minstrel sang (in free translation),

> I know the Yɔmeh as the prostitute knows the night. She walks about without stumbling against any body. She never steps on a snake, and no-one recognizes her.
>
> (Little, 1948, pp. 27–8)

The impression that the Mende also convey is that ' prostitute ' is a term of opprobrium applied to all women who live by themselves, or are not directly under the control of their families. Mende chiefdom enactments have frequently decreed, therefore, that under penalty of fining every woman, young or old, must have a husband or a ' caretaker '. Specifically, wives must not be allowed to stay away from their husband's house with their parents for more than a month; and if a woman did stay away in another chiefdom, it was the duty of her husband and village headman to inform the Paramount Chief immediately if she ran away (Little, 1951, p. 169). The resolution of a Sierra Leone Chiefs' conference in this connection was noted in Chapter 2. In effect, what Mende husbands fear – as is widely the case among other patrilineal peoples as well – is the loss of bridewealth. ' Chiefs ', remarked a member of this class, ' do not get wives for nothing ' (*ibid.*).

It is also the case that some peoples regard the acceptance of money for sexual services rendered as disgraceful and the women

---

[7] If Daniel Defoe is any guide this seems to have been the attitude also in England in the earlier part of the eighteenth century because in his *Moll Flanders* the term ' prostitute ' is applied very widely. Seemingly, it covered every kind of sexual relationship except the one that a man had with his own wife. Note also in this connection Bosman's reference to women who never marry being called ' Whores.' Bosman's work was published a few years before *Moll Flanders*. Also, the title of Forde's play, ' *Tis Pity She's a Whore* ', has reference to an incestuous relationship, not to prostitution.

trading in this way frequently change their names for this reason. A situation of this kind, according to Busia, existed in Sekondi-Takoradi where the women whom he studied appeared to have few ties with home and did not share any family obligations. Nor were they wanted by their kinsmen with whom, in some cases, they had lost all contact (1950, pp. 107–8). Some peoples, too, try to preserve their community's reputation by repatriating women who trade their sexual services and they also take stern measures against such practices when the women return home. Thus, clan unions among the Banyang of the West Cameroons debar such women from attending union functions, including the dance which accompanies the general meeting. They were also forbidden to wear certain types of dress, shoes, hats, or to carry umbrellas; and they were prevented, in addition, from organizing funeral celebrations, most of these ' laws ' carrying a fine of £5. These restrictions could apply only to the home area, but the clan unions also organized a ' drive ' against Banyang prostitutes working in the urban centres of the south, put the women on lorries and brought them back to their home village group alone where they were placed in charge of their own lineage kinsfolk. They had to obtain special permission if they wanted to leave the village-group area and were sternly told of their duty to return to their true role as wives and mothers. These measures and the pressure exerted persuaded some of the women to enter marriage again. As is the custom among other tribes, rites of purification were then carried out and the disability of prostitution status was formally removed (Ruel, 1964, pp. 1–14).

Also, as mentioned in Chapter 2, Caldwell found a strong resistance to female migration in Ghana. Except when women are joining husbands, going to form a marriage with a specific person, or when old women are extending their trading activities there is, he points out, a very strong emotional pressure exerted on girls to stay in the village. In fact, there was a rather extraordinary concentration on a single theme in the opposition to female migration. It is not destitution, crime or the loss of family ties which are feared; it is the temptation of prostitution (Caldwell, 1969, p. 103). On the other hand, in Acquah's survey of Accra (1958), the prostitutes spoke openly of their activities and seemed to suffer little, if any, disapprobation. This also seems to be the position in Dar es Salaam where, according to Leslie, the prostitute goes home when she has the amount of money for which she came. On her return she has, seemingly, every chance of making a good and respectable marriage on the basis of her proceeds which amount, in effect, to a dowry. These may include, in addition to money, a sewing machine, a gramophone and records, a bicycle, and good clothes and ornaments. She also brings with her all the polish of the town; and a number of women with whom the matter was discussed appeared to be in no doubt of their reacceptance into the society they had left. Indeed, like many of the ordinary male labour migrants, several of these prostitutes make regular visits home where, it is said, they are much admired as successful women (Leslie, 1963, p. 236). As will be explained later, the migration of certain groups specifically for purposes of prostitution appears also to be condoned in the women's home village. Indeed, it has been said of one large tribe that to their women 'prostitution . . . is merely a new calling like any other and that they become prostitutes as reasonably and as self-righteously as they would have become typists or telephone girls' (Leith-Ross, 1939).

And so the position remains unclear, especially in the 'modern' African town where what in the West may be called 'prostitution' overlaps other kinds of relationships. These may include intercourse when the woman concerned needs a male friend's financial assistance; or when she simply prefers a gift in money rather than in kind. Such a transaction may take place without it making any difference to the friendship, or either party regarding it as being at all derogatory. In fact, the first thing to grasp is the different cultural significance that 'money' itself has. To the Western economist money is a medium of exchange and a standard of value, but some literate Africans as well as traditionally-minded people use it in a variety of social transactions as well as economic ones. Bridewealth is the best known example; but in addition, when there is a bereavement, a donation of cash is the right way to show sympathy. Except in highly Westernized circles, a wreath of flowers, however expensive, will be neither welcome nor meaningful – except as a waste of good money. Also, even in the extended family the 'hire' of certain articles, such as a shirt, and the performance of certain personal services may sometimes be charged for and by members of both sexes (Little, 1951, p. 99).

In order, therefore, to avoid further ambiguity, it is proposed to confine the term 'prostitute' to women whose livelihood over a period of time depends wholly on the sale of sexual services and whose relationship with customers does not extend beyond the sexual act. This limitation is necessary because a large number of women who manage to subsist in other ways are willing periodically to provide sexual intercourse for money if, for example, they get into debt; if there are certain family obligations to be met; if they want badly to improve their wardrobe, and so on. In Euro-North American society there are plenty of 'good time' girls who are willing to oblige a friend, or even an acquaintance, provided he 'knows the ropes' and goes tactfully about the matter. For her 'co-operation' the Euro-North American girl is paid in kind, including entertainment in restaurants, theatres, cinemas, etc., whose actual cost may be a good deal greater than what the African girl is given. The difference is that the latter may see nothing wrong in accepting money; and, indeed, in an appreciable number of cases may expect as well as hope for monetary and material gain from the relationship.

A still further reason for limiting use of the term 'prostitute' is because, somewhat like seasonal labour migrants, the African girl may sometimes exchange sexual services for cash during a period of unemployment between one regular job and another. In the latter regard her position is somewhat analogous to that of the university student working as a waitress during the summer holidays and returning to her studies when the summer vacation is over. In the African urban situation, however, a good deal may depend on the nature and character of whatever 'openings' are available. It being an opportunistic environment,[8] some young women will readily throw over an existing job at a moment's notice if they catch the eye of a man who is influential and willing to improve on it. For example, although some girl secre-traries in government offices indignantly refuse the bait, there are others who yield to their bosses' advances in return for promotion (see, among others, Aluko, 1970).

Here again, there is the difficulty of defining norms [9] because a view quite widely taken is that life in the city being hard, people – including women – are entitled to make the most of their chances: that the method employed is sexual is regarded as inci-dental. Like the giving and taking of 'back-handers', it is an inevitable and unavoidable part of the effort to survive. This point is implicit in the comments of 'Fento', one of Ekwensi's male characters. 'Fento' – a junior civil servant in the Department of Labour – has just accepted money for making a false declaration on behalf of a person wanting a job. 'Nothing goes for nothing', 'Fento' exclaims, and he goes on to explain the 'reality' of city life, its opportunities as well as its drawbacks, and the need to accept things for what they are:

[8] Because, officially, one of my East African informants told me, such practices do not exist. He had been instructed by the department in which he worked as a research officer to prepare a report on staff relationships and had included references to what went on between some of the girls and the men for whom they worked. He was told that this would not do at all and that he must re-write this particular section before the document went on to a higher quarter.

[9] This point is elaborated on in Little, 1973a.

> Bribery is like prostitution : a private thing between giver and taker. Nobody knows about it, nobody can prove it, nobody is hurt. Why bother? This woman here, for instance . . . How can you prove she does not maintain herself and her children on the earnings of her body? She's quite attractive. True, she has a stall in the market where she sells imported European foods, but that may just be eye-wash to fool the police. She's come to me to help her get a stall licence. I know she has no money to bribe me, but I like her. If I make a demand, she has either to accept or refuse. If she accepts, she will not need to go on a waiting list like the others; the licence will be hers in a week instead of a year. So much for the licence. She gets it, then goes to the shop to buy controlled goods . . . the clerk is young, and she is in need. And so it goes on. She doesn't mind. Five years of that, and you'll be counting her among the richest women in the city.
>
> (1954, pp. 40–1)

A further consideration, pointed out by Ardener (1962) on the basis of his enquiries into the sexual dealings of Bakweri women with men in the Cameroons plantations, is that domestic privileges, such as the provision of meals, may be conceded to regular clients who may themselves help to provide firewood or other amenities. He suggests that this 'lack of anonymity or impersonality, in prostitution transactions in a "stranger quarter", gives the relations with the client some quasi-uxorial qualities'. Ardener therefore proposes the coining of some such term as *hyperpolandry* in order to isolate, for theoretical use, these aspects of prostitution as a category of conjugality (*ibid.*, p. 21). This leads, in turn, to his dividing up reported conjugal unions into six types which, in addition to including customary, inherited, church and civil as legitimate unions, included concubinary and casual as illegitimate unions. Altogether, Ardener interviewed 1,062 women and the figures, expressed as percentages, show that 7·6 per cent had contracted casual unions (as prostitutes) at some time during their lives and 7·4 per cent were engaged in prostitution at the time of the survey. (See table below which is based on data concerning Bakweri women who absconded to become prostitutes or to live with immigrants.) [10]

The advantage of Ardener's approach is that it avoids the kind of circular argument implicit in the distinction made by

[10]

	Legitimate unions				Illegitimate unions	
	Customary	Inherited	Church	Civil	Concubinary	Casual
Ever contracted	79·0	2·5	1·3	0·1	9·5	7·6
Extant only	80·1	2·7	0·9	0·3	8·8	7·4

Southall and Gutkind between prostitution and the occasional 'love affair'. Thus, according to these authors, Kampala prostitutes usually are paid in cash, whereas lovers are rarely given money. Another view, which our own data support, is subjective. It claims that what differentiates the prostitute type from all other categories of women providing sexual services is her professional attitude. Her livelihood depends on the job, and so she takes her work seriously, avoids dissipating her energies by being more sociable than she has to, and operates as mechanically as possible.[11] Competition is keen because the market is overcrowded already by the 'good-time girls' who, in addition to the women described in the next chapter, probably include another category, spoken of by Comhaire-Sylvain as *femmes 'faciles'*. These are happily-married women of Kinshasa who come into town for the easy money to be earned by the casual provision of sexual services (1968, p. 164).[12] Such practitioners are, from the point of view of the 'professional', just 'amateurs', whose activities affect the market.[13] The real prostitute's work is a full-time activity and she realizes that its success depends not only upon her having a wide clientele, but on her being available – 'on call' – at any time that clients feel the need for her.

This point is illustrated by a study of 'Tutu' prostitution made

[11] This point was made plain to the author who, on one occasion, spent a sociable evening, visiting Nairobi night clubs, in the company of such a woman, a Kamba. When, however, the tour ended and he indicated that all he now wanted was to return home, his companion made her own attitude clear. He had been wasting her time.

For the above reason, therefore, it is difficult entirely to agree with Ardener's further suggestion that 'the prostitute is not purely and simply an occupational category'. It is true that human beings are not like automata but the fact that commercial activities are carried on within a social context does not make them less commercial. A stockbroker, for example, has an occupation and it consists of buying and selling stocks and shares. He takes his client out, perhaps, for a round of golf and a pleasant and sociable time is had by both. Does this mean, in consequence of the 'social' part of the relationship, that stockbroking is not 'purely and simply an occupational category'?

[12] Hunt (1969) describes an analogous situation in New York.

[13] Needless to add, the activities of 'amateurs' are also resented in Britain. According to a report of the *Guardian* (6 August 1971) –

Two prostitutes had complained in an interview on Radio Teesside last month about the 'unprofessional' activities of teenage girls who board ships illegally and offer sailors 'sex' for a very small payment, sometimes taking 'only sweets'! . . .

They claimed that these girls were taken into the docks by taxi-drivers who hid them in their cars. The women . . . had said that these young girls spread venereal diseases and gave the professional prostitutes 'a bad name' because they steal from sailors.

87

in Accra and in some of the suburbs of Abidjan in the Ivory Coast. The name 'Tutu' is probably derived from the expression 'two-two' (two shillings, two shillings) and is indicative of the fixed price charged by this category of prostitute.[14] In Accra, they live in what is to all intents and purposes a separate 'red light' area,[15] and in the evenings they take up a position on the door-step, allowing the client to make his choice. In Abidjan, however, these prostitutes are more dispersed, although it is easy to recognize the 'Tutu' part of the street because a cloth curtain is lowered in front of the doorway when the woman is not occupied. She never leaves her house 'for business' and will only take a client for a short time; but in Accra, a 'Tutu' will visit a client and spend the night in his own room, the charge for this extra service naturally being higher. Quite a large proportion of the 'Tutu' apparently work first in Ghana and then move on to the Ivory Coast, Ghana being the normal stopping place for prospective 'Tutu' coming, say, from Nigeria. The Ghanaian women prefer to go directly to the Ivory Coast before starting work (cf. Rouch 1954, pp. 80–2, and Rouch and Bernus, 1959).

Young women between the ages of 20 and 30 constituted about 60 per cent of the sample taken in Abidjan, but there were also elderly women. This would suggest, according to Rouch and Bernus, that since youth is not an indispensable quality, the 'Tutu' provide for their clients a sort of mechanical prostitution. Out of 32 women who were interviewed, 23 claimed to be married, and 11 said that their husbands were in Abidjan. The group as a whole also claimed to have 54 children between them, and quite a large proportion of the married women had their husbands as well as children living with them. An informant explained that not only did the husbands know all about their wives' business but they themselves encouraged it. The husband also takes a job and when his day's work is over he comes and sleeps with his wife. Unmarried women are obliged to have a male protector for whom they provide food as well as sexual service. If a woman becomes pregnant the child belongs to the father, whoever he is, but unmarried women give children to their family. In fact, children are

[14] The 'Tutu' are also called 'English prostitutes' because they come exclusively from the former British colonies in West Africa, and include mainly Fante, Krobo, Ibo, Ijaw and Calabari women.
   Although in Accra itself the number of Fante women who are 'Tutu' appears to be small, this is possibly because the Fante people live so close to Accra.

[15] William Bosman (1705), the seventeenth-century Dutchman who travelled extensively on the West Coast, provides an interesting account of a 'red light' quarter in one of the Dahomey towns he visited.

an economic asset in the areas whence the women come and this explains why their own families do all they can to persuade their daughters to take up the trade (Rouch and Bernus, 1959).

The fact that prostitution is carried on in these terms with the husband's consent and that he continues throughout it to have sexual relations with his wife suggests, according to Rouch and Bernus, that the situation described is a traditional form of prostitution.[16]

A special feature of prostitution in Accra is the interest of certain groups in having children. Kotokoli women from Togo, in particular, come with this aim and hope, in addition to making money, quickly, to have by the end of their tour children by a client to take back to Kotokoli country (Acquah, 1958, pp. 72–4; Rouch, 1954, p. 81). A further reason for ' Tutu ' prostitution is the necessity of paying off debts, and Rouch and Bernus estimated that a ' Tutu ' in Abidjan is able to make a profit of between 250,000 and 400,000 francs out of a two years' stay. During that time, she sends money home by a friend returning to the village and she herself goes home at the end of her two years' tour. She returns, however, when her nest-egg has been used up, and three of the investigator's sample had been shuttling backwards and forwards over the past ten years. Five of the group had made their first trip in 1957; five in 1956, and seven in 1955. The average length of stay during which not more than one journey was made was one year, nine months (1959).

Another form of prostitution practised in both Accra and Abidjan follows a purely traditional pattern, and ' Karuas ' (*Karuwai*) who are Hausa, Fulani, Moshi and Zerma women, usually divorced, provide a well-known example of this. Their practice in Accra is to rent a small house in the *zongo*,[17] where

---

[16] This is an interesting idea, especially in the light of Bosman's report (1705), which includes a quite lengthy account of the initiation of girls as prostitutes in the coastal areas of what is now Ghana. Space does not permit even its summarization here, but my own reading of the institution described by Bosman is that it was a species of social service. Given that African society in the areas concerned was polygamous, there was probably a shortage of unattached girls and so the women trained as prostitutes provided the young unmarried men with a sexual outlet.

[17] Every Ghanaian town of any size has its *zongo* where African strangers live, and sometimes the *zongo* contains more people than the rest of the township. In Nigeria, the immigrants' quarters are known as *sabon-gari* (' new town ') (Steel, 1961, p. 273). The term *karuwai* is not adequately translated by its nearest English equivalent, prostitute, because it is also applied to male adults who are not married and are reputedly profligate (see Mary F. Smith, 1954, pp. 25–6 for further details).

they lodge and feed passing strangers. The young men visit them to talk and play music as well as to make love, and when a client leaves at the end of, say, a week, he hands over a sum of money (Rouch, 1954, p. 81).[18] In Abidjan, these Nigerian women live most often as courtesans for a long period of time with their clients and hope in this way to find another husband. They carry on their activities separately and are under the central authority of a *Magazia* (chief of 'free' women).[19] In Hausaland itself, although prostitution is part of the accepted pattern of life, attitudes towards it are ambivalent. It is formally disapproved of since all women should be married. On the other hand, many married men court prostitutes with offers of marriage and many married women declare their envy of the prostitutes' independence. As in the case, also, of the *femmes libres* (see next chapter), the relative success with which many individual *karuwai* maintain or maximize this undefined independence provides the basis of their status placement and differentiation (M. G. Smith, 1959, p. 246).

Prostitution is also an important economic activity for women in the larger towns of East Africa. In Dar es Salaam, as in West Africa, there are professional prostitutes who have come to the town, often from a great distance, specifically for this purpose.[20] They emanate from the 'Christian tribes', with the Haya in a huge

[18] By definition, all Hausa prostitutes have been previously married and they come from different social classes. Some are daughters of noblemen, some of commoners, and some of *malams* (Koranic scholars) (see Mary F. Smith, 1954, pp. 33–34, for further particulars).

[19] The term cited by Mary F. Smith (1954) in this connection is *Magajiya* and this woman is referred to as head of the prostitutes. This was a recognized status in the hierarchy of Hausa society, and at the end of the long ceremonial dance, which marked her installation, the local chief invested the chosen woman with a turban as the symbol of her authority. It was the *Magajiya's* duty to receive complaints from prostitutes who had been 'bilked' by their clients. She had the power not only to recover the fees due but to exact a fine.

It is also noteworthy that a hierarchy can be distinguished amongst Hausa prostitutes. At the head are the fashionable and prosperous courtesans whose establishments are patronized by wealthy and aristocratic clients. These women are known as *manya-manya kuruwai* and they are followed by the reasonably successful *kuruwai zaune*. At the bottom of the scale are itinerant prostitutes who travel from town to town, and who are clearly much worse off than their socially superior sisters.

In fact, Hausa disapproval of prostitution (or female independence) varies according to its fruit, and the Hausa equivalent of our film-stars enjoys a corresponding position (Mary F. Smith, 1954, pp. 225, 274: see also M. G. Smith, 1957, p. 35 and 1959, p. 246).

[20] Including, it would seem, some Arabs who are male prostitutes. Dar es Salaam is the only African town in which this writer has himself found evidence of male prostitution.

preponderance. Classed together with the Haya but rather above them are the Ganda, and higher still are the Indians, Arabs and ' half-castes '. The clientele of the latter includes all races but only the higher income groups, and such women are usually well dressed and live in rooms of considerable affluence. As a rule, these professional prostitutes (as opposed to ' call-girls ') band together and rent all the main rooms in a house, each taking one and being herself responsible for its rent. According to Leslie (1963, p. 232):

> it is not difficult for such women to rent rooms in this way. Though some landlords do not like to be mixed up with the type of clientele they bring, often drunk and quarrelsome and noisy, many are prepared to put up with this for the sake of the steady rent – prostitutes having a reputation for paying on the due date – and one well above the average. A room which by its condition and amenities deserved at present rates a rent of 20 shs. to the general public, will bring in 30 shs. from a prostitute, not to offset her ill-repute but because she is known to have the means to pay more than others.

Haya women, together with a few Ganda, are also the principal kind of professional prostitute in Kampala, Uganda. The Kisengi district there is characterized as a slum with a population density of 35.9 persons per acre. Roads, drainage and water supply are lacking, but at most times of the day Kisengi gives the impression of throbbing social activity. The sale of various kinds of beer is one of the principal forms of economic activity, and at most times of the day large groups gather to sit outside the rooms of the numerous sellers. Kisengi is the largest centre of petty trade in the whole of the Kampala area and equally active are the prostitutes. There is a concentration of them in what is known as the Kaziba quarter and the prostitutes there simply sit in their rooms and wait for customers to hire them. The agreed normal fee for a short time is 2s., and for the whole night or longer time during the day the cost is from 5s. to 10s. Southall and Gutkind have provided a number of case-studies: a Haya girl of 22 who had never been married and moved twice from room to room during the course of the survey, said that she came to get good dresses and money. ' I get money from men when they sleep with me, I charge three shillings for a short time and ten shillings for the whole night.' Southall and Gutkind point out, however, that the amount paid does not appear rigidly fixed. Almost all the men questioned said that they pay ' what we feel like '.

On the other hand, some men reported that the ' price ' was fixed by the women according to the time of day and duration of the visit. One woman, a Ganda prostitute, said that she charged according to tribe. This seemed to work out that some Bantu-speaking people were paying a good deal more than non-Bantu as the Acholi and the Lango.[21] It is also possible, of course, that prostitutes charge less in the case of clients whom they personally like. Three men came to the door during the interview and, seeing the girl engaged, said that they would return later.

> A Ganda girl of 23 was practising prostitution in the same area as the Haya, and while she was being interviewed a charcoal-seller entered. He had brought a lorry load of charcoal and had sold it for 900s. He said that he came to this area because he knew that women here allow men to spend the night with them provided they pay the fees. This woman had many mottoes on her wall: 'One who makes friends is better than one who quarrels.' 'A friend in need is a friend indeed.' 'Make friends with many, but trust only a few.' 'Money is my lord.' 'Welcome my friend.' 'To love without affection is not love.' 'Every day I wait for you, darling'
>
> (Southall and Gutkind, 1957, p. 8)

Another old Haya prostitute of about 40 was said to be 'still fat and clean'. She also sold millet beer, and in another area of Kampala – the temporary housing development area of Upper Kiswa – Parkin has reported that a number of prostitutes work in so-called 'European' bottle-beer bars. The proprietor employs a woman as a barmaid and no more. She carries on her own business of prostitution privately outside working hours, deciding the charges for her services. Since it provides the more expensive bottle-beer bars and woman, Upper Kiswa attracts a clientele of higher than average socio-economic status who are themselves not residents (1969, pp. 14–6).

An East African novelist has described this kind of resort and the contemptuous attitude of its habitués towards the barmaids:

> He looked at the bar girls dotted round the room. They looked like a huge mockery on all the men who were drinking and pinching their bottoms. They had completely, as it were, dispossessed themselves of their bodies. Their bodies were used like the old cushions around them, to be pinched and sat upon. Their souls felt like the stuffing that took the weight and the beating from the bottoms that fatted on them.
>
> (Rubadiri, 1967, p. 41)

---

[21] Sometimes there is also discrimination according to race. Thus, in Bo, Sierra Leone, European soldiers were charged more than African clients (Little, 1951, pp. 167–8).

As briefly mentioned above, some women combine prostitution and commerce, especially when the latter is intermittent. Pons found that in certain areas of Stanleyville this practice was carried on in the women's own compound (1969, p. 246); and Nadel has reported that numbers of women traders in the markets of Bida, Northern Nigeria, were also reputed prostitutes. In the latter case, trading often involved long journeys from home by train or canoe to the big towns and so led to the disappearance of all moral control of the husband over his wife, or the local community over its women. They, in consequence, claimed sexual licence for themselves; and so, not surprisingly, the women traders who go on these long expeditions and stay away from home for weeks, months, or even years, are commonly looked upon as ' loose ' women, who cannot help leading an immoral life. Yet at the same time, their profit from prostitution in the course of their journeys is regarded by the people as legitimate a form of earning as that from trade itself. On their eventual return home, husband and family receive them without question and no blame attaches to them for the life which they have been leading while away (Nadel, 1942, p. 333; quoted by Henriques, 1962, p. 389).

Somewhat similarly, although the attitude towards them is less sympathetic, there are women traders who in Sierra Leone also travel the country. These ' husbandless ' women (as un-attached women are derogatorily called) go from market to market and from town to town as their business in selling fish and produce and other interests, directs. In a sample of 34 women of this type in Bo, only 9 had resided in the same town for longer than a year. About three-fourths of the group were estimated to be below the age of thirty; 10 could read and write. About half the same sample were living with relatives; the others rented accommodation; 5 out of the group were married. Some 10 of them employed young boys whose duty, among other things, was to find and escort clients to them. Contacts with the opposite sex were made personally in other cases, or in the ordinary course of trading. The women were remunerated by ' drinks ' and clothes as well as in cash, the extent of the remuneration being left to the client (Little, 1951, pp. 167–8).[22]

[22] Where a group of such women share the same house, the arrangements approximate those of an organized brothel, with the exception that personal choice is exercised over customers, the sign of acceptance being a head-tie thrown over the head of the person accepted. Also, visitors were expected to be sociable, and to pay for a substantial part of the whisky and beer consumed. In one such house the women had more or less permanent ' friends ' who, however, gave way when business necessitated it (ibid.).

This was the situation in Bo, which is Sierra's largest town up-country, but prostitution in Freetown is on a wider scale, being largely the outcome of that city's function as one of West Africa's most important ports.[23] The women involved are know as 'rarray girls', and their presence there seems to have been one of the main reasons why Banton's migrant informants found life in the capital more agreeable than up-country. In the provinces, they complained, there was too much 'palaver' over women: husbands demanded £8, £10, £12 and more for 'woman damage' and were supported by the chiefs. In Freetown, on the other hand, there were plenty of women with whom they could go without being taken to court: 'Many women would take a lover and expect little in the way of presents, while there were others with whom one could have a "short time" for 4s. or 5s.' (Banton, 1957, p. 57).[24]

Moving across to Kenya, the Kipsigis, too, tolerate the presence of prostitutes, and the Kipsigis woman will leave her tribe and travel to a town for this kind of trade (Peristiany, 1939, pp. 5, 54, 83, 92). Its existence in this African country, it has been suggested, is partly due to the hiring of girls by European bachelors. Other prostitutes were wives who had been deserted, or girls in service with Europeans who had lost their jobs. Also, the European-type brothel has been reported from a number of Tanzanian towns where it is staffed by women from various tribes and patronized, sometimes, by Europeans,[25] as well as by the indigenous population, including some of their chiefs.

[23] In fact, Freetown has one of the finest natural harbours in the world, and during the last war it was quite common for more than 100 ships, collected in convoy, to be moored there at the mouth of the Sierra Leone river.

[24] Also, although many indigenous languages contain expressive ways of joking about or remonstrating at a display of the sexual impulse, Freetown is noteworthy for the lively and pungent way in which such matters are referred to, especially in Krio. Krio is the language of the Sierra Leone Creoles and its Rabelaisian flavour makes it most effective as repartee. For example, a relatively polite way of calling a lady a prostitute or a nymphomaniac is to say that she is '*man matrass*', i.e. always ready to respond to any man's demand for sexual satisfaction. Naturally such a term is rarely, if ever, used in genteel society; but other robust expressions include: '*Dam raray dog*' – you celebrated harlot'; '*mammay pimma*' – 'your mother's sex organ'; '*bamboat tin*' – 'this sex maniac'; '*basstar-pickin yasso*' – 'you child of no father'. Of course, an angry husband openly swears at his wife by her mother's genitalia in traditional society, also.

[25] Writing in 1962 in reference to the then Central African Federation (C.A.F.), Henriques wondered whether post offices and brothels were the two major meeting-places where the colour bar was not invoked (1962, p. 397). Tanzania itself did not, of course, belong to the C.A.F.

It is, however, mainly in the African townships of South Africa that the brothel exists. It is to be found in establishments known more politely as ' shebeens' which do, in fact, sell beer, illicitly brewed, but also employ girls to encourage the customers to drink by granting small sexual favours. Then, at various times in the evening a girl will take a man off, returning after she has had sexual intercourse with him. In some districts Coloured, as distinct from Bantu, men run these shebeens-cum-brothels, and in addition to paying 3s. 6d. for a woman, the customer is expected to buy a pint of beer. The Coloured owner takes 1s. of the prostitute's fee and the fact that at weekends a girl may make as much as £5 a day gives some idea of the trade's extent. In Malay Camp, outside Johannesburg, there is a variant of this pattern. Any backyard premises are likely to be used for prostitution, and if a number of customers are waiting, anyone willing to pay more than the others is allowed to jump the queue (Longmore, 1959, *passim*).

The numerical preponderance of adult males in the African population of South African towns is probably greater than anywhere else in the African continent. In fact, not only does the entire edge of cities like Johannesburg tend to be predominantly male, but thousands of men are quartered in compounds and hostels separated by hundreds of miles from any home influence and restraint. Consequently, there being no communal voice to condemn behaviour, no sanctions and no penalties, so many unmarried women have borne children that it seems to be accepted as an everyday occurrence and to cause little untoward comment. This was the case in all sections of township life, but especially in the notorious Sophiatown [26] where many Bantu parents encouraged their children into prostitution in order to help make ends meet in the family: girls of only fourteen or fifteen years earned money in this way.[27] Also, wives in co-operation with their husbands became part-timers, the husband keeping watch outside the house in case the police might come on the scene. Since in the latter situation liquor is also included in the charges, it has been estimated that such women make as much as £20 a day (Longmore, 1959, p. 43). As elsewhere in Africa, there is also an apparently more independent type of prostitute. These women,

[26] I write here in the past tense because the district known as Sophiatown when Longmore's book was written has been demolished in the meantime.

[27] The resemblance in this connection is obviously very close to nineteenth-century conditions in London and other British cities (see, among others, Mayhew, 1861-2 and Pearsall, 1969).

who are at the top of their profession, cater mostly for European, Chinese and Indian men (Henriques, 1962).[28]

Dar es Salaam is another port town that has some similarity to Freetown in respect of both prostitution and an effective vocabulary of slang terms applying to the fair sex (Leslie, 1963, pp. 148–9).[29] The prices charged there by professional prostitutes appear to be about the same as in Kampala. In Dar es Salaam, however, there is no real 'red-light area' and the houses containing the trade are scattered fairly evenly in the more likely positions. Most newcomers to the trade enter through the help of an established friend or relative, and the end of such a career comes usually when the prostitute has made the amount of money for which she came. Leslie found that, like the 'Tutu', Dar es Salaam prostitutes also have children, although the proportion of those women who had never borne a child rose from the mean of 33 per cent to 48 per cent in the case of prostitutes. On the other hand, more than half had borne a child, mostly (29 per cent) a single child; and 10 per cent had borne four or five children (compared to 12 per cent in a sample of all married women).

Of course, some prostitutes never do go home. On retirement they may, as in Stanleyville, become small shop keepers (Pons, 1969, p. 248). Others become prosperous enough to acquire houses which, sometimes, they let to others of their trade. A steady income is to be made in this way, and, as illustrated in *Jagua Nana*, some of these older women like to have younger husbands much in the position of 'kept men'. Thus 'Jagua' who subsidizes her lover's further education has marriage with him in view, both

[28] Henriques' suggestion is that since sexual intercourse between European and Bantu is now a serious criminal offence in South Africa, there may be an incentive for those whites who seek prostitutes (1962, p. 400).

[29] Some of the less rude expressions include a semi-political phrase that has been diverted to use by a woman thus: '*Alani taabu, bwana ninaye akili hana*', to mean, 'I have a husband (or lover) but he does not satisfy me and he won't notice if I go off with somebody else'. Used as a greeting and invitation together, this, Leslie remarks, is said to be very effective. '*Kibiriti ngoma*' ('dance-flame') describes a loose woman; she is probably referred to as a '*koo*' ('dame'), and described as an '*mtoto shoo*' ('show-girl'), '*wa kisura*' ('pin-up'). To attract her one must show oneself a real '*mwana-heramu*' ('son-of-sin'), dressing as a cowboy in a '*koti la kigai*' ('a guy's coat'), with '*nchinjo*' ('knife-edge') tight trousers, or perhaps '*siruali ya njiwa*' ('ring-necked dove trousers'), with '*kilipa*' ('crepe-soled shoes'), and '*gaistait*' ('United States guy or cow-boy's tie'). One must be generous with presents, lest she say one has '*Mkono wa ganzi*' ('pins and needles in the hands' [meanness]), even if it means that in the end '*akukanshe*' ('dries out'), she squeezes you dry (Leslie, *ibid.*).

for the prestige of having an eligible young man attached to her and in order to provide companionship in old age (p. 6). There are also the women who, though not actual prostitutes, come close to qualifying as such. This type of person has been used to having men about her ready and anxious to render a 'helping hand' whenever she is willing to receive it. But the source of this un-solicited economic support grows progressively smaller as age overtakes her and the stage is eventually reached when such a woman finds it necessary to demand cash payment for sexual services. In Dar es Salaam these 'ex-amateurs', as Leslie calls them, are from the same main tribes as form the bulk of the population. The Zaramo predominate and they are collectively referred to as 'Swahili women' in a slightly derogatory sense. They operate or try to operate from a rented room; but, being new to the game and inexperienced in a professional sense, they have either to depend on taxi-drivers or go outside themselves in order to find clients. It is for this reason that, according to Leslie, the newest and the biggest taxis are to be found in the more African part of Dar es Salaam (1963, p. 236).

Besides their taxi-driver scouts, prostitutes who are not, as yet, established go out to look for their customers in dance halls, bars and hotels. Some loiter in or walk certain streets, usually in pursuit of non-African custom. They are easily recognized by their heavily powdered make-up and by a brisk glance and a lively reply to an enquiry. Their companionship is purchased by an entrance ticket to a dance, or a bottle of beer and a cigarette. After the party they can be taken to a room, of which there are many kept vacant for such an eventuality, and some rooms can be hired by the hour.

In Sekondi–Takoradi and in other seaport towns of the West Coast the boy or young man who procures customers is known as a 'pilot boy', and, in addition to directing customers to the prostitutes for whom he works, he often gets money by stealing or by acting as a guide to sightseers (Busia, 1950). 'Pilot boys' first became of significance as a group in Sekondi-Takoradi during the Second World War when the port was full of American and British soldiers. Busia's report of these activities was published in 1950 and at that time he estimated that a 'pilot boy' earned between £3 and £6 per month. This was on the basis of his being paid 8s. for each pound earned by the prostitute herself (pp. 96–7; see also Banton, 1957, pp. 186–7).

In Freetown these touts are known as 'rarray' boys and, in general, each professional prostitute employs her own pimp whose fee is known (following Naval parlance) as the 'tow-rope' (Little, 1951, p. 168). In Lagos, pimping is also done by car-park attendants. These *jagudas*, as they are known, make the introduction. For example, a customer who does not 'know the ropes' can walk into a hotel after speaking to the attendant outside and the latter will bring a woman to his table. If she and the client agree to go back to her flat the *jaguda* receives a fee from both parties. Acting in this way as the woman's broker, the *jaguda* controls a good deal of her activity because, as explained, girls new to professional prostitution need contacts. This applies particularly to those whom the *jaguda* himself picks up in provincial towns and who, as mentioned earlier, are only waiting for an opportunity to abscond (Little, 1972*a*).

Characteristically, however, instead of relying upon a ponce, many prostitutes form associations to consolidate and protect their position. Such measures are necessary because usually a room has to be rented, a plentiful supply of clothes is needed, and, as explained, the young men who solicit custom or act as go-between have to be paid.[30] Since, moreover, prostitutes are often fair game for criminal gangs as well as being in trouble quite often with the police, they rely upon their associations to intervene on their behalf with the authorities as well as in disputes with other women. 'Tutu' prostitutes, for example, were the object of a good deal of jealousy because they entertained not only migrant men but the husbands of women in Abidjan itself. This so incensed the local Abidjan prostitutes as well as the Abidjan wives that on one occasion when a fight broke out between a 'Tutu' and an Abidjan wife, a number of non-'Tutu' prostitutes joined in and ransacked the 'Tutu's' house. Her associates called in the police and laid a complaint with the authorities (Rouch and Bernus, 1959).[31] Also, there are many 'good-time' girls, just referred to, who are equally accessible to men.

This category will be described more fully in the next chapter; and since some of these 'amateurs' are better dressed and sexually more attractive than the 'regulars', it becomes necessary for the latter to show that they have superior services to offer. Especially are young 'civilized' girls in demand, and this side of the trade being particularly lucrative, competition is correspondingly keen. This makes it essential to maintain a proper standard of professional conduct and so some associations formed by these would-be courtesans help them to advertise and to discourage unprofitable

[30] In a report, which I am unable to check, it is said that prostitutes' associations in eastern Nigeria petitioned the Government to allow the above expenses against income tax.

[31] This led to the position of the 'Tutu' being officially recognized and to their leader being permitted to represent them officially in the same way as other professional bodies.

competition. This is done in Brazzaville by providing at the society's own expense musical and other public forms of entertainment. One of the girls, specially chosen for the quality of her voice as well as her good looks, leads the singing. A high standard of elegance is aimed at, and older women of experience and taste choose the girls' dresses and instruct them in deportment. These societies – they are picturesquely styled by such names as ' Violette et Elegance ', ' Dollar ', ' La Rose ' (incorporating ' Stella ') – also seek a good name for themselves by limiting membership to carefully selected girls. The principal officers are the president, treasurer and a commissioner, and a committee rules the association and insists on proper professional conduct, including the avoidance of casual prostitution. There is also a common fund out of which members in financial straits are helped and their funeral expenses paid should they die.[32] In the latter event, the society behaves as if it were the family of the deceased; that is to say, every girl goes into mourning, giving up her jewellery and finer clothes for six months, and at the end there is a night-long celebration in some ' bar-dancing ' establishment hired for the occasion (Balandier, 1955, pp. 145–8; Little, 1965, pp. 131–3).

These practices encourage the girls to regard each other as sisters instead of rivals. Off-duty, however, they are less glamorous to the eye, and of an informal gathering observed in a Poto-Poto (Brazzaville) bar Balandier remarks :

> In one corner some young women seated around a table formed a noisy group; they were drinking beer, munching roasted peanuts and smoking. They wore long dresses of printed cotton and scarves of the same material on their heads. Their toe nails were painted with dark red polish, as were their finger nails and hands, which opened occasionally like that sinister flower, the black tulip. They were surrounded by some men of too studied an elegance, who were disdainful, seemingly indifferent to their chatter   (1969, pp. 192–4)

Balandier was told that out of her profits a girl may send back to her parents four to five thousand francs a month.

> She has no objection to being a courtesan but she does resent being an object of exploitation. Her surrender, therefore, to commercial ' love ' causes her some bitterness, although the young women concerned don't give way to depression.
>
> (Ibid.)

---

[32] In Sekondi-Takoradi, also, prostitutes' unions provide proper facilities for funeral celebrations and burials (Busia, 1950).

They dress in costly fashion, vie with one another in the purchase of jewellery; and they dance and they sing to such an effect that, as Balandier puts it:

> The provocativeness of their movements gives commercial eroticism a glamour in which our [Western] societies are no longer even interested:
> 'Come! Whom do you fear?
> I no longer have a husband.
> I married very young,
> Thinking there were no other men.
> If only I had known !
> Let me love you. You're just my type.'
> *(Ibid.)*

Some of the above category of women are *femmes libres* who, as will be explained in the next chapter, are often very much sought after. Most prostitutes, however, have to be content with whatever custom they can get and, unless backed by a regular lover, need to reserve every penny earned against the day when they will be too old for 'service'. It is not surprising, therefore, that many such associations, like those of women who market foodstuffs and other commodities, are primarily designed to safeguard their members' livelihood, especially the maintenance of prices. The difficulty is that women who are older and physically less attractive than their fellows tend to accept a lower fee from customers. This naturally causes dissension and Rouch and Bernus have described how, on arrival in the 'Tutu' prostitutes' street, they found most of the doors closed because the women were on strike.

> The reason was a 'palaver' the night before when one 'Tutu', who had refused 150 francs was undercut by her neighbour. A meeting of the association was immediately called and the president, trying to calm the women down, pleaded for unity. They were all in the same boat, she said: since the profession they had taken up was tough as well as unconventional it was essential to have a single tariff. If they did not, those who were neither young nor beautiful would have to lower prices in order to earn their own daily bread. She advised everyone to return to the job, charge 200 francs a time, and see how that worked. The following evening nearly all the 'Tutus' were working at the proposed rate, but two Krobo women cut their price to 175 francs. There was, therefore, further 'palaver' with the association's leader bitterly pointing out that she had one customer because,

despite being older and more ugly than the rest, she had insisted on 200 francs. Opinion was clearly divided over the idea of flat rate; but the president in the end firmly decreed that 200 francs, no more and no less, was the price that everybody must charge. (1959, *passim*)

Rouch and Bernus looked in again on two successive evenings and this was the amount uniformly asked for irrespective of the women's physical appearance which the investigators classified as toothless (1); very shabby (3); shabby (11); passable (8); beautiful (13). Such then was the position in Adjamé, but it did not appear that in Treichville, another district of Abidjan, prices were standard.

Finally, it appears as if the differences between the position of women in towns where they dominate the trade sector and in towns where they stay indoors is also reflected in patterns and kinds of prostitution. In countries where women are traders, prostitution is centred on markets and bars, and it is either unorganized or the prostitutes have their own mutual voluntary associations, as mentioned above. In those countries, on the other hand, where men dominate the market place while their wives stay at home, the prostitutes also live in secluded quarters and houses (Servais and Laurence, 1965, quoted by Boserup, 1970). Except, however, where Islamic influences are strong, the latter conditions are not characteristic of sub-Saharan Africa as a whole. Nor is prostitution the most favoured sexual relationship open to men outside marriage. On the contrary, while prostitutes are patronized mainly by migrants and other temporary visitors, there is also a wide variety of additional arrangements of an extramarital kind which are, for the most part, a normal feature of town life. These contacts, as the next chapter will show, often bring monetary and other material advantages to the women concerned, but they involve a more personal kind of relationship and, on the whole, are not regarded as derogatory by society in general.

7 The world of lovers

A favourite resort at which women can meet members of the opposite sex are the night clubs which provide an expert band. Such places vary in appointment and style and a few of them have an almost exclusively élite clientele whose taste in dance music is the latest European 'hits'. In the less expensive clubs, however, the popular 'high life' music is played,[1] and entrance, typically, is gained through a wooden door and narrow corridor into a piazza-like enclosure open to the sky. The chairs and tables are wooden with iron legs and they surround space for dancing. There is a festoon of coloured electric bulbs but lighting is pro-

[1] This statement is in the historical present because varieties of 'pop' music appear now (i.e. 1972) to be more in favour than 'high life'. Nevertheless, high life has not been entirely deserted by its devotees and its considerable significance for social life during the period when most of this book's data were collected merits its technical description as a syncretic form of music-dance. It uses many elements of European or American music such as scales (to their nearest approximation) and harmonies (some are conventional church harmonies), or instruments (piano, guitar, trumpet and drum set). But Yoruba bands apart, few high life bands in the urban areas employed indigenous African drums. For instance, a high life band would make use of maracas instead of the gourd rattle, and the Congo drum instead of the barrel drum (Kinney, 1970, pp. 3ff.).

The dance form is a couple dance. Couples usually begin to dance face to face and holding each other. They may separate to dance facing each other, alongside each other, or in single file. Movement is not on a flat plane, but, as in traditional dance, the body 'bounces' on every pulse. The posture when dancing apart displays a slightly forward inclination, and the dancers tend to move in a circular formation, counter-clockwise, as in traditional dance. The torso moves smoothly as a unit, from right to left, four times the speed of each foot. The male partner may move the woman's torso for her by placing his hand on her rib cage. Hip movement only results from the action of the torso. Hands sway with the body or are slightly balled and held at waist level. Footwork is the basic two-step (step-together). The degree to which the body moves varies

vided mainly by the moon.[2] Drinks may be fairly expensive, and there may or may not be a nominal charge for admission, many of the girls who come being admitted free. Most of them arrive quite early (say, between 10 and 11 p.m.), sit in groups at the tables, or on chairs around the room, sometimes with a male in attendance. The band plays almost continuously, and the place gradually fills up, largely with European men wearing white shirts and neck-ties. The Africans who come are usually more formally dressed. There are also a few European women, some of whom have Africans as escorts. The African girls are all smartly dressed. Most of the younger and slimmer wear pyjama suits or tight skirts and nylon blouses or frocks of the cocktail type. Those who are plumper and older wear an 'African' form of dress, which is of richer material and of a more theatrical design than what is conventionally worn. These women also have jewellery and trinkets sparkling on the neck, ears and arms and sometimes in the hair, in addition to being heavily pomaded and having an elaborate make-up to match (Little, 1972a).

Ekwensi's description of a well-known Lagos club (fictionally called the Tropicana) aptly conveys the atmosphere:

> Jagua saw them now as, with white collars off, they struck a different mood from the British Council: the expatriate bank managers, the oil men and the shipping agents, the brewers of beer, and the pumpers out of swamp water, the builders of Maternity Blocks, the healers of the flesh, German, English, Dutch, American, Nigerian, Ghanaian, they were all here, bound together in the common quest for diversion. Bouncing off the roofs, Jagua heard the trumpet choruses from the adjacent club reaching out to the Tropicana with a kind of challenging virility . . .

with the speed of the dance. Variations including dancing backwards, arching, and so on.

The high life was greatly influenced by West Indian sailors who went to the West African coast, taking with them the calypso, and much high life music is almost identical in style to calypso, i.e. rhythmic accompaniment, harmony and instrumentation. Also, the high life can be danced to calypso music.

It is also relevant that a particular and popular high life style has evolved among prostitutes, and their peculiar dance style distinguishes them from those who are not in the trade. As already mentioned, prostitutes are a mobile group who frequently travel from city to city. This, naturally, distributes their style, which nevertheless exhibits local variations (*ibid.*).

[2] We are speaking here, for the greater part, about the more popular West African 'night-spots'. The more exclusive are housed in buildings, as are most night clubs in other parts of Africa where the temperature is cooler but the weather less reliable.

Jimo Ladi and his Leopards always played well, though rather loudly, but dance high life must be loud to fire the blood. White men and black men, they all arose and crowded the floor. The black men chose the fat women with big hips, the white men clung to the slim girls with plenty of collar bone and little or no waists. There were girls here and women to suit all men's tastes. Pure ebony, half caste, Asiatic, even white. Each girl had the national characteristic that appealed to some male and each man saw in his type of woman a quality which inspired his gallantry. So the women enticed their victims and the Tropicana profited.

(Ekwensi, 1961, pp. 11–12)

The etiquette is for a man to invite a girl to dance. Usually, she accepts. While dancing they make a rapid assessment of each other. He has to decide whether the contact is likely to cause him subsequent embarrassment; she, whether he is in a position to be generous and, if so, what prospects the relationship will offer. After a time, if he has sized things up in the girl's favour, they return to his table or he sends over drinks to where she is sitting. If she accepts what is offered (which she usually does) it is understood that she is his girl for the evening and that he will accompany her to her room or take her back to his own place. However, they do not necessarily leave at once. The younger woman has come to dance as well as for business and so she may take the floor from time to time with another partner provided her client gives permission. Also, before joining the former person on the dance floor, she will slip into her client's hand the key to her room. This is the token of her agreement; it also signifies that she does not intend to go off with any other man (Little, 1972a).

Girls who attend night clubs of the above kind are generally able to follow a conversation in English or French. They also have some acquaintance with Western ways which has been gained in school or through contact with European men. Indeed, girls who lack this experience would be at a disadvantage because many of the men present are only out for a convivial evening. What they want is an amusing and attractive companion, and a number of these young women-about-town fill the bill. They have travelled in several countries, usually know intimately the gossip and scandal concerning local personalities and are able to talk, even if superficially, about political and other matters that their partners are interested in. Nor, provided the position is made clear to her, does the girl herself object to limiting her role to that of dance hostess if at the end she is given a good tip. However, that such night clubs are not the place for impecunious students is made clear in Ike's *Toads for Supper*. When the hero, 'Amobi' visits one of these resorts, none of the girls will dance with him because he refuses to buy them drinks. He resolves never again to attend such a place 'without a decent partner' (1965, pp. 29–30).[3]

Quite often these women-about-town have a particular 'friend' of their own age group or are kept by an older and richer man. However, since the girl's main interest is in fine clothes, costly jewellery, and expensive entertainment, a particular attachment rarely lasts for very long. Either the present 'friend' or patron objects to her consorting with other men, or she herself decides to transfer her affections to a more handsome or more generous swain. The significant thing is that the men with whom these girls associate must please them, and the older men who have been hoping that their lovers will make a home fail to understand this.

> They do not recognise the fact [remark Southall and Gutkind] that most women treat their love relationships as convenient, temporary and rewarding unions. One Ganda man, a *dhobi*, has had seven lovers in nine months. He has given them expensive dresses, shoes, handbags, pearls, scarves and money. They have all left him. He is bitter about this, saying: 'all women are unfaithful and they are all robbers'. He does not recognise these women for what they are. (1957, p. 163)

The elusiveness of 'town-women' is also illustrated by Ekwensi's 'Jagua Nana'[4] who infatuates an up-country Chief. He is rich and wishes 'Jagua' to marry him, promising her anything she

---

[3] In Onuora Nzekwu's novel, too, the hero has stopped going to Lagos dance halls because the men bringing their girl friends made sure that they danced only with well-known friends (1961, pp. 9–10).

[4] 'They called her Jagua because of her good looks and stunning fashions. They said, she was Ja-gwa, after the famous British prestige car' (Ekwensi, 1961, p. 1). It is interesting in this connection that a term frequently used in the Copperbelt was 'champion'. This is a highly ambiguous expression, and it seemed to have referred initially to a particular kind of bicycle that was very popular in early days. The term 'champion' of course suggests prowess, excellence, etc., someone to be emulated. On the Copperbelt it was used to refer to a woman who was skilled in ballroom dancing; perhaps one who had won prizes at such competitions. But by easy extension it also came to indicate a sophisticated woman in the modern idiom who had gained some notoriety for her sexual skills. Such a woman stood in sharp contrast to the 'respectable house-wife' who was, of course, always modest and faithful to her husband (personal communication from Professor A. L. Epstein). The personality and qualities attributed by Ekwensi to his character 'Jagua' are virtually identical with the latter connotation of 'champion', and it is also of interest that the Champion bicycle, as well as the Jaguar motor car, is a prestigious object.

desires. But 'Jagua' only wants to get back to Lagos. When she announces this her would-be husband is dismayed and points out that he has already paid 'Jagua's' bride price. Her pride deeply wounded, 'Jagua' promptly offers the Chief his money back:

> Is all you thinking about! You think you kin buy me with money? Am a free woman. An' I already sleep wid you ten night an' give you experience of Lagos woman you never dream. (Ekwensi, 1961, p. 74)

What, in fact, is at the heart of such typical attitudes is quite often expressed in words like the following:

> I like men who are modern. I like the men who do things. I like men who are elegant and civilized, and not just those who think their money can buy me.[5]

And the women co-operate with each other and scheme in order to attract the kind of man they think they want. For example, it is reported from Johannesburg that a woman may hesitate to say to a man, 'I love you', but will arrange instead for an indirect advance to be made on her behalf through another woman. Also, love affairs may develop between a man and some-one else's wife simply because the man is a friend of that particular woman's husband. The wife finds ways of letting her husband's friend know that to win her may not be impossible and so he learns to go to his friend's house even during his absence. The wife persuades herself that she has been love-starved for years and that in consequence 'her blood is stagnant'. She has been denied the pleasure to which she is entitled through preserving herself for a useless husband. At this stage she gives her now would-be lover the signal to go right ahead (Longmore, 1959, pp. 266–7).

In fact, there was general agreement in the African townships of Johannesburg that every man had a *nyatsi* (paramour), but the practice was more risky than in the rural areas where there was seldom more than one *nyatsi* involved. In the urban township the trouble arose in many cases by the woman having a number of *nyatsis*, so that they collided over her. This situation largely results from the women's avariciousness having outpaced their men's earning capacity. They become dissatisfied with what they can get from their 'husbands' and parents, and are easily enticed by men who can supply their wants. The large number of men available exerts strong temptations and pressures on the women and there are, in consequence, many stabbing and assault cases.

[5] More is said about this point in the next chapter.

This happens despite the necessity of keeping such affairs secret and the efforts of the women concerned to avoid arousing their neighbours' suspicions (*ibid.* pp. 269–70).[6] Although there is public protest against such behaviour, casual unions are widespread even among those who most strongly oppose it. The consequence, according to Longmore, is that the African urban society that no longer practises polygamy is developing a type of disguised polygamy/polyandry. The women claim that if their husbands think it is a grand game to have more than one wife in *nyatsi* form, there is no reason for them to remain attached and faithful to one man. They maintain that fidelity is a thing of the past and they contend that the word 'fidelity' does not occur.

> In short, the African woman in Johannesburg . . . is not afraid of being divorced.[7] She welcomes any change from her husband, as long as she does not have to finance a divorce case, as long as she is able to work for herself, and as long as she has somebody else to admire her. As far as she is concerned, married life has so many restrictions; so many responsibilities; and such boredom.   (*Ibid.* p. 271) [8]

And so, in announcing that she would not marry again, one woman said: 'it is so boring . . . One man before you every day. I shall never agree to that type of thing any more'. Like the girl in Dipoko's novel about the Cameroon (Chapter 2) who, being still young, wanted to go on 'playing with life', this Johannesburg woman felt that she was 'so young to be bored ! ' (p. 273).

[6] The Shoeshoe women, however, speak openly of their *nyatsis*, and it seems to be a generally accepted pattern of behaviour among them to have more than one such lover. These women accept money in exchange for the sexual services they provide, but each particular woman has her own particular *nyatsi* and so this aspect of the relationship cannot be classed as prostitution. If her *nyatsi* makes such a woman pregnant and she cares more for him than her own husband, she may run away with him. In any event, the break-up of a 'union' was usually preceded by a period of violent conflict, chiefly over 'outside' men and women (*ibid.* p. 270).

[7] A woman had a serious quarrel with her husband after getting drunk and sitting on a strange man's lap. She was very keen for a divorce but was not prepared to finance it, and so she was playing for time. In the meantime, she went to weekend parties more often than before, boasting that there was no monotony in a free single life (*ibid.* p. 271).

[8] Longmore comments in this regard that there are women 'who desire a new love affair, merely for the stimulus and excitement of the unknown. They consider it adventurous to sleep with someone else's spouse. Such people derive even more satisfaction from it if they can keep their affairs going without detection' (p. 270).

In Johannesburg, educated as well as uneducated people rely greatly on love medicine obtained from the ' doctors ' (professional magicians) in order to gain or retain the attention of the object of one's affections (Longmore, 1959, pp. 2–6). For example, one young girl wanted a love philtre in order to attract the attention of men. The ' doctors ' to whom she went asked her to cut some of her pubic hair. This was mixed with other charms and she was told to pour some of this concoction into a glass of beer and to offer it to the young man in whom she was interested. This she did, and very soon he had fallen for her, it is said.[9]

Kampala, too, according to Southall and Gutkind, has its ' world of lovers ' which is also one of considerable competition and jealousy. The women concerned try to cultivate an intimate, more or less permanent, circle of men friends, and a woman would certainly think twice before she accepted the offers of a man who was known to her as ' belonging ' to another lover (1957, p. 160). She would be in fear of physical assault as well as verbal injury. *Jagua Nana* illustrates a similar situation in a comparable stratum of West African society when ' Jagua ' discovers that ' Freddie ' has been attracted by ' Nancy ', a much younger woman and is, as ' Jagua ' suspects, carrying matters to their logical conclusion. To make things worse ' Nancy ' is the daughter of ' Jagua's ' rival for male admiration at the Tropicana; and so ' Jagua ' crashes into ' Freddie's ' room, lunging straight at ' Nancy ' and calling her names. ' Nancy ' retaliates in like fashion, declaring that she loves ' Freddie ' and that on his return from the United Kingdom, he will be her ' England man '. Whereupon ' Jagua ' springs at her.

---

[9] Another such love medicine is a preparation known as *sauslaudela*, which is administered in powder form. It is sprinkled into a handkerchief and, when the young lover approaches the girl he desires, he blows his nose when he is near her so that the fumes are inhaled by her, whereupon she cannot fail to fall for him immediately. In fact, the use of magical substances to win the hearts of either sex is so common that at a certain school, it is said, the girls refused to share seats in a classroom because they had been warned that the boys were in possession of *sauslaudela* (Longmore, 1959, pp. 42–6). Stimulants are also taken to increase sexual desire, and one of the most popular is known as ' Spanish Fly '. Either sex may use this, and it can be obtained from any chemist. If put under the armpit or rubbed against the sexual organs it is said to make them very active, and it is also said to be able to influence any woman to love a man or any man to love a woman (*ibid.* p. 45).
Longmore was told that European women are also among the people who practise these arts. These women move about under pretext of being fortune-tellers, and they are said to charge exorbitant amounts for their substances (*ibid.* p. 42).

Freddie scarcely saw the flash of her hand but he heard the smack and saw Nancy wince and place a hand on her cheek. The two women clinched, and it was Nancy who screamed, 'Oh! . . . Freddie, she bite me! De witch woman bite me!' (Ekwensi, 1961, p. 31)[10]

Needless to say, it is not only the women who like to make conquests. In Johannesburg, according to Longmore, a young man may have two, three, or four girls, running at the same time. For example,

the boy may bring (say) Dora to his home one night and free her at 4 a.m. the following day. He may have a number of girls, so Lizzie may be taken to his home the following evening. Lizzie may be working in the factory and from the boy's home she goes straight to work the following morning. Maisie is next after Lizzie. Dora may decide the fourth day to find out why her boy friend has not turned up to invite her to his home. Dora may invite herself to the boy's home where, on arriving, she finds that she has to sit in the kitchen until he is informed of her presence. Then she is greeted by her boy friend, accompanied as far as her home, and told that she should not call except when she is fetched. The boy then goes back home to get busy with Maisie. (1959, p. 25)

An *affaire* can be ended as quickly and as casually as it begun,[11] and from the young man's point of view relationships with women are only entered into ' for the fun of it '.

[10] In another of Ekwensi's stories, 'Ajayi', the hero, has a 'friend' 'Bintu', who provides him with domestic as well as sexual services, including cooking. He is more attracted sexually, however, to 'Konni', a prostitute whose clientele also includes 'Nwuke', one of 'Ajayi's' work-mates. 'Nwuke's' wife knows about 'Konni's' goings on with her husband, and so she picks a quarrel and physically assaults 'Konni'. 'Konni's' cheeks are so badly scratched that she has difficulty in covering the marks with face powder (1966b, pp. 1–45).

[11] The usual overture is the offer of a small present – even a cigarette may be sufficient for illiterate girls. Thus, in the recital of his adventures the Mende minstrel mentioned above (Chapter 6) wants the 'lovely girl' he has met to 'befriend' him. But the lady's husband is in near proximity – and so, 'she took me into a corner, where she agreed to be my "friend" and accepted the two shillings' (he had offered to show that he 'loved' her).

Note, also, Ekwensi (1945, p. 15): 'Every Sunday in this city, men met girls they had never seen and might never see again. They took them out and amused them. Sometimes it led to a romance and that was unexpected; but more often, it led nowhere. Every little affair was a gay adventure, part of the pattern of life in the city. No sensible person who worked six days a week expected anything else but relaxation from these strange encounters'.

Eric is a young (23) Ganda clerk in an office in Kampala. He rents one spacious room in Mulago where he has lived for 14 months. His income is 167/– per month. He pays 17/– rent and his food costs him another 55/– per month. He tries to save so that he can take a correspondence course in book-keeping and accounting. He came to Kampala because his father had no money to continue his education beyond the Secondary 2 level . . . After he had been in Mulago for three weeks he met a Ganda girl, an *ayah* to a European, at a dance in Katwe. He brought her home and she cooked for him for some weeks. He started to abuse her and she abused him, and the girl left. He did not mind that she had gone. For a while he cooked for himself or invited another young boy to live with him for a few days. Often he went out to eat in a hotel. After some weeks he found a Toro girl and lived with her for four weeks. He is always cheerful and says ' I am just a young boy. I do not want to be married for another three years. If I do not like the woman I tell her to leave me. I know that there are many young girls in Kampala who would like to come and live here with me. I never give them money, but we go out dancing and drinking together.'

(Southall and Gutkind, 1959, pp. 164–5. These authors provide a large number of similar examples.)

Sometimes, in Freetown as elsewhere, the mere ' smell' of money is enough to start things off:

Koroma boarded a bus and . . . [at] Brookfields a young woman got on, swearing and looking very angry. A man who was already on board moved over to her seat. The lady's ill-humour continued at first but began to abate when the man told her that he was going up-country to . . . the diamond mines. She then began to ask him questions. Was he married? How long would he be away for? Would he like to look her up on his return? Eventually she gave him her name and address on a piece of paper and rode a mile past the stop for which she had originally booked. Her new friend paid the extra twopence for her.

(Koroma and Proudfoot, 1960, p. 47)

Similarly, meetings can easily be arranged in Dar es Salaam, too. The man may have to set his fancy on this particular face:

he may be working a ' tour ' before going home to marry, and be amusing himself meanwhile; he may have a wife cultivating his fields at home, and be filling in the time; or he may, like many, be anxious to try many flowers, and willing to pause so long as the taste is sweet. If he is already married he will not wish to go through the formalities again in Dar es Salaam; and even if not married (and 39 per cent of the men in the 16–45 age group are single) it is cheaper, less tedious, and less of a commitment to form a liaison than to go through a formal marriage. On the woman's side, her price as mistress is higher than it would be as wife, for she holds continuously the spoken or unspoken threat that, if presents are not sufficiently frequent and expensive, she will move on to a rival. In her status as mistress she cannot be forced to do the menial jobs that a wife would have to do . . . This threat diminishes if the relationship turns into that of 'living together', for the woman ceases to live with him because he is the highest bidder, and begins to do so because they suit each other; a more dependant status, and a weaker bargaining position, but one of less tension and more content.

> (Leslie, 1963, p. 229)

But that there is male resistance to young women moving in to the latter position is shown by the East African novelist, Rubadiri.

Miria had walked into Lombe's life with the ease of most city girls. He had picked her up at the Astronaut, slept with her for a day and decided to employ her as a housekeeper . . .
Everything had gone on splendidly so long as Miria played her part of being house-girl during the day and mistress at night. But all of a sudden the arrangement changed because Miria was tired of playing at girl housekeeping; to all intents and purposes, was now mistress of the house, and was beginning to show possessiveness.

This irritated 'Lombe' and since 'Miria' was getting 'too many fancy ideas he decided to chuck her out'. To make matters very much worse Miria announces that she is pregnant and the doctor has told her to expect twins. This is too much for Lombe. He pushes Miria out of the bedroom and shouts, 'How do you know that they are my babies anyway?' (1967, pp. 7–9).[12]

[12] Girls who are easy to seduce are accused – sometimes correctly – of attempting to pin their pregnancy on an eligible bachelor. Ike (1965) illustrates this in his description of the easy-going Lagosian girl, 'Sweetie', whose mother complains to the university authorities that 'Amobi' has made her daughter pregnant; she wants a signed statement from 'Amobi' to the effect that he will marry 'Sweetie'. In due course, 'Sweetie' gives birth to a child, but the child is mulatto and its father presumably the European official with whom 'Sweetie' has also been consorting.

Ekwensi's *People of the City* depicts the same kind of male attitude and indicates that the girl's most effective way of countering it is to keep the opposite sex guessing. This novel also shows that there are different types of 'town-girl' – the emotionally dependent as well as the emotionally independent. In the story, 'Amusa Sango' is an ambitious young journalist who plays in a band. The previous evening he 'picked up' and slept with 'Aina', an alluring young woman, but feels very guilty the next morning. This is not because he has seduced an inexperienced girl, but because he does not want to be compromised. On top of it all, 'Aina' herself calls at his room [13] and begs 'Amusa' to reassure her: she wants to be sure that he loves her.

> 'Amusa . . . I want to ask you . . . Amusa, will you always love me as you did yesterday, no matter what happens ? '
> Yesterday ? To Sango, yesterday was past. You made a promise to a girl yesterday, but that was because you were selfish and a man who wanted her – yesterday. Why could she not undestand that it was over ?   (1954, pp. 14–6)

' Amusa Sango ' also meets ' Beatrice ' in whose case, however, the boot is on the other foot because ' Beatrice's ' attitude to men is objective and completely self-assured. She takes her ability to captivate for granted and is in a position – she knows very well – to pick and choose. ' Beatrice ' is the wife by native law and custom of a European engineer, ' Grunnings ', with whom she has lived for several years, and had children. ' Grunnings ', ' Beatrice ' admits, has treated her very well, but ' Grunnings ' is not taking her out enough. He spends too much time working, and things are too quiet. ' Beatrice ' likes noise, not silence. She enjoys ' high life ' and drinks and music. If she lived on her own she'd be happy because she came to Lagos to live and enjoy life . . . she always wanted to be ' free '. This was before she met ' Grunnings ', but she is now, in effect, looking for someone who, while supporting her, will allow her to live in the way that suits her.

And so ' Amusa ', in whom ' Beatrice ' has confided, introduces her to an elderly but wealthy African who already has eight

---

[13] ' Aina's ' uninvited call at ' Sango's ' room suggests that some girls in Lagos are as ready as those in Johannesburg to make advances to boys they fancy. Longmore cites, as a typical example, a young man who was asked by a girl in the latter city to give her private coaching in English. When he arrived the room was highly scented; he was given an expensive dinner, and when he was leaving the girl offered to do his washing. The next time he called the girl was in her nightdress. She put her arms around him and kissed him calling him darling. The boy told Longmore: ' I could not resist the temptation and I just surrendered ' (1959, p. 36).

wives. He – 'Lajide' – is attracted by 'Beatrice' and immediately offers her accommodation in a good quarter of the town. 'Beatrice' is not keen on the implications of this offer and on the way out meets 'Zamil', a Lebanese, who is thinking of buying the house in question. All three of them drive over there in 'Zamil's' large American car, and from 'Beatrice's' point of view it is a more convenient place than the one outside Lagos where she lives with 'Grunnings'. But where in all this scheme did 'Beatrice' fit in ?

> She decided not to accept a room here if Lajide gave her one. She might as well be Zamil's mistress.

After 'Lajide' and 'Zamil' have completed their business they all go on to a department store celebrated for its stock of women's fashionable clothes. In the restaurant there 'Zamil' proffers a snack all round, but 'Lajide' leaves and 'Zamil' offers to buy 'Beatrice' anything she fancies. She declines his offer and walks over to where 'Amusa' is sitting. 'Amusa' advises 'Beatrice' to stick to 'Grunnings', but the next time he sees her she has apparently taken up with a Ghanaian transport owner. 'Amusa' and she are attracted to each other but neither is disposed to take things further. They both know that 'Amusa' cannot provide the luxuries that are 'Beatrice's' life blood; nor does he move in the sort of milieu that 'Beatrice' loves – 'the world of glamour and seduction' (Ekwensi, 1954, pp. 113–19).

It has been suggested that Ekwensi's characterization of 'Beatrice' symbolizes the materialistic aims and values of the city.[14] Another view might be that 'Beatrice' is an African version of the 'career girl'. She has no occupational aspirations in the ordinary sense of the term, but in line with the Western stereo- type of such women is 'Beatrice's' cool and well-controlled determination to get what she wants. To provide her with the things she desires, men must be rich; and so, despite 'Amusa's' attraction for her, 'Beatrice' realistically rejects any idea of becoming emotionally involved with him.

In the French-speaking countries women of 'Beatrice's' type are called *femmes libres* because, unlike the ordinary prostitute, they do not necessarily take any man who comes along.[15] To do so

---

[14] See Tucker (1967) who provides an interesting discussion of the writings of Ekwensi and other African novelists.

[15] However, the primary connotation of this term is legal because in the former Belgian Congo *femmes libres* were women who qualified for residence in African townships – known as *centres extra-coutumiers* (or C.E.C.) – in their own right, and who thus had their own identity cards. Such women are also spoken of as 'independent women', quite often with the implication that women who live on their own and do not share a house with husbands, relatives, friends, or lovers are prostitutes.

would, quite apart from personal feelings, do damage to their reputation.[16] On the whole, therefore, they choose whom they will favour, are unwilling sometimes to accept a stranger, and are unlikely to continue an affair unless the lover satisfies their standards of personal conduct and generosity. According to studies made in Cotonou, Stanleyville and elsewhere, a *femme libre* has usually been married but now lives independently, sometimes with her children. She loves luxury and has liaisons with high-ranking civil servants. She is quite often a wealthy trader, but other women of this category are employed in offices and shops during the day. In Stanleyville (now Kisangani), *femmes libres* were locally centred mainly in the fashionable and lively part of the town, where they constituted an élite, setting modern or 'urban' standards for the masses (Pons, 1969, *passim*). Also, for a politician to be seen in the company of *femmes libres* is a useful way of advertising his qualities. If he demonstrates in this way that he is acceptable to a circle of notorious beauties, he is admired for his virility and personality (La Fontaine, 1970, p. 204).

Many, though not all, *femmes libres* in Stanleyville – Kisangani led relatively independent lives as the mistresses of wealthier African men, and in a minority of cases, Europeans. Some of them were semi-prostitutes whose small, changing sets of 'lovers' or clients ordinarily gave them 'presents' in return for sexual favours granted regularly over a period of time, rather than strictly contracted cash payments in return for intermittent sexual encounters. In contrast to the male *évolués*, members of this fashionable female élite were not usually involved in social relations of direct subordination to European men and women. The secret of their success, it is said, lies in the *femmes libres* having brought coquetry to a fine art, thereby giving clients the illusion of having made a most difficult conquest. Also, such a woman has a special taste for love and sexual experience (Comhaire-Sylvain, 1968, pp. 162–3). These, then, may be the reasons why the supply and demand for the favours of 'civilized' women were such that a *femme libre* was normally able to establish or break off relations with a lover or client according to whim and fancy (Pons, 1969, pp. 215–6). In other words, she was in this respect relatively independent of individual African men – a situation which has prompted Balandier to write:

> Il est révélateur des bouleversements survenus dans la situation de la femme à la faveur de cette société nouvelle qu'est la centre urbaine; elle choisit alors qu'elle était choisie, elle

---

[16] Hence, as already explained in Chapter 6, one of the main purposes of courtesans' voluntary associations.

cherche à obtenir le plus d'avantages possibles alors qu'elle était source de profit et richesse capitalisée, affirmant ainsi un véritable renversement des rôles. (1955, p. 148).

Balandier also makes the related point that for this female 'élite' the designation *heitaira* is more suitable than prostitute. Apparently, Balandier has in mind the special position of the *heitairae* in classical Greece which included their being sought after by the most eminent of personages. Their favours could not be bought by all and sundry (see also, Henriques, 1962, pp. 65–6). Moreover, in some of the Francophone countries concerned there are common factors in the role of the *heitairae* and that of the *femmes libres*. These include the low status of the wife as well as the cultivation of the arts of coquetry and love. There is also the courtesan's prerogative to pick and choose her lovers, and this has often aroused critical and sometimes resentful comment (Pons, 1969,). Pons quotes the following free translation from Swahili of a song by a local guitarist. It illustrates a regular theme in discussions on the relationship between a *femme libre* and one of her 'lovers'.

I. '*Chérie*, you wander about the town; *chérie*, why do you roam around ?
You have a lover, why do you hang about ? '
[The woman laughs.] 'I am not a fool to wander about for nothing.'

II. 'Dear woman, you are always out and about;
I come at mid-day and you are not there;
I come in the evenings and you are not there;
Surely you must have been with other men.'
[The woman laughs.] 'I am not a fool to wander about for nothing.'

III. 'Madam, you are always in the town;
You ask me for a cloth of *mapomboli* [17] and for a head-scarf and a necklace too;
Do you take me to be a supplier of goods for the benefit of other men ? '
[The woman laughs.] 'I am not a fool to wander about for nothing.' (Pons, 1969) [18]

[17] *Mapomboli* is a cloth of a particular design.
[18] The song goes on:
IV. 'Daughter of a father, ask other women who have seen the daylight;
When you meet them, you will see that they have all they want;
You will smoke, you will drink beer and you will eat well;
(*continued on page* 116)

There is also some resemblance to the *heitaira's* role in the fact that *femmes libres* are invited, sometimes, to official parties. Thus according to a report in *New Society*:

> At a recent Presidential ball in Elizabethville . . . the European and African guests were sitting primly in the garden of the ornate salmon-pink mansion formerly occupied by Tsombe, sipping beer and waiting for the music to begin so that they could dance. Diplomats and leading Congolese personalities were wearing dinner jackets. The occasion was a formal one: the visit of President Diun of the newly established Luajaba province to President Balandwe of East Katanga. Suddenly the *chef de protocol* strode purposefully through the crowd. He pointed first to a pretty African woman, then another. They followed him modestly to the table where sat the two presidents. The music struck up and the ball was opened by Presidents Balandwe and Diun dancing with the two prostitutes. No-one looked either surprised or shocked.[19]

> *New Society*, 1963, pp. 4–5; cited also in Little, 1972*a*)

A related grade of 'independent women' in the Congo (now Zaire) is the *femmes libres sérieuses* (Mair, 1971, pp. 205–6). These are women with some professional qualifications which bring them an independent income. However, as Mair points out they are not too serious to take lovers and many have a permanent association with one man that is somewhat similar to the informally established marriages described later in this chapter.[20]

As all this implies, the *femme libre* tradition flourishes largely because in the countries concerned, few wives are educated enough to play the kind of social role that, nowadays, is required in

> And you will see that they all have one lover only;
> To such a woman I would give everything, to give a *mapomboli* would be nothing;
> I would give whole-heartedly, and do nothing but give;
> What you have asked for is nothing as to what I would give.'
> [The woman laughs.] 'I am not a fool to wander about for nothing.' (*Ibid.*)

[19] This article points out that in this context the current price for a *femme libre's* favour was more than a third of an unskilled labourer's monthly wage.

[20] Though documentation is lacking, the existence of this further category of *femme libre* suggests that some Zairean (Congolese) men who are wealthy as well as enterprising enough may be enjoying the same specialized relationship with the opposite sex as did Spanish gentlemen during the seventeenth century. It is said that the latter had, in addition to a wife who upheld their social position, two other women: one to provide sexual satisfaction and the other aesthetic conversation (Sturtevant, 1917).

'upper class' African society. A corollary is that in several ways the ordinary educated man may have more in common with his Westernized 'girl friend' than with his own wife. Paradoxically, therefore, in such cases, it is the latter extra-marital relationship rather than the conjugal one that comes nearest to the egalitarian ideal regarded by Euro-North Americans and increasing numbers of Africans as the proper basis of marriage.[21]

However, it should not be inferred from the above description of city 'high life' that all contacts involving sexual relationships are of a temporary kind. Casual as many such relationships are, there are also some associations, which, though casually begun, result in a longstanding friendship (in the Western sense) and, in the end, take the form of marriage. Since, however, they value their independence greatly, marriages with *femmes libres* are probably rare, and this is apparently the position, also, of like-minded women in Dar es Salaam. They, too, Leslie says, are reluctant to exchange their 'freedom' for formal marriage, and this attitude has raised the status 'or at least the bargaining position of women in the town'. A woman of this type usually entertains several lovers; nevertheless, she may also remain faithful – after her own fashion – to one particular paramour. He, ironically enough, is probably to be regarded more as a friend than a lover !

In addition to these relationships in which the woman plays the role of mistress there are several forms of concubinage into which women of varying degrees of education enter. One such type which may involve non-African as well as African men is reminiscent of colonial times when it was the practice, quite often, for a European official to pay a sum of money for a girl who became his temporary wife for as long as she was wanted.[22] Such an arrangement constituted a species of marriage by native law and custom; but, more often, the arrangement was less formal and was made either with the relatives of the girl or with the woman herself.[23]

---

[21] See later chapters. Hennin (1965) and Bernard (1968, p. 102) provide some interesting examples of this point.

[22] According to Henriques, it was also customary in Ghana to 'buy' female servants in the Northern Territories. The parents were paid a sum and it was your responsibility to feed and clothe them. What purpose you put your servant to was your affair, and the edge of the European quarter in Tamale was always crowded with potential prostitutes. It was not unknown for Europeans to visit the Territories for the express purpose of obtaining a woman in this way (1962, p. 386).

[23] In a visit to Gabon, Balandier found that in Libreville, 'capital of the free life', the 'marriage of colours' still goes on. The archives bear witness to this tradition. They testify that in 1918 out of '935

Sometimes, in the latter case, the girl having attended a convent, or a mission school, was able to speak English or French, and already possessed a smattering of European ways. To men looking for companionship, this knowledge made her a more acceptable partner than a girl straight from the bush, and so some of these liaisons continued for a number of years or until the man was posted to another country.[24] When the time came to part, it was customary for the man to make his temporary 'wife' a 'good-bye' present[25] in the form of money, or even property. It depended on how long the relationship had lasted. The purpose of this settlement was to let everyone know that the woman was not regarded as 'cheap', thus enabling her to be married later with no loss of status to a suitable African husband.

This writer is unable to say if the custom of saying 'good-bye' in the way described above is still carried on. It was certainly followed in Ghana and Sierra Leone in colonial times, and, as indicated earlier, the arrangements made involved a species of social contract recognized by the man as well as by the girl's kinsfolk. Nowadays, inter-racial alliances based on what the European man regards, or chooses to regard, as friendship, occur quite frequently and are normally tolerated by the girl's family who seem to look upon them as a variant of the older practice. From the European's point of view, however, these relationships, though often intimate in a physical sense, do not necessarily imply any deeper or moral involvement. So far as he is concerned, a short-term (or even longer-term) alliance *without* social recognition, for which payment is expected, is degrading for the woman involved. It reduces her, in fact, to the status of a woman who can be had for money; and, since the payment plays a negative role, the procedure is strongly suggestive of paying off a mistress or of paying a fee to a prostitute. If the girl herself presses for payment, this may seem tantamount to extortion, or even black-mail. For the girl herself, who extrapolates from the socially

native women of marriageable age, more than 400 remain single'. Of these single women, '65 cohabit with Europeans, while about a hundred actually live by prostitution' (1969, p. 179).

In the earlier history of European contact with the West Coast, there is also at least one reference to a European-run 'brothel' whose personnel, according to Skertchly (1874), comprised the daughters of the incumbent of a Wesleyan mission station at the Dahomeyan town of Whydah.

24 If it was merely a temporary absence, while on leave, the man might ask a friend 'to look after' the girl until his return. The present writer was made this proposition, but is unable to say if the custom was widespread.

25 This is termed *awangyadze* in Accra, and in 1950 it might have amounted to as much as £200 (Crabtree, 1950).

recognized alliance, the payment is an emotional necessity. It allows her to preserve her self-respect by enabling her to demonstrate her rising status in society (Trutenau, 1968, pp. 199–222).[26]

A close personal relationship sometimes developed in these interracial liaisons, providing the girl concerned with a deeper understanding of the values and goals of Western culture than most of her sisters obtained through formal education.[27] Also, it gave such a person an advantage over other women who, despite their attendance at school, were unaccustomed to dealing and conversing on terms of equality with the opposite sex. These attributes naturally made such a woman attractive to the élite, highly Westernized individual but more in the capacity of a kept woman than a wife.

[26] The wide difference between Euro-North American and African attitudes in respect of the above kind of situation has been explained in the previous chapter. However, elaborating on the above points, Trutenau suggests that the different moral evaluation of the settlement may account for the frequent offers to European expatriates of female kinsfolk. The same writer correctly reminds us that this question is linguistic as well as sociological because semantic difficulties arise over such expressions as 'love-like' and 'hear-understand' where English words are often used wrongly, obscuring rather than clarifying what the English-speaking Ghanaian wants to convey. Also, the varieties of African 'marriage' contain patterns of mating which do not in any way fall under what is meant by the English word 'marriage' (*ibid.*).

[27] According to Henriques (1962, p. 382), an interesting aspect of such African-European liaisons is the design of bungalows and houses for white people. I myself was unaware of it, but Henriques says 'that often there will be a side door leading out of the bedroom, traditionally known as a "Mammy Door", which enables female visitors to arrive and depart unseen from the main part of the house'.

In fact, any such attempt to maintain secrecy could only be the merest pretence because, needless to say, the movements and activities of all European officials were of the greatest interest to the African population, especially in 'the bush' where the entire European complement of a station might not number more than six or seven persons. Since, therefore, it was impossible to hide the comings and goings of visitors from servants, news travelled very rapidly by the grapevine of house-boys from one European bungalow to another. Possibly for this reason, or because it was found more satisfactory in any case, individual Europeans lived openly with their African mistresses. This practice was, however, more common in the 'African' than the 'European' section of the town, partly on account of the attitude of European women. After the 1930s the latter accompanied their husbands to the African colonies much more frequently, and the presence of European wives produced – as happened at a much earlier date in India – a marked change in the attitude of European 'bachelors'. They became much more self-conscious of their relationships with the local girls.

Nevertheless, the former role was often quite advantageous. Certainly in colonial days, she could often do quite well for herself. Receiving a generous allowance every month and with housing provided, she probably enjoyed a real income which was high by local standards and only equalled among Africans by what highly skilled people could earn. In addition, the likelihood was that her wardrobe and her trinkets and jewellery surpassed in variety and quantity what her women friends owned. In this kind of situation, therefore, an attractive and intelligent woman might – like the *femmes libres* in the Francophone countries – achieve a large measure of personal independence. This was the more likely if, during her various liaisons, she used profitably the money given her in trading or saved it up in order to open a small hotel.

Since it is possible in this fashion to acquire house property or start businesses of their own, such women are relatively secure. They must, however, choose their partners very carefully and also be circumspect in their behaviour. As, in particular, it is essential not to arouse gossip and the public attention of other men, a woman of this category will rarely be seen in night clubs, dance halls and hotel bars except in the company of her regular patron, unless she is in need of a fresh one. In that event, she will find ways and means of indicating that she is available, usually by frequenting such places as the better class of night club, where the right kind of patron may be met.[28] A 'pick-up' there provides an opportunity for the preliminary exploration of terms and conditions, so that the situation is somewhat analogous to a 'hiring fair'. Alternatively, having heard news of a potential patron's arrival in town, an enterprising woman may call, perhaps escorted by a male relative, in order to ask if there is a 'vacancy'. If the girl is shy, the role of her male escort is to discuss terms and to answer questions about her health.

[28] 'The right kind of patron' is one who can be trusted to fulfil his obligations. In addition to being a man of some social standing who is generous with his money, he is expected to stand by his temporary partner in the event, for instance, of pregnancy. For this reason a sharp distinction was drawn, sometimes, in colonial times between European civil servants, who had a stake in the country, and Europeans 'in transit'. The former, who could generally be expected to fulfil their obligations, were referred to simply as 'Europeans' – a term which commanded respect among the African women with whom they consorted. The latter category, as represented, for example, by European soldiers, posted locally for a short time, were characterized as 'unreliable'. They were regarded quite differently from the civil servants and were spoken of as 'temporary Europeans', the implication being very similar to that of 'temporary gentlemen' in British military parlance.

The attitude toward such women varies, but provided their behaviour in public is circumspect their position is not socially unacceptable. Indeed, there are homes in Lagos under the control of prosperous women who may make or break their daughters' marriages because the existing husbands lack position or prestige. These ambitious women would prefer their daughters to have temporary liaisons with well-to-do men rather than accept men of lower social status as sons-in-law. They wish to boast that they are connected with such and such wealthy or socially respected families, who will be represented at their family functions and ceremonies (Izzett, 1961, p. 307).[29] In such a relationship the man is generally much older than his mistress and so the feelings of the girl may be ambivalent. On the one hand, she gains luxuries that she cannot herself afford, and it is glamorous to be wooed by a person of wealth and power. This is some compensation for her common or garden routine in real life as, perhaps, a salesgirl. On the other, she may come to dislike herself and her lover on account of her own role.

In a short story illustrating this point, 'Mercy's' well-to-do and influential 'friend', 'Mensar-Arthur', is driving his big car 'with a super-smooth engine' towards the beach. 'Mercy' has the fanciful idea of the car's tyres touching the edge of the water; but, fearing a fatherly rebuke, keeps the thought to herself. Things would be different, she muses, if she had a handsome lover; younger, but well enough off to own a sports car. 'Mercy' tells 'Mensar-Arthur' that her sister knows about their affair. She informed her just in case she ('Mercy') got into trouble. Her sister did not like the situation at all, but 'Mensar-Arthur' tells 'Mercy' not to worry. He is going on a delegation to London and will bring back something for 'Mercy's' sister that will smooth things over. In the meantime, he has arranged for 'Mercy' to have a Government estate house if she'd like to leave her sister's place. 'Mercy' duly moves and her sister is pleased with her present, but

[29] This is also the attitude quite often of the women themselves when their business is concubinage, because if the patron is of high standing, word soon travels round and the woman herself gains kudos, especially among other women similarly employed. Her prestige is further advanced if her patron agrees to use his good offices on behalf of her relatives and friends in, for example, securing promotion for them, obtaining special licences, and so on. If there are children they are likely to be brought up by the woman's own family, but a lot depends on the kind of relationship existing between their father and his legal wife. As will be explained more fully in a later paragraph, there are occasions when 'outside' children are brought up and reared along with a man's legitimate children. In either case, as they grow up the children concerned will be treated as ordinary members of the community.

there is a military coup and 'Mensar-Arthur' goes to jail. 'Mercy', however, is not inconsolable and the story closes with her being driven home by a new 'friend', an officer with an important post in the new regime. She is cock-a-hoop; but on hearing this man's name, 'Mercy's' brother asks: 'Wasn't there a picture in *The Crystal* over the week-end about his daughter's wedding? And another one of him with his wife and children and grand-children?' (Aidoo, 1970, pp. 87–102).

In the above story, 'Mensar-Arthur' would like to keep his *affaire* dark, and it can be more accurately categorized as one between 'casual lovers' rather than concubinage or any other. In western Nigeria, on the other hand, there may be no public objection to a husband having an extra-marital union with a single woman. Popular parlance calls such a woman an 'outside wife', not a mistress or a concubine. If such a union persists for some time, it receives social acceptance and may form the basis of an elementary family. Man and woman regard themselves as husband and wife, and the woman is expected to be faithful to the man. Any children born are usually recognized as their father's children by all concerned – the father, his kinsfolk, and society in general – and he often spends as much money on those women and their children as he does on his legal wife and her children (Bird, 1963, pp. 68–70). The explanation of this liberal attitude is that among the Yoruba, at least, marriage by cohabitation, and the birth of children has always been recognized, and a society accustomed to polygamy does not change its values overnight. In so far, how-ever, as the 'outside' wife will not have the high personal status of an official statutorily married wife, she stands in a 'second class' position (Bird and Baker, 1959, pp. 115–16).[30]

---

[30] Under Nigerian law a man is liable for a charge of bigamy if he marries under statutory law and then contracts a customary marriage. Many 'outside' wives are therefore married by co-residence and cohabitation only, but forms of 'marriage', socially accepted and even religiously blessed – though without legal sanction – are coming to be accepted. If the 'outside' wife then remains either with her own or her husband's kin, her position may be similar to that of a woman in the indigenous system. If she is living on her own, she will be forced to rely on her own activities for the major part of the upkeep of herself and her children. Instead of having that degree of security and status of the wife in the small family unit, she is a member of the same smallest domestic unit of wife and offspring found in the indigenous polygamic compound system. Being, how-ever, isolated in her existence from the support of the rest of the members of the compound, she is even more dependent on her own resources. It is as though the minimal unit of the polygamous compound were separated and scattered through the society. This places the mother concerned in the virtual position of head of the household (Bird and Baker, *ibid.*).

The latter kind of relationship varies, in fact, between concubinage (in which there is co-habitation) and what Southall and
Gutkind term 'lover relations'. Generally, such arrangements are
made individually and, since they are common in all classes of
society, many men and also a large number of women have
several such unions before contracting marriage. They may lead
to marriage, but there is no special expectation that they will do
so. In Monrovia, according to some of Fraenkel's informants, it
was traditionally acceptable for either a married or a single man
to keep such a lover, or *megi*, and many married men in the
suburbs have such arrangements – usually, but by no means
always, despite their wives' disapproval. A man may bring his
megi to live with him but this is relatively unusual; more often he
pays her an allowance for food and clothing and sometimes she
cooks for him (1964, pp. 113–14). Some women prefer the *megi*
arrangement to marriage, since it can more easily be broken off.
Where much employment is of a casual kind, a man's income is
subject to many vicissitudes; when he is unemployed, his wife may
be expected to provide for the household out of the proceeds of
her trading. A *megi*, on the other hand, can simply look for a
wealthier man to attach herself to. The *megi* relationship, therefore, is not a prerogative of the well-to-do. It exists among all
economic classes (Fraenkel, *ibid.*).[31]

In these terms 'friendship', as it is widely called, is frequently
entered into to meet an expediency, as among the kind of low
income groups described in Chapter 3. 'Friendship' made in such
circumstances may be merely a matter of mutual convenience and
has no greater emotional significance than the engagement in
Euro-North American society of a housekeeper. Thus, in one
household described by Fraenkel (1964, p. 138), the *megi*, it was
expected, would soon return to her family, and her lover was
already paying bridewealth for another girl whom he hoped to
marry. On the other hand, sometimes a woman stays with one
man for such a long time that their association passes over into

[31] Although a disguised type of polygamy/polyandry may exist in
Johannesburg (see comment above) there are no signs in African
upper class society of the roles, epitomized in Liberia and in western
Nigeria by the 'outside' wife, being reversed or taking a form
similar to marital life in some European aristocratic circles during the
baroque and rococo periods. True, the *femme libre* and others of
her kind may have more than a single lover at one and the same
time, but this is a different situation from Vienna in the early
eighteenth century. In that city, according to Lady Montagu, every
woman of social standing had two men, her husband and her lover.
Everyone knew of it and it was a serious offence to invite a lady
to a party without asking both of her men (Carrière, 1916).

the simplest kind of marriage relationship. This is an arrangement whereby a man and woman live together without having gone through either a tribal, a Christian, or a Moslem ceremony. It is referred to as 'free marriage' in Uganda (Southall and Gutkind, 1957, pp. 165–6) and is also widespread in the French-speaking countries. In Dakar, for example, it has been estimated that some 29 per cent of the Christian population live in consensual union of this type. To some groups an arrangement of this kind appears to be a sort of pseudo-marriage. Some people contract it in preference to a permanent commitment, while for others it is considered to be the beginning of a union that will become legalized later in life (Martin, 1968, pp. 362–95).

Somewhat similarly, when a Liberian whose *megi* bears children continues to provide for, but does not marry her, the arrangement may gradually slide over into the type of union known as 'outside marriage' (see earlier paragraph). More usually, however, the (English) term 'outside wife' refers, in Liberia, to the long-term extra-marital unions of 'civilized' men living in Christian marriage (Fraenkel, 1964, p. 114). In this case, the 'outside wife' is usually a 'tribal' woman from a lower social stratum than the man. Sometimes, however, she may be an educated woman; for, apart from questions of affection and sentiment, an educated woman may be able to do better for herself and her children by remaining the 'outside wife' of a rich and influential man than by marrying lower in the social scale. She has a recognized social status, and although she is rarely, if ever, admitted to the man's home, her children are often taken over by the man when they reach school-going age: they may be reared, perhaps, by him and his official wife. Such unions are widespread and contracting them often adds to, rather than detracts from a man's prestige (*ibid.*).

From the woman's point of view both the *megi* relationship and 'free marriage' combine the advantages of a more or less settled existence of being looked after by a man with the freedom to leave his house at any time. The man, in turn, may feel less tension than in a more casual affair because, as a Ganda informant put it, 'You can be sure that your wife is at home when you come back from work'. Also of importance to many of the men is that in a 'free marriage' the woman may agree to have children, while the willingness of the community to recognize this kind of sexual contract gives it a certain seal of respectability. In Kampala this is gained, as a rule, when the man and woman have lived together long enough for neighbours and kin to award their cohabitation the title 'permanent'. The birth of children is usually essential to this title, before which the union is called 'temporary'. If both spouses are of migrant tribes pressure is brought to bear by both sides to legitimize the union through payment of bridewealth. If, however, the man is migrant and the woman 'host', the man's kin and friends usually dissuade him from taking the matter too seriously. They say 'she is wasting your blood, because soon she may run away' (cf. Parkin 1969, pp. 97–8).

A 'free marriage' also provides both parties with the opportunity of trying out a spouse before they settle down and have a 'real' marriage. This is important because:

> If you take the first woman you find in a bar or on the street you may not get the right woman. She may not have been educated and perhaps she does not want to obey. I think that all woman should do what their husbands want ! A woman may want to have a Christian marrige, but the husband does not want to spend all that money. Some men want to have a tribal marriage because they can send the woman back to her father and get their money back if they find that she cannot cook, cultivate food, or if she lives with other men.   (Southall and Gutkind, 1957, p. 165)

There was also, however, a case of a man and 'wife' who lived happily together for well over six years. This kind of arrangement suited them rather well for reasons that they refused, at first, to give. Later on, the husband said of his 'wife' that he 'was still trying her out' and that he liked the freedom of 'being able to send her home'. When it was pointed out to him that his marriage had lasted more than six years, and that some of his neighbours who had made 'legal' marriages had separated from their spouses in considerably less time than this, he replied that that was exactly the reason why he had never taken a 'legal' wife (*ibid.* p. 166).

Southall and Gutkind also report that a number of the women who were living in 'free marriage' relationships were the daughters of important chiefs, well-to-do peasants and equally well-off independent traders (*ibid.* p. 167). However, in a sample of unions studied by Gutkind the number of 'free marriages' was not high. It comprised 21 per cent of the unions in which 30 per cent were Christian; 55 per cent tribal; and a percentage Moslem. Gutkind's data also indicate that 'free marriages' appear to last as long as Christian, Moslem or tribal unions, and on the whole there is no evidence that the 'Christian' form of marriage may perhaps have a better chance of survival than common law unions (1962–3, pp. 191–3).

For Africans in Johannesburg, getting married is a confusing, expensive, taxing and laborious procedure. A man pays *lobolo*, goes to the Native Commissioner's office for one ceremony, goes to the minister of his religious denomination, calls his relatives to a feast, buys clothing and the rest of his essentials, and soon finds himself short of money. As a consequence – as in many other urban areas of Africa – many men and women have thought it better to take the easier way out and simply live together without undergoing any of the formalities and trappings. Some of the 'illegal' unions formed are brief and casual; others continue for a long period between the same man and woman (Longmore, 1959, p. 61). In other words, these 'free marriages' are very similar in kind to the Kampala unions referred to in the last paragraph.

A particular species of this 'free' kind of relationship, however is the system of *kipita* unions which, in Johannesburg, is the commonest form of liaison among the domestic servant population. It is also found very frequently in the larger municipal African townships, and the advantage is that, as in the Liberian *megi* relationship, it can be dissolved at the will of either party. In other words, if the love of a man for a woman dies, it is not difficult for him in such a union to tell her bluntly to find herself another 'husband'. Then, again, if the 'wife' carries on with another man, the husband seldom worries: he has not paid *lobolo* for her, and so there is no injury to his pride which might oblige him to divorce her were he legally married to her. Moreover, the men realized that they will not be called upon to provide maintenance if there are any children because few women know that unmarried women as well as legal wives are entitled to claim this from the fathers of their children. From the woman's point of view an important advantage is that she is free to go the moment her 'husband' illtreats her.[32] Domestic servants, however, frequently fall victims of the system because most of them come directly from the rural areas and are not sufficiently on their guard against 'city slickers'. This kind of person often has no place to sleep and so, having seduced the girl from the country, he proceeds to live off her, spending the night in her employer's back yard and being fed and provided with clothes. The girl and the man never marry, and if she becomes pregnant he runs away and finds another domestic lover prepared to take him in (Longmore, 1959, pp. 68–9).

The extra-marital relationships reviewed above have ranged through those with courtesans, mistresses, concubines, kept women, 'friends', 'outside wives' and casual lovers. Nevertheless, despite this wide variety there is a common element which needs to be

[32] Apparently, however, the churches are strongly opposed to *kipita* unions and excommunicate their members if such unions are discovered (Longmore, 1959, p. 70).

stressed before concluding the chapter. This is the fact that although both traditional and modern norms operate in this general 'world of lovers', a subtle but mutually understood set of rules exists for the 'game's' control. For example, a husband may be carrying on an *affaire*. His wife knows about this and he is aware that she knows, but so long as neither of them deliberately ventilates the matter, marital life may go on harmoniously. The pact is likely to be broken, however, if the wife's pride or *amour-propre* is affronted. This may occur if, for instance, the husband omits to provide sufficient cover for his actions by offering 'reasonable' excuses for his absence from home, or if dealings with his girl friend assume too ostentatious a form. In the latter case, what the wife will dread, especially if she is an educated woman, is the possibility of the girl friend making a scene by, for example, confronting her in public. However, as explained above, the 'outside' woman's own reputation depends upon her being circumspect and discreet and so the wife herself will usually prefer her husband's *affaires* to be with women whose status is about the same as her own. She knows that if the latter have a similar social background and education they will have almost as much to lose as the wife herself in the event of a scandal. Of course, there may already be an estrangement between husband and wife; or the husband may feel no need or obligation in any case to take his wife's point of view into account. Otherwise, he will do his best to keep his extra-marital activities officially out of sight and will expect his wife to be equally careful. According to Clément, few Stanleyville husbands were convinced that their wives were entirely faithful to them. Nevertheless, they desired and appreciated a wife who, when she deceived them, did so secretly or at least discreetly, so that neighbours and, above all, her husband's family might not notice or hear about it (1956, p. 435).

As explained above, the jealousy of 'unattached' women players of the game is aroused very readily, partly because their pecuniary as well as emotional interests are involved. Also, they too are sensitive to the loss of personal prestige, and so it is a very serious breach of the rules for one woman to poach on another woman's preserves – especially if they are personally acquainted. Since most such 'outside' women accept their role as 'natural', they do not generally experience feelings of guilt. Usually, they accept 'their place', and have little or no ambition to supplant the legal wife, least of all if she is an educated woman and they are not. They may resent somewhat her superior status rather in the same way as junior wives may regard the head woman in the polygynous compound, but they have little or no animosity. This is reserved for any other 'outside' women to whom their unofficial consort may show even slight attention.

Wives themselves have naturally to exercise more care than their husbands, and it may be almost impossible for a wife who is house-bound to keep a lover. As explained, the position of women trading is different, and a professional woman may have a car of her own and so be able, if necessary, to drive as far as the next town.[33] Failing this, a wife's best opportunity of entertaining a male friend is when her husband is away. Provided she can depend on the discretion of her domestic staff he may come to her house, or she may meet him at the house of a woman friend or of a male relative. Generally, such expeditions are made after dark. They may involve a good deal of subterfuge as well as the coming and going of house-boys with messages, faces hidden beneath head-ties, and scurryings through the darkest streets and by-ways. There is the general air of a Restoration comedy, which is enhanced by the presence of the accompanying house-boy or girl. Especially if making her journey on foot, a woman will rarely venture forth without him or her. In addition to providing an escort, the latter's function is to spy out the land and to make sure that the coast at the trysting-place is clear before his mistress enters the house.

Naturally, wives band together to keep each others' secrets, and the husbands' girl friends are generally in touch and are at pains to keep up-to-date in respect of each others' movements and latest lovers. They watch the latter as well as each other very closely and have their own informal 'clearing-house' of information. This includes a fairly complete dossier of the more élite individuals with whom the girls have, or have had, dealings, including an estimation of a man's present financial position, his career prospects, his relations with his wife, his previous girl friends, personal idiosyncrasies, etc. In addition, they collect and sometimes pool information about an élite newcomer and his potentialities as a prospective patron or lover. The first girl to start an *affaire* with him is careful to announce the fact and thus to stake a claim in rather the same sense as a miner would make known that he has started digging at a particular place. Also, these women band together in opposition, in turn, to the wives as a group; and, needless to add, the fact that any one of them is in a position to reveal to a particular wife the identity of her husband's

---

[33] Among the many novelists who have referred to or described the infidelities of 'civilized' married women are Achebe (1966); Ekwensi (1961); and Ike (1970). Ike also includes in his theme the less-often-mentioned subject of European wives and African lovers.

current mistress serves as a very strong sanction on these ' outside '
women's own behaviour in respect of ' poaching '.

The men, too, keep each other's secrets and sometimes form a
clique which holds convivial parties to which the only women
invited are the men's respective girl friends. Naturally no
husband would dream of taking his own wife to such a gathering.[34]

---

[34] Nevertheless, according to Harrell-Bond (1971) this has happened,
presumably through ignorance on the man's part. It is not difficult
to imagine the acute embarrassment that a misunderstanding of this
kind would cause to all present, except, perhaps, the man's wife
herself.

8 Courtship and social mobility

Women's desire for 'independence' is also reflected in attitudes towards courtship and marriage. They want, to an increasing extent, to choose their own spouses, and this is also the wish of many of the young men. As a result, although parents continue to regard marriage as a union between two groups, personal choice is nowadays more frequent than in the past. For example, all the fiancés interviewed by Lombard in Cotonou had chosen their partners themselves (1954, pp. 3, 56), and few of the Nigerian élite in Ibadan had their marriage arranged by their family; most met their spouses during their student days (Lloyd, 1967). In Porto Novo, too, almost all the men in a sample had chosen their wives themselves (Tardits, 1958, p. 60); while in Ghana, 86 per cent of 275 students said they had gained their girl or boy friend by their own efforts and 24 per cent declared that they would reject their parents' choice. Thirty-one per cent, however, were uncertain and as many as 41 per cent would accept their parents' wishes. The latter respondents were mainly girls and so there are signs that although the 'modern' young woman wants to please herself, she is more influenced by her family and often married to a man she would rather not have married (Omari, 1960, p. 204; *idem*, 1962, p. 125). Moreover, although the influence of parents often consists only in the formal agreement to a choice already made, there are still educated young men who accept their parents' choice. This is because they can then obtain financial assistance to get married or because their sense of loyalty to their parents or kin is still strong.[1]

In other words, it is often more difficult in practice than in theory to disregard parental wishes; a point frequently made by

---

[1] Speaking of Ghana, Jahoda says that an uncle would be gravely offended if the offer of his daughter was refused by his literate nephew to whose education he had contributed (1958, p. 156; *idem*, 1959, p. 180).

contemporary African novelists. They show characters traditionally engaged by their family who happen to fall in love with another partner. In Ike's *Toads for Supper* (1965, pp. 9–10 and 80–5), for example, 'Amobi', the hero, is an Ibo whom his father betrothed as a child to the daughter of one of his father's closest friends. Since 'Amobi's' parents know this girl's family very well and the girl herself has been brought up in the best traditions of village life, they are very disturbed when news comes to their ears that 'Amobi' is courting a Lagos girl. In addition to the embarrassment breaking off the marriage will cause them, they are genuinely concerned about 'Amobi's' own welfare because in their opinion only immoral girls are to be found in Lagos.

On the other hand, there is evidence that the percentage of inter-tribal unions increases at the higher levels of the social ladder and in Harrell-Bond's sample of Sierra Leonean professionals (1971), 40 per cent of the provincials had married provincial women of another tribe. Also, in Dakar, professional men, skilled workers and senior civil servants marry outside their own group more often than do farmers, fishermen and unskilled workers (Mercier, 1954, p. 29). But the relative scarcity of educated women may be a reason for such inter-tribal unions because the Ijebu-Ode of western Nigeria, having many educated girls, tend to marry endogamously (Lloyd, 1967). Possibly, therefore, a lot of educated young people still prefer spouses of their own group, especially when tribal prejudices are strong. *Toads for Supper* illustrates this point as well because when 'Amobi' confesses his love for a Yoruba girl, one of his compatriots immediately scoffs at him. He remarks, 'Let me cut the matter neatly like a scarf. That girl is Yoruba and you are Ibo. The twain cannot meet!' He goes on to recite the story of the Yoruba girl who, at a study group meeting of the Student Christian Movement, swept an Ibo boy off his feet by her defence of inter-racial and inter-tribal marriage. This, she asserted, was a practical demonstration of the truth that in Christ there is no East or West. But 'the oaf, that this Ibo was, forgot that the Yoruba girl had spoken from the pulpit, and so his romance was nipped in the bud because Miss Solanke refuses to see him when he calls' (pp. 9–10).[2]

Also, some of the evidence is contradictory. For example, among Bernard's Kinshasa sample (1968) only 5 per cent of all marriages were inter-tribal, but two-thirds of the teachers concerned said that they would have married a girl from another tribe if the opportunity had arisen. Only 61 per cent thought that inter-tribal

---

[2] The implication is, of course, that the Yoruba regard themselves as socially superior, especially to Easterners.

marriages were morally wrong; and 49 per cent stressed that only *love* (my italics) counted.

This is a common attitude among the girls as well. Harrell-Bond's group of Sierra Leone students, for example, considered 'love' to be the most important criterion in choosing a marriage partner and in answer to the question of how they expected to be treated by the man they married, a further sample of Sierra Leone girls, both Creole and provincial, mentioned 'love', followed by 'kindness', more frequently than any other thing (1971; Little, 1966a, p. 142–3). Among educated Yoruba, too, the ideal for two partners is to get married because they are in love (Bird and Baker, 1959), and similar attitudes are reported from Ghana (Omari, 1962, pp. 14, 43). Commenting there on the fact that in contrast to the traditional pattern, 'love' is becoming nowadays an initial requirement for mate selection, Omari says:

> While in grandfather's time he was lucky if he was permitted to edge in a word as to whom he would rather marry; today a young man wants to do everything for himself. Grandmother had even less to do or say about these things; she only found herself with a husband. She did not know anything about 'love' and never expected her husband to say 'sweet things' to her. She knew she had to get along with the man – for her own happiness, and for the happiness of her family which had taken 'head money' (*ibid.* p. 5).

This is not to suggest that there is a lack of romantic attachments among young people in traditional society. Among the Mende of Sierra Leone, for example, the marriage of a man to his first or to a subsequent wife may sometimes be the result of mutual physical attraction and she will be known specifically as his 'love wife' (*ndoma nyaha*). There are love songs too; and a Mende one begins with the not unfamiliar strain of 'Where has my dark boy gone? I left my dark boy crying for another's sake !' In addition, although her motives may be commercial as well as amorous, a member of the polygynous household will elope with or enter, sometimes, into an illicit relationship with a man much younger than her husband. Also, another West African people, the Gonja of northern Ghana, have a species of trial marriage (*jipo*) (Goody, 1963, p. 20), and among the Tallensi it is a point of honour for a boy to find a girl for himself (Fortes, 1949). Courtship, though often formalized, is also a common institution; and the many people for whom it is part of the preliminaries of marriage include the Yakö of south eastern Nigeria, and the Hausa (Forde, 1941).

The contemporary situation, therefore, is different only in that the young Africans concerned want to 'fall in love' before they marry. In other words, romantic values are now socially emphasized to a much greater extent. This point is illustrated by Jahoda's study of letters addressed to the advice column of a Ghanaian newspaper in 1955. One problem, often mentioned, was how to recognize true love, and be sure of one's partner's feelings. Letters written by unmarried young men (mainly clerks and teachers) referred principally to two kinds of difficulty. First, the man states that his girl has ceased to care for him and asks how he can win her back; a rival has appeared and the girl has started 'playing'; the question is, what can be done about it? A twenty-year-old clerk wrote about his telephonist wife-to-be: 'I love this girl to the bottom of my heart.' However, as she lived far away, he unfortunately made two other girls pregnant and consequently is, to quote his own words, 'perplexed mentally'. He asks. 'What can I do to repel these two girls . . . and get hold of my own darling as my ever and one wife ? ' (1959, pp. 177–90).

However, as the above quotation implies, although many educated young men are apparently just as keen as the girls to marry for 'love', the notion has not the same meaning for all. Thus, among a sample of school leavers in Elizabethville, Hennin (1965) found that for some 'love' was a true affection which may or may not be a modern phenomenon. For many, however, it was a physical attraction, which is not a new conception. In fact, although one-third of the men interrogated did consider love as the essential element in their choice of a fiancée, they thought of it rather as a sympathy which would eventually develop into reciprocal affection. They get to know each other later, during the engagement and above all after marriage. This is the point made in Nzekwu's *Wand of Noble Wood* (1961) in which the Nigerian hero is looking for a suitable girl to marry. He is certain that if he finds such a girl and moves along with her for some time he will be able to win her love. When, however, he reports his decision to a woman in-law who is helping him in his quest, she says:

> True love has rarely influenced the choice of wife here. My observation is that if you treated a girl well she remained a good and faithful wife. If you treated her badly, she became troublesome, unfaithful and mean. That is why, on my list, I had love as the last item.   (p. 89)

She goes on to explain that their people's traditions did not allow for 'love' in its modern form. In the past the period between the first and the last stage of courtship was fairly long and was spent in 'trying the girl out'. The difficulty she says is that:

> Today you have no opportunity to move along with a girl
> a considerable length of time without someone butting in
> and snatching her from you. If the opportunity does present
> itself, parents will begin to suspect your good but undeclared
> intentions and order their girls to shun you.   (*Ibid.*)

What, therefore, this may mean is that the emotional bond
implied when the young men speak of 'love' is not always
identical with that in Euro-North American societies. Thus, the
newspaper correspondence mentioned above was marked by the
frequent request for reassurance. Some sign was required that
'love' is really true, and so it may be that very many young
people are in fact groping for the full meaning of what is
symbolized by the word 'love' in some criterion by which they
could judge that it is really there. Comhaire-Sylvain's findings have
a similar implication. Of the young women she interviewed in
Kinshasa, 83 per cent said that they wanted to see love films,
sometimes because of a genuine romantic desire, but more often
for practical reasons 'to learn about love' or 'to adapt oneself to
love' (1968, p. 97). Bernard (1968), studying letters between fiancés,
also found that amorous vocabulary in French was often used as
'make believe' of modern passionate love, in order to hide from
oneself the absence of real communication (p. 153). Furthermore,
whereas in the West the concept of romantic love carries the
connotation of exclusiveness, the usage frequently exemplified in
the correspondence analysed by Jahoda shows that this is not
necessarily true of the writers. In short, as he remarks, 'It appears
that, although Western influences have given a wide currency to
the language of romantic love, its actual content of meaning
remains encumbered by the existing matrix of social values, which
can alter only gradually' (1959, p. 184).

The above may imply that in courtship it is the man who takes
the initiative, but this is not invariably so. For example, the
Zairean (Congolese) girl plays a much less active part than in
some other countries, but even she will, in rare cases, use an
intermediary, a common friend, to let a young man know she
likes him (Bernard, 1968, p. 68). In Freetown, the customary
method among Creoles is for the man to write to the girl's parents,
asking whether he may visit her at home. When accepted, he pays
the girl frequent visits, escorts her to public functions, but in
fact there is little privacy for the couple (Jellicoe, 1955a). In Ghana,
as explained, to have a 'date' is a recent pattern. It is only
when the man has given the girl a ring and a Bible that he is
allowed to take her out, and so the engagement often precedes

dating and courtship except when these have been carried out secretly (Omari, 1962, pp. 37, 41, 44, 45, 53).[3]

Once engaged, a girl will often have regular sexual relations with her fiancé, and even if virginity at marriage is the ideal it is not expected in Ghana, where few boys and girls are chaste when they reach twenty-one (Omari, 1962, p. 55; Crabtree, 1950). In Johannesburg, today, girls refuse to be examined, and it was considered by some of Longmore's informants that possibly a townsgirl could stay a virgin until she was fifteen. After that it was difficult for parents to keep an eye on her (1959, p. 49). This situation alone, however, does not necessarily signalize a change in the women's position because among a number of indigenous peoples cohabitation is acceptable as a prelude to marriage proper. Among the Asante, for example, a relationship may begin in this way and be approved by the parents of the couple.[4] This is regarded as proper marriage for all practical purposes (Forte, 1962, pp. 279–80) although in such cases the man does have exclusive rights in the wife. Often, too, the girl's fiancé will not come to the marriage before she conceives a child (Omari, 1962, p. 57). Sterility, indeed, is regarded as the worst thing that can happen to a married couple, and in Johannesburg, for instance, many men stressed that the usefulness of a woman lay in her ability to bear children; even if she was beautiful and came from a good home she was useless if she were barren (Longmore, 1959, p. 50). Since, therefore, a man wants to be sure that his future wife is capable of bearing children,[5] cohabitation before marriage is regarded very often as a test of fertility. Many of the younger people in Hennin's study of Elizabethville considered this practice reprehensible; nevertheless among the adults some 80 per cent had cohabited

[3] In Cotonou, there are 'trial marriages' among young *évolués*; afraid of the cost of marriage payments and the fact that marriages in the Roman Catholic Church are indissoluble, young men prefer to have a trial with their possible wife-to-be for one year or more (Lombard, 1954, p. 162). In Hennin's (1965) Elizabethville survey, 3 people out of every 5 were engaged for less than four months, but a fifth were engaged for more than one year. The tendency to have a prolonged engagement is most marked in literate Christians, especially in the case of young people. Among the latter the boys wish to prolong the period for over a year, but the girls consider a period of two to six months to be enough. For reasons that will be explained later it is significant perhaps that they apparently prefer to acquire a job before thinking of becoming engaged.

[4] The Red Xhosa are another people who did not expect a girl to be sexually abstinent before marriage. However they insisted upon her technical virginity being safeguarded and so she was not supposed to take off her undergarments during intercourse (Mayer, 1961, p. 253).

[5] Especially when he contracts a statutory marriage which is mono-gamous and may be difficult and expensive to dissolve.

before marriage,[6] while in Johannesburg it is apparently taken for granted. Thus, according to Longmore's informants, out of every 100 urban families there were 95 who had children before marriage, and this state of affairs was found 'even in the "best" homes, including those of pastors and school teachers' (1959, p. 50).

The latter situation, however, is extreme. In other countries, girls are worried about this matter because to have a baby would be a burden in view of their hope for independence and a career (Omari, 1962, p. 118). Also, their claim to enjoy sexual relations as of right may be modified by their desire for a high status husband. The result, Harrell-Bond found in Freetown, was an exacting pattern of behaviour whose rules were ambiguous and sometimes contradictory because, as one informant put it, 'In order to get a good husband you have to be good, but you have to be careful not to be too good !' (1971).

Such concern is understandable because the widest and most general channel for women's upward mobility is marriage. Of course, the same broadly applies as well to Euro-North American society, but the African situation is exceptional. This is the case because political and economic development, followed by Independence, have naturally multiplied many times the number of important places which are now filled by Africans themselves, in government, the senior civil service, business and all modern sectors of the economy. Taking the Nigerian Civil Service as an example, whereas even in 1956 two-thirds of the men in 'A' scale and super-scale posts were expatriates, by 1967 there were 650 Nigerians in super-scale posts against about 150 expatriates (Lloyd, 1967, pp. 129–50). Out of the resulting opportunistic situation (see Peil, 1965 and 1972) virtually a whole new class of 'élite' and high-ranking individuals has arisen, thereby adding an extra dimension to the marriage market. This is the greater because, with the exception of some trading communities and a few women belonging mostly to wealthy families, principally in the coastal towns of West Africa, the most common place of women was previously on the farm. Today, numbers of those who, in the former situation, would have been junior wives in a polygamous household are married monogamously to professional and other successful men and have charge of luxurious and up-to-date homes equipped with every modern electrical and other appliance.

---

[6] In Kinshasa, out of 283 teachers, 103 said that in the event of their wife being sterile they would keep her as their only wife, 29 would take a second wife, 2 would try to have children by a concubine, 76 would seek a divorce and 73 did not know what they would do (Bernard, 1968).

There are spacious halls and lounges and rooms are furnished and decorated as richly as in the 'plushier' avenues of, say, Hampstead. Often, also, there is a special suite for guests; a chauffeur is kept to drive the larger car, and other servants are employed to cook, mind the children, clean the house, tend the garden, and wait at table. In addition, there may be young relatives sent to the wife for domestic training. She, as mistress of this quite considerable establishment, enjoys respect and prestige to an extent unheard of in the rural compound except among women of rank and the 'big' women who sometimes head large kinship groupings (Little, 1972b).

However, a girl's prospects of marriage are inevitably bound up with her particular country's social and economic development. For example, Longmore reports that in Johannesburg many educated urban women, especially teachers, prefer to marry other teachers. But Longmore was also told that a trained nurse (considered a very high-class woman) would be quite prepared to be courted by an ordinary labourer, or a teacher by a jail-bird or a woman doctor by an uneducated man, provided in all these cases that the man had plenty of money.[7] In West Africa, too, some civilized women will accept a semi-literate 'money man', as such persons are called, who already has one or two wives but can afford to house each of his spouses in separate quarters.[8] But, as explained, other such civilized women may prefer to have an illicit relationship with an educated man if the only alternative is an uncultured husband of low status. Indeed, most of the evidence is that this type of woman will not be happy about a prospective spouse unless he has at least a secondary school education. She will also look for some of the social graces because, as one of Ekwensi's characters who wants 'a gentleman' puts it, 'A man can have money and still be crude'. Indeed, it is not perhaps an over-statement that in West Coast towns the acquisition of a well-to-do, much-travelled young husband has become part of the African girl's 'dream' as summed up in the 'high-life' ditty:

[7] Well-dressed men as well as money were preferred by the majority of urban women, and so professional women in Johannesburg will often marry ordinary labourers who dress in most expensive clothes when not at work and look very handsome and presentable. For these reasons, one of the most regular habits of many men is their weekly visit to the dry cleaners to ensure that their weekend clothes are spick and span. It is probably the case that a man would rather buy clothes, often of superior quality, than save his money, or even spend it to feed himself adequately (Longmore, 1959, p. 33).

[8] See Leslie in this connection. The 'horrors' of polygyny under urban conditions when the wives share the same house with the husband are graphically depicted in Okpewho's novel (1970).

What shall I do to get a man of that type ?
One who is a been-to,[9]
Carfull and fridge full [10]
What shall I do to obtain a man like that ?

Such a girl will also have visions of marrying her well-educated fiancé by statute, partly for legal reasons given in the next chapter, but also because it is the 'civilized' way of marrying. Not only does it entitle the wife to call herself 'Mrs' or 'Madame' and command respect, but it also implies that she and her husband are 'progressive' and have sufficient means to live in a modern up-to-date style. This is so much the case that members of well-to-do and highly Westernized families marry in church as a matter of course (see Harrell-Bond, 1971; Little, 1969*a*; Little and Price, 1967, pp. 410–12; and Omari, 1960), and wedding cards are sent out. In some parts of the sub-continent, including the Francophone countries, Western fashions in clothes, hair styles, etc. are assiduously followed by all concerned (cf. Bernard, 1968, pp. 78–80),[11] but in other countries only the bride and bridesmaids wear a Western type of wedding dress. In either case, the occasion is marked by a great deal of conspicuous consumption. Money will be lavishly spent on the bridal gown, the clothes of bridesmaids and pages, food and drink and musical entertainment for a large number of invited and uninvited guests and the distribution of presents (Little and Price, 1967, fn. pp. 418–19). In this regard, too, bridewealth often continues to play an important part, and although some educated parents refuse any money, or give it to their daughter, the amount is usually higher for an educated girl. There may also be many traditional expenses prior to the wedding itself, including maintenance of the girl during the engagement period. Sometimes the cost can reach a sum equivalent to the bridegroom's total salary for a year (*ibid.*).

This, then, is the kind of picture into which the ambitious young girl would like to fit her matrimonial aims. The difficulty

9 A 'been-to' is a person who has lived and/or studied in the United Kingdom. Meillassoux (1968) reports that in Bamako, Mali, young people of the literate class have the same respectful attitude towards fellow Africans who have lived and/or studied in France, especially Paris.

10 I.e. possessing a car and a refrigerator (cf. Busia, 1957).

11 Thus, in the Congo (now Zaire), according to Bernard, it is a matter of whisky and beer replacing palm wine, and modern dances the traditional ones. The two types of marriage – Western and traditional – are juxtaposed (the traditional one only concerning the kin in the village); and even when sexual intercourse has taken place after the traditional marriage, the couple is referred to as 'fiancés' until the religious ceremony (*ibid.*).

is that she may lack the requisite Western training because men of the type she is after usually want a wife who will bring social distinction and be able to support their position (cf. Mitchell, 1959, pp. 128–31). Indeed, one of the common complaints made by young men is that their traditionally-oriented parents wish them to marry illiterate girls (Jahoda, 1959, p. 178), when they are in fact looking for a woman of roughly similar educational standard. Such a man, if ambitious, requires a wife who knows enough about modern tastes to furnish and decorate his home in up-to-date style. She should be at ease in society and know how to entertain his guests and impress with her Western sophistication his own social superiors. Unlike the Westernized intelligentsia and *évolués* of the West Coast, many such men have themselves been reared in purely traditional homes. For example, in Ibadan two-fifths of this ' new ' élite with post-secondary education had fathers who never attended school and between two-thirds and three-quarters had illiterate mothers (Lloyd, 1967, pp. 135–6ff.; see also Jahoda, 1955, Leith-Ross, 1956, Little 1973a, Peil, 1965, and Van den Berghe, 1969). Since therefore he himself lacks Western training in the social sense this kind of person is all the keener to have a wife who knows the appropriate etiquette and upon whom he can rely to act as hostess and see him through at official parties and receptions.[12] Also, most such men being ambitious for their children wish them to be suitably reared, and this is facilitated if their mother understands modern practices of child welfare; she should also be capable of checking their homework.

Consequently, in order to make sure of getting an educated wife, men in western Nigeria often get engaged to school-girls and pay for their education [13]: but the girl, once trained, often marries a younger man (Bird, 1963).[14] Sometimes, when educated girls are particularly rare, men travel abroad to find a countrywoman who is educated (Omari, 1962, p. 52); and it is not entirely accidental that numbers of top-ranking men have married West Indian, Euro-

---

[12] As implied above, for related reasons many less socially prominent men as well – a tribal chief or an illiterate trader wealthy enough to support a polygamous household – include a literate woman as one of its members. Her role is to cook meals to the taste of his educated visitors, as well as to write his letters (Little, 1951; Ottenberg 1959, p. 213).

[13] In *Toads for Supper*, ' Amobi ' is himself at the university but his fiancée, to whom he has been betrothed since childhood, is only a village girl. Being concerned about his own career ' Amobi ' insists on her being sent to a secondary modern school and from there to a four-year higher elementary teachers' training college – ' nothing less ' (1965, pp. 11, 12).

[14] See President Sékou Touré's comment on this point (Chapter 5).

pean and North American girls whom they met as students while overseas. Others have African wives but from a different country from their own. For example, the low level of women's education in Central Africa seems to have prompted Rhodesian men to seek brides in South Africa where there are many more girls with an education equal to their own (Mitchell, 1959). And even more significant in this regard has been the role of the Sierra Leone Creoles who have constituted, both locally, and for the former Anglophone colonies, a social élite. As a result, girls brought up as members of these ' old families ' who lived in or emanated from Freetown were looked upon as arbiters of civilized manners and styles whom it was prestigious to capture (see appendix; also Little, 1950, pp. 308–19; and Porter, 1963).[15] In the Congo, it appears from Hennin's data that the young men showed then a preference for girls who have taken a course in domestic science or done a junior secondary course at school.

That the women themselves are alive to these requirements of a wife's modern role is shown by the relatively large amount of space given to social matters in the popular press. For example, leading newspapers often carry a column that includes social notes. There are references to well-known personalities and 'socialites' and to persons going overseas. Sometimes, articles discuss the proper kind of relationship between persons of different sex and there is frequently a column answering readers' enquiries about etiquette. In a well-known Nigerian journal, for instance, among the problems raised are such apparently trivial questions as how much food a person who is a guest can leave untouched on her plate; when it is proper for the veil a bride wears over her face to be lifted, etc. Advice on how to play the host or hostess is frequently given, and one such article warned the housewife against meeting guests in her kitchen clothes. She was advised to have food prepared in readiness for them and to see that utensils and tumblers were clean; it pointed out that the husband as well as the wife has duties as a host. More and more magazines are being designed specifically for African readers and some of them provide fashion notes and dress-making hints as a regular feature. Photographs of African women illustrate the use of cosmetics, and even problems of deportment have been dealt with in detail in the now defunct *West African Review*. After explaining how a woman can sit elegantly on a low seat when wearing a tight skirt, or sit

---

[15] Attitudes have changed in more recent years; but among the older generation, Creole parents regarded not only men from up-country but from Nigeria and Ghana, for example, as too ' uncouth ' for their daughters, even when such suitors were well-educated individuals.

cross-legged on a straight seat, this article warned against standing akimbo as it displays too much of the hips. It went on:

> the West African woman still has something to learn from the deportment schools of London and Paris. She can learn, like the girls in Europe, that a large stride has something of the masculine quality about it; a small one, feminine charm . . .

> What other things does a girl who wants to charm and please and be acceptable in society need to know? She needs to appreciate that even when doing nothing, there is a graceful way of doing it; to learn how to stand in a relaxed manner . . .

> The rules of good deportment are simple, but to carry them out in an effortless manner needs continual concentration . . . only then will they become second nature and make one graceful and attractive. (Little, 1965, pp. 159–60)

Through these and other relevant media a lot can be learned about the niceties of social etiquette and deportment and ' drawing-room behaviour '.[16] So magazines and newspaper articles help; but in order to hold her own in the circles to which her husband aspires, a wife needs personal experience of top-level society. She requires not only to pass muster with his male colleagues and friends, she has also to show women of equivalent rank, too, that she cannot easily be snubbed: that she is, in fact, the kind of person with whom they and their husbands can be proud to associate.

One important way whereby a socially conscious and ambitious woman may achieve these objectives is by gaining membership in the appropriate type of women's organization. Several such associations exist and some of the most relevant and most useful for purposes of acquiring the requisite social skills are dining clubs for women which are exclusive. These enable members to dine together once a month, a guest speaker usually being invited. In Accra, the women's club is restricted to equal numbers of African and European ladies, and in Lagos there is a similar division.[17] The aim being to recapture the social atmosphere of a high-class club in Europe, the meals taken together tend to be highly formal.

[16] There appears to be quite a close analogy here between the situation of these contemporary African women and that of English women among the rising middle classes of the Victorian era. In the latter case there was a proliferation of books on social etiquette.

[17] Such being the prestige of these mixed dining clubs in Lagos, the allocation of ' African ' vacancies is said to engender fierce competition among socially ambitious ladies.

Ostensibly, of course, the occasion is simply a sociable gathering of well-to-do women. But what, sociologically, is important, is the opportunity provided for the uninitiated but would-be élite woman to observe in detail the way in which more sophisticated women behave. How, for example, they apply make-up, enter a room and engage in small talk, and how they select their clothes for particular occasions. For the woman who is already married, the main difficulty is entertaining. Her husband may be well enough off to employ male servants, including a cook, but she herself knows nothing about the appropriate ritual. Membership of a dining club, therefore, enables her to learn this by watching what is done, including the setting of the table, selection of menus, etc. To belong to such company not only brings prestige, it also provides her with a practical demonstration of the 'right' way in which to run an evening party. In addition, the necessity at such formal gatherings of speaking correctly will improve her knowledge of English, including socially important expressions and phrases that are 'U' but not learned at school. It goes without saying that this greater fluency is valuable for occupational as well as social purposes.

What also confers prestige in a somewhat analogous way in some West African cities is an invitation to join one of the informal companies of élite women who support each other as a group at the anniversaries and other ceremonies of their relatives and friends. Each such company consists of six to a dozen persons and the women concerned turn out wearing the same style of dress and accessories in terms of gown, smock, lappa, head-tie, sandals, necklace, etc. This custom, which is widely known by its Yoruba name – *aso-ebi* [18] – signifies close friendship, and so to be associated in this quite intimate way with socially prominent women naturally marks out the individual herself as a woman of distinction. It is also a measure of personal affluence because *aso-ebi* involves rivalry between the various companies, each group seeking to out-shine the others in the quality, richness and originality of its particular 'uniform' each time a convivial party brings them all together.

The social significance of clothes is the greater because nationalism has completely altered the trend in some countries. Previously, European attire was *de rigueur* for formal occasions; but, as the above remarks imply, it is frequently the practice, nowadays, for élite women to wear an 'African' style of dress. This is especially incumbent upon them at official receptions and parties, and so there is scope here for the woman with a flair for clothes. Those who already possess some social *cachet* and are

[18] Harrell-Bond (1971) contains an interesting note on this custom.

able to combine it with the successful adaptation of traditional dress to modern styles stand out as leaders of women's fashions.[19]

However, these sartorial responses to Independence apart, the social prestige of Western custom is still strong. This is especially so in the Francophone countries; and, in Bamako, for example, even part-traditional organizations have celebrations which include a dinner party in the European fashion. Members of both sexes belong to these associations and after between thirty and forty tables have been set out in the street with plates and silverware, it is the girls' duty to prepare the food (Meillassoux, 1968, pp. 112–16). For the latter another socially useful skill is dancing, and among the circles into which an ambitious girl hopes to enter, the preferred style is often 'ballroom'. In order, therefore, to keep up to date she belongs to clubs organized specifically for this purpose. These associations also teach their members the latest version of jazz and jive, and there are expert male and female performers to demonstrate steps. The most select of these clubs is known as the 'Casa Antica' because the majority of its members are educated. For both the girls and the young men the social advantage of membership is the opportunity afforded of 'keeping in the swim'; and, above all, no effort is spared in the exact imitation of modern dances. Consequently, in accordance with the world to which both sexes aspire, women members are expected to be well dressed in the fashionable Western way in addition to being educated and good dancers. In fact, a new feminine social type has been created by these clubs. She is the *écolière*, that is to say, a girl who dresses well, though provocatively, and is, for both older men of position and the younger men, a symbol of cultural achievement. 'She is desired both as a wife and as a mistress because she offers the double promise of modern social distinction and sexual licence' (Meillassoux, 1968, pp. 140–2).

In the above ways, therefore, a girl may be able to equip herself more adequately for the marriage market and the only drawback to her efforts is the men's preference for both the 'modern' type of woman and the 'traditional' at the same time. In other words, although men wish their wives to be good looking and smartly dressed, they have a stereotype as well of educated women as troublesome, demanding, insubordinate, neglectful of children and husbands (cf. Jahoda, 1958, *passim*; Little and Price, 1967, *passim*).[20]

[19] An article in *Nigeria* by Eve de Negri (March 1962) describes the technicalities of style and design in Yoruba women's fashions.
[20] This ambiguous attitude sometimes affects the position of university-trained girls of whose advanced education there are signs that the men appear to be afraid. Thus, according to Harrell-Bond's study in

Finally, we have already mentioned that women come occupationally to the fore in the professions, and so those who are barristers and doctors have élite status in their own right, and this applies to the relatively few women who are members of the senior civil service. Women prominent in the political parties also belong to the élite category, and for related reasons so do the leaders of the national federation of women's organizations. This is the case because within these federations are grouped most of the women's societies and clubs which have usually been formed by educated women. The framework is usually quite simple and consists of each affiliated society being represented on the federation itself by a number of members who elect an executive committee. One example, among many others is the West Cameroon, where there were, by 1964, more than 125 registered women's organizations with a total membership of over 3,500. The federations' own activities include active participation in international conferences and seminars concerning the welfare of women. In addition, as indicated in Chapter 5, these federations often play directly, or indirectly, an important part in politics, mainly as pressure groups and as the main-spring for movements in the direction of women's emancipation. This also applies to other broadly-based women's organizations of which an important example in Kenya is 'Maendelo Ya Wanawake' (Swahili for 'women's progress'). Its ostensible aims are to improve domestic standards by educating women in home-making, child care, nutrition and hygiene; but it also campaigns militantly for women's rights and among its leaders is Margaret Kenyatta, daughter of Kenya's President.

The result is that the women in control of these federations and other widely spread associations possess a good deal of political influence. Quite often their services are given public recognition and they are singled out by the Government and appointed as representatives of national delegations (see Chapter 11; also, Burnley, 1964, pp. 34–5; Wipper, 1971a, pp. 429–42).

Freetown (1971), these girls have difficulty in finding suitable husbands. In the sample she collected, only a quarter of the professional men had wives with university degrees and so – as she points out – the small proportion of women graduates is not, perhaps, the only factor in the disparity between husbands' and wives' educational standard. On the other hand, Lloyd (1967) found that in Ibadan half of the men with university education married women with secondary education.

9 Wife versus lineage

In the last chapter it was pointed out that although the women's desire for 'independence' finds expression in courtship, in the actual selection of a spouse a good deal depends upon how far a girl, as well as a man, are in a position to decide on this for themselves. This state of things is exemplified by a number of marriages reported from Stanleyville. One of these unions began as a clandestine relationship between two lovers, Lusaka and Antoinette. It later continued as an open association between a man and a woman, Antoinette having been registered as a *femme libre* [1] by her father. Finally, payment of bridewealth was negotiated and handed over by the man himself, converting the relationship into marriage. Yet, the arrangements were made over a considerable period of time and it is clear that they deeply involved members of the families of both bride and groom. Some time after the couple had begun to cohabit in the man's house, the marriage was registered at the offices of the C.E.C. (*Centre Extra-Coutumier* – African township) and thus gained the formal recognition and protection of the urban courts (Pons, 1969, pp. 219–22).

In another union which followed a substantially different course, the marriage was arranged in the countryside between the man's father and members of the girl's family. The betrothal took place in the man's absence and without his knowledge or consent. The bridewealth was paid in full by his father and family and was partly in cash and partly in kind. The marriage was registered in the couple's *chefferie* and, being registered in the countryside, it did not fall under the jurisdiction of the urban courts. Consequently, the girl's status in town was solely that of the wife of a man who was himself living there *à titre précaise*. In the event of a divorce she would not have been accorded the status of a *femme*

---

[1] The legal implications of this have already been explained in Chapter 7, footnote 15.

libre and would not have been allowed to continue residence in the *C.E.C.* A third case, also, involved some measure of consultation and negotiation between members of the families of the prospective bride and groom. However, although the couple were not lovers prior to the marriage, the initiative in arranging the union was entirely individual rather than familial. The man's father provided the bridewealth but only after the marriage had been negotiated at the groom's instigation. Registration took place at the offices of the administrative outpost near to the mission station where the couple had met and married; and finally, in addition to being contracted according to customary law, the marriage was celebrated according to Roman Catholic rites. It was thus governed by ecclesiastical law and there were in the territory no provisions for its dissolution or for the legal recognition of any dissolution which the contracting parties might have arranged with their families according to custom (*ibid.* p. 219).

The above were all marriages with clearly defined legal status, and between them they exemplify three types of marriage common in Kisangani – Stanleyville. The second marriage described may be thought of as typically traditional in that it involved betrothal before marriage, the maximum involvement and the most explicit alliance of the families of bride and groom, individual initiative being minimal. By the same tokens, the first and third marriages may be thought of as typically modern or 'urban' in that they were largely instigated and arranged by the individuals concerned. In both these cases, however, family consent and involvement remained essential features of the process and fact of marriage. Consequently, since the differences between traditional and modern or 'urban' marriages conceived of in this way were largely differences of degree, the two types represent the opposite poles of a continuum rather than discrete categories. In effect, Pons' classification of such unions as marriages is based primarily on the main feature which the vast majority of the inhabitants recognized as sanctioning marriage, namely the payment of bridewealth.[2]

The latter consideration has an important bearing upon the woman's position as a wife because of bridewealth's traditional function in the cementing of marriage as a compact between two

[2] This, it appears, was also the attitude in Mulago, another district of Kampala, on which Southall and Gutkind reported. There, tribal marriages were considered 'good' marriages by most of the residents, and there was some feeling that the great number of unhappy marriages was due to omission of the procedures customary in tribal marriage. Not only was a 'tribal' marriage considered to be a 'good' marriage, but in contrast to a Christian marriage, it was regarded as more convenient (1957, p. 155).

groups of kin. This means, if interpreted literally, that the relationship of the spouses is regarded as of secondary significance – a
situation which is wholly incompatible with the educated
woman's expectations of marriage. Thus, in Oppong's study of
observed and reported marital behaviour among a sample of élite
married couples in Accra, not only were most of the women
agreed about the importance of the conjugal relationship but they
also stated categorically that companionship between husband and
wife was the most valuable purpose of marriage. Indeed, 84 per
cent of the female respondents absolutely agreed with and only
2 per cent absolutely disagreed with the statement that 'companionship between husband and wife is the most valuable thing
marriage can offer' (Oppong, 1973a and 1973b). A similar impression is gained from the attitudes of educated young Creole
and provincial women in Freetown. They say that the wife is to
accept her husband's leadership (stressed more in non-Creole than
in Creole responses), and is to play her accustomed role as
housewife and mother. The man is to be the main provider and
marriage is to be a true union of husband and wife as well as an
economic partnership. The fact that there was general agreement
about the need of wives being as well educated as their husbands
and a general expectation as well that husbands and wives should
share common interests appeared to emphasize the latter point
(Little, 1966a, pp. 139–62). It is in this regard, therefore, that the
'civilized' girl – especially if she has gone as far as secondary
school – differs most sharply from her unlettered sister. This type
of woman wants her husband to make her comfortable (in a
material sense), to be kind and considerate, and to show respect
to her senior relatives. But she does not expect her husband and
herself to be 'partners'; still less that they will share each other's
interests.

As already implied, quite often this is also the orientation, at
heart, of the husbands of educated women, and so such women
may have to face the existence, beneath their spouses' veneer of
Western sophistication, of a strong feeling that wives should
be kept in their traditional place.[3] True, Ghanaian evidence
suggests that an appreciable proportion of educated men are disposed to contract a monogamous marriage.[4] However, although

---

[3] Documentation from Dakar as well as elsewhere suggests that dis-
illusion sets in *after* marriage. An educated *single* girl sees merely the
difference between the cloistered position of her illiterate sisters and
the prerogatives she herself expects to enjoy – a job, if she feels like
working; access to the same jobs as men; an equal voice in domestic
affairs, etc. (communicated).

[4] In his study of secondary school students, Omari found that 66 per
cent of the men against 83 per cent of the girls preferred marriage

75 per cent of the men in Oppong's sample agreed absolutely with the statement cited above, a wider look at statements regarding marriage's underlying purpose, whether procreation or conjugal companionship, throws a somewhat different light upon the matter. Thus, while Oppong's women respondents are significantly more inclined to state categorically that companionship between husband and wife is the most valuable purpose of marriage, the men tend to emphasize more than the women the traditional instrumental aspect, i.e. the birth of children. Moreover, in response to the further statement that 'legally a man can only have one registered wife but she should accept the fact that he may have one or more customary wives as well', only 55 per cent of Oppong's male respondents absolutely disagreed, in comparison with 69 per cent of women (1973b). Somewhat similarly, in a study made by Omari, polygamy was rejected by 86 per cent of Ghanaian secondary school girls as a backward practice, but only 61 per cent of the boys shared this opinion (1960). Again, while in Little's Sierra Leone sample only 5 girls out of 119 expressed a preference for polygamy, one-third of the young men felt that they were entitled to more than one wife. In addition, in a Zaire (Congo) survey only half as many men as women were opposed to polygamy (Hennin, 1965, pp. 16–18).

The explanation of this apparent paradox seems to be that many educated men favour monogamy, not for its own sake but because it is virtually incumbent on professional people. This applies irrespective of religion. Thus, in Dakar, Mercier found that not only was monogamy regarded as the ideal among both senior civil servants and members of the professional occupations, but only 15 per cent of these educated classes practising it were Christians (1954).[5] In fact, it is a common pattern to marry first for a number of years according to native law and custom. When, later, a man feels sufficiently advanced in his career to afford the expense of a church wedding and to maintain an educated wife, it represents a definite achievement of social prestige. A case-study supplied by Oppong (1973b) illustrates this point:

> Mr Amoah and his wife are both Eastern Akan, he is in his early thirties and she in her late twenties, a middle-school

under the Ordinance. Since this type of marriage makes bigamy a crime, it is to be presumed that this particular group opted for monogamy. In a further, more detailed sample of university students, only 16 per cent preferred customary marriage (1960, pp. 197–210).'

[5] Mercier differentiates in this regard between 'a monogamy of fact' and 'a monogamy of choice'. In other words if unskilled workers were monogamous it was because they could not afford polygamy, but professional men *chose* (my italics) to be monogamous (1960, pp. 40–1).

leaver from the same village. He was a certificated teacher working at a primary school in Accra when he married his wife. His parental half-brother was sent by his father to see his wife's parents and matrilineage head. Two bottles of whisky and money, in all about £10, were given to them. His wife did not join him immediately but stayed to get her cooking utensils ready with a further £10 he gave to her. She joined him after a month or so and then, when it was time for her to deliver her first child, she went to stay with her mother for six months, returning later with their son. During the next five years of marriage two more children were born and Mr Amoah studied at home, gained entrance to University and took a degree. While he lived in the University for three years his wife went back to stay with her mother. After graduating he got his present post as secondary school teacher, with bungalow provided with his job. His wife and three children joined him there. He now says that the second stage of the customary rites remains to be performed. He expects that it will cost him about £18. After that he hopes to have the church blessing and may subsequently decide to have the marriage registered.

The fact, therefore, that despite apparent similarities educated men and women have fundamentally different expectations makes it difficult for the latter to achieve their companionate ideal. These differences arise because what Jahoda (1959) has referred to as ' the existing matrix of social values' is based largely upon the traditional family system. In this the primary obligations of both spouses are to their respective kinsfolk which may mean that, as among the matrilineal Akan people of Ghana, a man's first duty is towards his sisters and their children rather than his own elementary family. Perhaps even stronger, as implied in the closing paragraphs of Chapter 3, is the bond in many cases, between a man and his mother. Having been reared in a traditional home, most young people have learned to give attachments of this kind a high degree of priority,[6] and kinship ties are the more meaningful because of the absence of other safeguards. African countries do not have statutory schemes for social insurance to cover sickness

---

[6] Harrell-Bond's material (1971) strongly emphasizes the importance of the kinship sentiment, and even residence overseas appears not greatly to alter it. West African students in the United States were interviewed by Zalinger and no less than 45 per cent of the sample said that the fulfilment of one's family obligations was still the proper thing; only 5 per cent claimed that they would have absolutely nothing to do with such obligations (Zalinger, 1960; see, also, Little and Price, 1967, p. 416, fn.).

or disability, or pensions for widows, orphans and old people: nor is there any public assistance to provide for the destitute or the unemployed. Civil servants have their pensions but only a very few men are wealthy enough, in every such crisis, to shoulder the financial burden of sickness and unemployment on their own. Many people prepare for the rainy day by joining friendly societies which organize mutual aid, including benefit in case of illness and bereavement (Little, 1965, Ch. 3). On the whole, however, these associations are patronized by, and cater for, the less literate and well-to-do sections of society; and so, in general, a person's kinsfolk, even in the case of an élite man or woman, are still the main standby. He or she knows that so long as the kin group's goodwill is retained, practical and moral support will always be forthcoming.

Naturally, all such assistance has to be reciprocated when relatives in turn need help, and the result is that few married couples of the first generation find it possible to make the break from their familial ties sufficiently complete. They tend, for the reasons given, to compromise. In other words, although a husband's main concern may be the education of his own children he may also feel it necessary for the sake of peaceable lineage relations to see that his nephews and nieces receive a good schooling as well. A fifth of a man's income may be spent in ways of this kind (Lloyd, 1967), in addition to remittances made to his mother and other maternal relatives.[7] The wife, too, will spend money on presents for her brothers and sisters and for her mother (Crabtree, 1950) when the available cash could have been used to provide her own children with clothes or to decorate the home. Again, rather than offend his lineage's sense of propriety, the husband may insist on his wife making customary obeisances to female relatives younger and much less educated than herself (Bird, 1958).

Educated wives resent the continuous draining away of money from their own children which such customs involve and many of them feel insecure in consequence of it. Some of them, too, suffer from a constant dread that on their husband's death they and their children will be turned out homeless and penniless by their husband's kinsmen (Busia, 1950). What is more, since the traditional family system is more concerned with procreation than with the husband and wife relationship, the husband's lineage is

[7] In Lagos, for example, 70 per cent of the heads of households gave some regular help to at least one member of their natal family; 55 per cent of them gave an average of over £1 (out of a monthly earning of £20); 25 per cent spent regularly £4 on relatives, and 12 per cent £6. These sums did not include gifts and expenses of family ceremonies (Marris, 1961, pp. 36–8).

more likely to encourage than to condemn his relations with other women. This may happen when conservative kinsfolk, particularly the man's mother, resent the wife as an interloper who is seducing the boy from them. If she proves unsatisfactory in any way the mother-in-law seizes on this avidly in order to try to prejudice the husband against his wife. If her fault lies in her infertility they may 'marry' a young girl for him by customary law, paying the bridewealth and installing her in another house. As explained in Chapter 7, such women are known as 'outside' wives (Bird, 1963). Circumstances of this kind reinforce, in turn, the tendency of husbands to take a traditional view of 'sex' after their monogamous marriage. Since, generally speaking, such behaviour is not publicly criticized and the double standard is applied, the question of moral scruple need not arise. If it does, there are additional rationalizations to justify the husband's extra-marital conduct in terms of men having greater sexual needs than women. As explained in Chapter 6, men themselves do not deny that some women, too, have strong sexual desires. But such women are regarded as 'bad'. Being 'bad' they are available for illicit 'sex' whereas 'good' women like mothers, sisters and good wives are different. They do not openly manifest evidence of their sexual feelings and they are not available for sexual relations with anyone other than their marriage partner (see Bernard, 1968, *passim*; and Comhaire-Sylvain, 1968, *passim*).[8]

Harrell-Bond (1971), who also makes the above point, suggests the existence of a further relevant factor. This is the effect of extra-marital affairs on a man's relationship with his male friends and the association of his manhood with his potency. A man's position and prestige in traditional society was measured largely in terms of the number of wives, children and other dependants he could acquire. Since this prestige associated with procreative power persists among educated men, involving a strong motive for a man to beget as many children as possible, the result is

---

[8] An attitude of this kind is analogous with the ideas held of middle-class women during Victorian times. Also, the notion of love being connected with marriage seems to have been forged in the intense heat of the Industrial Revolution. Previously, love was mainly conceived of in extra-marital terms and, according to the eighteenth-century novelist, Daniel Defoe, money was the important thing. It took precedence over everything else, and what mattered in marriage was not love but the amount of money that marriage brought. In his *Moll Flanders*, Defoe wrote: 'That marriages were here the consequence of politic schemes for forming interests and carrying on business and that Love had no share, or but very little, in the matter' (1924). (See, also, Little, 1966b. Pearsall, 1969, *passim*, has a good deal to say about the Victorian era in this connection.)

paradoxical. For, while the wife's discovery that her husband has had an illegitimate child may give rise to intensive conflict *within* the marriage, *outside* the event will be celebrated. The man's male friends will sympathize with him over the trouble his wife is causing, but another birth evokes their own sincere and enthusiastic approbation.

A tendency to look outside a marriage itself for satisfaction would explain why, according to Bernard, the most frequent kind of adultery is the 'short adventure' in a bar with a *femme libre*. It would also be in line with the fact that Kinshasa teachers apparently behave with the more sophisticated women they keep as concubines in a different way from their relations with wives. With a concubine they go out and drink, eat and dance together, are 'extrovert' and behave in a 'European' way (Bernard, 1968). In the Anglophone countries, too, it is by no means unheard of for a member of the élite to leave his wife at home if she lacks *chic* and modern *savoir faire*. At formal receptions and other parties attended by go-ahead people he may be seen, instead, with a smart up-to-date young woman who is usually his mistress. The way in which the men concerned see this situation is made very clear in Aluko's novel, *Chief the Honourable Minister*, in which 'Alade Moses', a former headmaster, has been appointed a Minister of State. There is a celebration in his honour and the principal speaker refers to 'Alade's' 'indefatigable, amiable consort, Mrs Hannah Bosede Moses' . . . 'Alade' wonders why this portion about his wife had to be brought in.

> Everyone that had eyes to see knew that Bose was not beautiful and that she was not a wife that the headmaster of a grammar school would be encouraged to introduce to his friends. It was obvious that she was going to become an even greater embarrassment to him now that he had become a Minister. He had married her when both of them were pupil teachers . . . She had no parents to object to him on the grounds of his obscure family background, as Lola's people had done before he settled on Bose. In the five years in which he studied and improved himself academically before going to University, Bose settled down to the wifely duties of cooking the family meals, producing babies – three girls in five years – and getting fat. When he came back from his overseas studies she was waiting for him, still fatter than when he left her four years before. The gaps between their outlooks had grown correspondingly wider. In the nineteen months that he had been back she had produced a set of twin girls and was now expecting another baby . . .
>
> (1970, p. 19)

And so, 'Alade's' emotions direct themselves, instead, to the more glamorous 'girl friend' who, a number of African novelists imply, is practically one of the perquisites as well as requisites [9] of ministerial office.[10] She is the cynosure of all eyes at gatherings of diplomatists and 'Alade's' ministerial colleagues, and so serves him as a status symbol as well as a mistress. Aluko describes the effect created in the following words:

> The ambassador took two steps back noisily and subjected Gloria to a more formal, critical examination, the way you step back to admire more effectively a work of art hanging on the wall. Gloria was truly attractive and attractively dressed, the obviously exaggerated observations of Dr Mose Selisha notwithstanding. She wore a cream Afromacolese blouse over a blue velvet lapper, the contours of her breasts showing invitingly through the blouse. She wore a striped silk head-tie in the famous 'onilegogoro' style. Her white handbag went very well with her white, stylish sandals. She did not have on excessive jewellery but her gold necklace and her earrings were obviously from the famous Hooper works. (pp. 98–9)

In Aluko's story, 'Gloria' has a good job as a nursing sister, but the economic price of having in tow girls of such sophistication and charm is often high. Since circumstances of this kind including the cost to husbands' incomes, are widely known, this is another reason why educated women are anxious to contract a statutory marriage. They want the satisfaction and kudos of a 'proper' wedding, but, in addition, this statutory union entitles a woman 'in principle' (as Phillips and Morris put it) 'to an enhancement of legal status and to relief from any customary disabilities or obligations which are incompatible with the ordinary standards of civilized society' (1971). In other words, it not only makes a wife free of her husband's lineage, but gives her the right to sue him on the grounds, *inter alia*, of adultery as well as the right to inherit property from him, etc.

In this regard, therefore, changes in the social position of the women *seem* now to be reinforced by improvements in their legal position. This, at least, is the appearance of things. There are, however, drawbacks because, in the first place, many wives do not

---

[9] See Achebe (1966) as well. His description of 'Chief Nganga's' acquisition of a 'parlour wife' is particularly illuminating (p. 43 and *passim*).

[10] Note, in this connection, the analogy with the traditional position of the 'big' man whose prestige depends quite largely upon his having a number of wives.

know how they actually stand. Further, while in some places
divorce is evidently easy,[11] in other countries implementation of
the wife's matrimonial rights often involves in the courts a very
difficult, protracted and costly procedure. Sometimes, too, there
are loopholes and although, as a rule, adultery is grounds for
divorce on both sides, the law may condone or tolerate matrimonial behaviour on the part of the husband that it does not
accept as justifiable when it is the wife. Especially, therefore, in
the latter kind of situation, a wife is likely to hesitate if she feels
that public opinion is not sufficiently on her side. Of course, when
the wife comes from a wealthy family, has money of her own,
or is professionally well-established, riddance of an adulterous
husband may be felt as well worth the trouble. But wives less
fortunate than this may have more to lose than gain from a
legal victory. Not only will they forfeit their position as married
women, as Mrs X, the wife of So and So [12] – an important consideration in the emerging class system – but there are also difficulties over alimony and maintenance. These may be crucial
because few men are well enough off to afford the upkeep of two
Western-style establishments – one for themselves and one for a
former wife. Consequently, even if the court is sympathetic and
awards as much as the wife asks for, the chances of such a ruling
being enforced are small and she will probably be obliged, when
the divorce has gone through, considerably to lower her own
living standard. A further drawback – if she wishes to remarry –
is that her having sued and won on grounds of adultery will
naturally be known and is likely to frighten off any further suitors.
True, her education and any physical charms she possesses may
make her attractive to members of the opposite sex, but more
readily as a mistress than as a wife. Most of the men whom she
herself may regard as suitable mates will be already married or
affianced, and those who are bachelors will, in the circumstances,
hestitate to jeopardize their own 'liberty' as they themselves
construe it.

On the other hand, there is, as implied above, some evidence of
wives making increasing use of the courts. This happens in
Ibadan through the weakened role of the patrilineal descent group
which is no longer able to exert control over its members. The
women, as a result, enjoy more autonomy than they were

[11] According to Pons, Stanleyville was one such place. See later
paragraph.
[12] Achebe's exposition of 'Chief Nganga's' wife's position and attitude
to the introduction of a new young 'wife' is particularly relevant
in this regard (p. 43).

traditionally entitled to,[13] and they employ it to seek a divorce when the husband fails to satisfy them as a breadwinner. Previously, under customary practice, the only grounds on which a wife could appeal were her husband's laziness, indebtedness, insanity, disease or criminal behaviour. His adultery was not accepted as sufficient reason, and in any case the woman's lineage could stop action by refusing to repay bridewealth. Nowadays, a woman who wants to initiate divorce action on grounds other than the above can proceed without reference to her patrilineal kin because there is generally a prospective husband in the wings ready to redeem financial obligations (Okedijis, 1966, pp. 151–63).

Perhaps more typical of the kind of matrimonial dispute that arises under urban conditions is the case of Lusaka and Antoinette reported in the last chapter. This union took place despite the strong disapproval of Antoinette's father and it was successful until the death of the second child. At this point, however, Antoinette began, according to Lusaka, to turn against him and to side with her father. She had also, he said, followed her relatives' advice to ' have her stomach closed ' and had, in fact, admitted these contraceptive intentions to him. Finally, although – according to Lusaka – Antoinette was now going with other men, he received very little sympathy when he complained of Antoinette's adultery to her father. The latter merely said that if Lusaka spent nights away from home, there was no reason why Antoinette should not do the same. Lusaka was outraged by this tacit admission of Antoinette's infidelity and stopped entrusting housekeeping money to her. He also called his mother in and consulted kinsmen and other members of his immediate social circle about sending Antoinette away (Pons, 1969, pp. 181–2).

In the end, a mediator was brought in. He, after giving Antoinette and Lusaka a general homily on marriage between ' civilized ' people, suggested that the urban court was the best place for airing their differences. Both parties accepted this advice and Antoinette accused Lusaka of neglect and of wanting her to leave him. He admitted the latter charge, but Lusaka said it was impossible to be happy when a man's in-laws were always dissatisfied with him. He added that he and Antoinette were agreed on wanting to end the marriage.[14] In other words, Antoinette

[13] The significance of structural change in this regard appears to be borne out by the findings, also, of a somewhat similar enquiry carried out by Sofoluwe, also in Nigeria. This research, although conducted in a rural area, showed that the typical divorcee was, to an extent, relatively ' urbanized '; she had been away from lineage influence and control from one to fifteen years (cf. Sofoluwe, 1965).

[14] Lusaka's marriage to Antoinette had lasted nearly seven years and

might have made a much better wife from Lusaka's point of view had her family, instead of opposing it, given the marriage their whole-hearted support. On the other hand, it is doubtful if Lusaka himself was disposed to treat Antoinette as an equal.

In the above case, the husband's attitude was not apparently extreme, but what is demonstrated is the wife's fundamental disadvantage. Husbands are allowed to kick over the traces; but wives, irrespective of educational status, are not. This means that, when unable to check her husband's infidelities, the 'civilized' wife has to take action on her own if, in addition to off-setting insecurity and safeguarding her children, she wishes to remain 'independent'. This may involve her, too, in 'outside' relationships and so result in an uneasy compromise between a 'modern' and a 'traditional' solution. In other words, the marital path of the literate woman may be beset with many vicissitudes and this point is exemplified by the following case of a Ghanaian woman we will call Mary. It will be noted that in the first instance Mary apparently 'married' for love:

> Mary's father, an educated man, had three uneducated wives whom he formally divorced on his subsequent Ordinance marriage to an educated girl. Mary, whose own mother was one of the uneducated wives, lived with her father while attending school but on leaving she joined her mother in order to help her business as a petty trader. When Mary reached the age of 18 an offer of marriage was made for her by a non-Ghanaian West African, but her father rejected it. Mary, nevertheless, had intercourse with the man, became pregnant and decided against her parents' wishes to live with him. She resided with him and she and her child rejoined him after he had returned to his own country. They remained together for over a year but during this time Mary complained in letters to her mother about her consort's neglect of

> during this time his family and domestic responsibilities had appreciably increased. After Antoinette's departure, therefore, he became aware of the difficulties of living in town without a wife, especially as he could not entertain marrying an 'uncivilized' woman. She would be no companion, would be unable to welcome his guests, handle his money, or take messages. Nor could he easily contemplate marrying a young but inexperienced 'civilized' girl. You had to be very cautious, he said, because 'the ways of Stanleyville women are often wayward', and there were very few women who, being both civilized and experienced, were prepared to give up the independence enjoyed by *femmes libres*. For a man in his position, the most prudent course was 'to take a fiancée [*sic*] into his home so as to have the opportunity of watching her conduct and her ways very carefully'. And this – six weeks after Antoinette's departure – is what Lusaka eventually did (Pons, 1969, pp. 183–4).

her and of his association with other women. A second child had arrived in the meantime, but, fearing a possible visit from Mary's mother, the man sent Mary and the children back to Ghana. There, she obtained a well-paid office job, made 'friendship' with one of her work associates, a Ga like herself, and became pregnant by him. Though there was no marriage contract Mary and he lived together; but after a short time she returned to her mother's home.

Later on, Mary met another Ga who wished to marry under native law, a proposal that did not appeal to her. The man's customary presents, however, were accepted by Mary's parents and so she went to live with him, there being two children of this union. Mary continued to ask her husband for an Ordinance marriage and after ten years of married life he agreed.[15] Mary wore the white bridal attire and had a typically expensive wedding.

The husband's work takes him to remote parts of the country for long periods of time, and he often has to reside in a tent or a village hut. During the early part of their life together Mary travelled about with him but did not enjoy these rural experiences. After some years, therefore, she decided to settle in her native town with the children, leaving her husband to trek about the country on his own and only seeing him during his biennial leave.

Mary assists her mother and her mother's mother when they are in financial need because she has now four sources of income. These include, in addition to a monthly remittance from her husband, profits from petty trading and from property and money inherited from her father. Also, she receives material benefits from occasional sexual services to men other than her husband.[16]

As explained in the next chapter, an important factor in conjugal relationships between educated people appears to be the difference in age. The reasons for this gap are that, since statutory marriage is likely to be costly, many men delay marrying. The need for further education also causes a postponement because, due often to irregular attendance at school, a youth may sometimes not finish his secondary education until he is over 20. If he embarks on higher education it will be several years before he is in a position to earn his own living, let alone keep a wife. Initial

[15] For a further interesting and illuminative description of the woman's own initiative in this kind of situation see Nicol (1965).

[16] From Crabtree, 1950. From a case-study compiled by the late Mrs Acquah, quoted with the permission of Mr David Acquah.

salaries are low and with every increment will come fresh demands, not only in terms of social display, but from relatives who may have partly paid for the man's education and now expect a return in the form of the partial support of a yet younger relative while he is at school. Further, it may be clear to the young man that marriage is an obvious risk. He may have observed the break-up of unsuccessful marriages which have involved the husband in the extra expense of supporting wife, children and himself in different homes, and divorce itself is difficult to obtain. Also, if he married an educated girl, she is likely to demand a degree of consideration and faithfulness which he is unwilling to concede. Why hurry the inevitable day of settling down, when in the meantime mothers and sisters are ready to look after one's material comforts and a temporary or permanent mistress is so easily obtainable? Even children need not be foregone; for a small expense one's mistresses' children can be christened in one's own name and their custody claimed at some more convenient time (Jellicoe, 1955a, *passim*).

Consequently, although Sierra Leonean respondents said that the best age for marriage is twenty-four (Little, 1966a), the actual evidence is that statutory marriages are not contracted by most men until they are twenty-five or much older. Somewhat similarly in a western Nigerian sample most of the men were over rather than under thirty years of age, while their brides were on the whole in their mid-twenties (Bird, 1958). In Accra, too, more men marry between thirty and forty than between twenty and thirty (Crabtree, 1950), and in a sample of Ghanaian 'lecturers', Date-Bah (1973) found that there was more than five years' difference in age between husbands and wives in fourteen out of twenty-five respondents. Some of these men have children by illiterate women with whom they have cohabited or married by customary law, and although there was an absence of 'hard' information about this particular point, seven out of twenty-five of the sample had children with other women before entering into marriage with their present spouses. This means, since the latter unions may have lasted for ten years or more, that on their statutory marriage [17] the men concerned have already strong ties and obliga-

[17] There is also some reason for believing that under urban conditions marriages by native law and custom as well as by statute are contracted much later by men than women. For example, it was found in a ward of Cape Coast, Ghana, that, whereas some 90 per cent of men were still single at the age of 20, some 58 per cent of the women were married at that age. Also, whereas 9 out of 10 women in the 21–30 age group were married, only about 30 per cent of the men in that age group were married (Rado, 1956, p. 39). Also, in Banton's (1957) Freetown sample, only 2 men out of a total of 78

tions that cannot be ignored. Relationships with their former customary wives or concubines may have ended, but the bond with children invariably continues; and, in addition, there are the husband's relatives with whom he keeps closely in touch. This includes attendance at family councils at least once every month, as well as birth, marriage and other ceremonies. It is also in line with the traditional pattern for him to spend leisure time with men friends as well as with other women. He and his male associates may spend the evening together in each other's homes, attend parties with their respective girl friends, or meet in social clubs modelled on European lines which are formed for dining and drinking (Bird, 1958; Crabtree, 1950; Plotnicov, 1967; Smythes, 1960). The result, in short, is that familial activities tend to be organized on the basis of the husband's and the wife's social networks.

This kind of marital situation has been analysed and its components categorized by a number of writers, notably Elizabeth Bott (1957). More recently (1970, pp. 676–80 and 1973a), following a study she made of Ghanaian senior civil servants, Christine Oppong has suggested that where the relationship of a couple involved separate decision-making and continual tension under the surface, it was characterized by *autonomia*. This meant that there is an obvious lack of trust and a latent fear that the husband or wife is being disloyal in some way, either by giving too much to relatives, spending too much on friends, or, in the husband's case, taking on a girl friend as one or two of his associates have done. Oppong provides the following illustration :

> The Frampongs spent their first few years of married life separated from each other in Ghana or separated from their children when they were in England. Each gained much more moral and also economic support from kin and friends during the periods of separation : the wife lived with her own parents for two years and the husband formed firm friendships with colleagues from the home region.
>
> When they set up home together each had numerous financial and social obligations to kin and friends continuing from this period. The wife had two junior relatives staying with her. The husband still spends much of his leisure time with associates instead of at home. He continues

in the 16–24 age group had wives (p. 198), and among 26 Creole men there were 5 who married between the ages of 18 and 20, 14 who married between 23 and 31, and the remainder married at 34 or later. Among 55 Creole women, on the other hand, 49 married before the age of 27, 4 at the age of 28 or 29 and only 2 after the age of 30 (Jellicoe, 1955a).

to support one or two patrikin and his children by his previous wife.

Partly as a result of this the wife complains that her husband does not give her enough money for shopping each week, nor does he take her to town at all or discuss the financial situation with her. On the other hand, he complains that she keeps her money to herself, though he admits that she has occasionally helped him when he has been in difficulty by lending him money till the end of the month. In addition, she regularly adds some of her money to the food bill and buys all her own and the children's clothes.

The wife also complains that her husband does not spend enough time at home with herself and the children. He admits that he prefers to spend his leisure time at an hotel bar drinking with friends, rather than coming home to the overcrowding and noise of the children. They both usually visit their home towns alone once a month or so. If either has a problem he or she tends to discuss it with friends or kin rather than husband or wife. (1973*a*)

In the case-study thus cited, some of the wife's and the husband's activities complement each other; but, in the main, man and wife have a considerable number of separate interests. This kind of relationship in which complementary and independent types of organization predominate involves a segregation of roles between the spouses. Elizabeth Bott used this phrase in describing variations in the ways that the husbands and wives she studied in London performed their conjugal roles. She found that these families that had a high degree of segregation in the role-relationships of husband and wife had a close-knit network; that is to say, many of their neighbours, friends and relatives knew one another. Families, on the other hand, that had a relatively joint role-relationship between husband and wife had a loose-knit network; few of their relatives, neighbours and friends knew one another. Bott's suggestion is that the degree of segregation in the role-relationship of husband and wife varies directly with the connectedness of the family's social network. In other words, the more connected the respective networks of man and wife, the greater the degree of segregation between their roles.[18] At the

[18] Bott explains that the social relationships of other people with one another may affect the relationship of husband and wife in the following way:

When many of the people a person knows interact with one another, that is when the person's network is close-knit, the members of his network tend to reach consensus on norms and they exert consistent informal pressure on one another to con-

other extreme, however, was a family in which husband and wife spent as much time together as possible. They stressed that husband and wife should be equals; all major decisions were made together, and even in minor household matters they helped one another as much as possible. To the latter kind of family in which joint organization is predominant Bott applied the term joint conjugal role-relationship (1957, pp. 52–61).

The fact that social distance between spouses is prescribed by custom is one reason why it is often difficult usefully to apply these formulations to the African situation.[19] Also, as stressed in a succeeding paragraph, among traditionally minded people the whole conception of conjugality is different from Euro-North American society – at least in the latter's urban middle-class circles.[20]

Bott's approach is mentioned, however, because of the apparent interest of educated young people in establishing a companionate type of union. The sharing of activities which this implies corresponds to the notion of a joint conjugal role-relationship and, as described in the next chapter, this pattern of marital behaviour is found in certain social circumstances.

However, it is also necessary to view in perspective conflicting tendencies in the African wife's position especially as, according to several observers, successful and durable marriages are the exception rather than the rule among the educated class (Bernard, 1968; Bird, 1958; Busia, 1950; Crabtree, 1950; Ekwensi, 1967). A large number of marriages do not necessarily end in the courts and, so far as civil marriages are concerned, the divorce rate appears in many cases to be low by Western standards. The same applies to Christian marriages; and in respect of the African urban family in general, Gutkind says that on the whole there is no evidence

> form to the norms, to keep in touch with one another and, if need be, to help one another. If both husband and wife come to marriage with such close-knit networks, and if conditions are such that the previous pattern of relationships is continued, the marriage will be superimposed on these pre-existing relationships, and both spouses will continue to be drawn into activities with people outside their own elementary family (family of pro-creation). Each will get some emotional satisfaction from these external relationships and will be likely to demand correspondingly less of the spouse. Rigid segregation of conjugal roles will be possible because each spouse can get help from people outside. (1957, p. 60)

[19] This point emerges strongly from Harrell-Bond's data (1971).

[20] This reservation is necessary because there is reason to suppose that in sections of the Euro-North American working class and in peasant communities a 'segregated role-relationship' may be the accepted pattern without implying marital misunderstanding or discord (see, among others, Littlejohn, 1963).

that the latter form of marriage may, perhaps, have a better chance of survival than common law unions (1962–3, p. 193). Naturally, however, the situation varies a great deal not only between one country and another but also between towns in the same country. Thus, in Cotonou, according to Lombard, divorces seem to be quite frequent; whereas in Porto Novo, also in Dahomey, Tardits (1958) found a lower incidence among educated people than illiterate. In the Sierra Leone Colony during 1941–2 there were only 53 divorces compared with 3,700 Christian marriages, 39 civil marriages and 701 Moslem marriages (Banton, 1957, pp. 40–1). In Stanleyville, on the other hand, Clément (1956) reported that in two districts respectively 54·5 per cent and 59·2 per cent of adult persons had been divorced one or more times. The frequency of divorce was made still more evident if one remembered that the figures referred to a youthful population (p. 423). The situation, therefore, is variable and in the area of Dar es Salaam, for example, frequent divorces and re-marriages are characteristic of the coastal people in rural as well as urban areas (Leslie, 1963, p. 287). But what is of more immediate relevance, is the high degree of marital instability in certain districts which, although rural in the ordinary sense of the term, are demographically marked by urban characteristics. Reference has already been made (Chapter 1) to the considerable incidence of immigrants in the Southern Cameroons plantations, and Ardener, who studied divorce, found that out of 1,821 legitimate unions

(a) *ever contracted* by the women, 42 per cent had ended in divorce or separation; of the 1,159 legitimate unions reported as

(b) *completed*, 66 per cent had ended in divorce or separation; and of the 1,429 legitimate unions reported as

(c) *ever contracted excluding those ended by death*, 54 per cent had so ended.   (1962, p. 37)

Taking all legitimate and concubinary unions reported, and excluding periods of prostitution, 36 per cent were still extant, 20 per cent ended by the death of the male partner, 36 per cent divorced and 8 per cent otherwise separated. Ardener restricted the term 'divorced', however, to legitimate unions, while the term 'separated' [21] applies primarily to the breaking of a con-

[21] It is also of interest that 41 per cent of ordinary customary unions were ended by divorce, compared with 24 per cent of 'inherited' marriages (representing the perpetuation of marriage within the husband's kin-group), and 11 per cent of the church marriages; while 60 per cent of the concubinary unions ended in separation (*ibid.* pp. 35–6).

cubinary union and to a small proportion of legitimate unions in which divorce is not complete (p. 35).

However, in considering data of the above kind it must also be remembered that even when there is no question of divorce or separation, husbands and wives may, for traditional reasons, not live together (see, among others, Fortes, 1962): and so their occupying separate residences does not necessarily betoken a broken or unhappy marriage. Also, a man who has several wives may not have them in the same house. Thus, in his study of a Lagos suburb, Marris found that 11 per cent of the married men were not living with any of their wives and half the men with several wives lived apart from at least one of them. In all, a quarter of the wives were not living in their husband's household, and a third of these were still in Lagos – from lack of space, or because he could not afford to maintain her, the husband had sent his wife to live with his parents or her own family, or rented her a room of her own. Two-thirds lived outside Lagos altogether (1961, p. 51).

Possibly, also, the divorce rate in towns varies between one occupation and another. For example, in the Ibadan study mentioned above it was found that traders with enough available cash were enticing wives away from their husbands. The consequence of this behaviour on the part of the husband-trader is that a higher divorce rate is reported among traders than any other occupation group. The reason, seemingly, is that on discovering that they are economically no better off, the women who have divorced their previous husbands initiate divorce action in turn against their new ones. Thus, of 112 women divorcees, 41 stated that their husbands were traders, and 40 of these women instituted divorce actions. Why is it, then, that more actions are instituted against traders than against men who are employed in other ways? The reason, the Okedijis suggest, may be that their work makes traders more innovative and individualistic and so more prone to experimentation with women. Also, being economically independent as well as physically mobile, they are less subject to lineage pressures which might be brought to bear on their marital relationships (Okedijis, 1966, pp. 151–63).

It was also found that in 110 out of 112 cases the husbands of the women divorcees concerned had more than one wife and that the rate of divorce among Moslems was the highest as compared with other religious groups (about 89 per cent). A contributory factor in this regard may be the liberal attitude of Moslems to divorce as well as marital and familial trouble. It also appeared that all the women concerned had contracted previous marriages before seeking divorce from their present husbands. Almost all of the prospective husbands, too, had been married before, the range of previous marriages being one and five. In other words, seemingly, divorcees tend to marry divorcees.

Needless to say, figures for divorce do not cover all marriages that have failed because, as one of Harrell-Bond's informants put it

> Westerners take divorce too lightly. In Africa we always hope that things will work out, will improve. Even if an African couple separate we keep hoping things will change.
>
> (1971)

Consequently, in a great many cases urban couples do not trouble to get a legal divorce. As mentioned already, the procedure, especially for the wife, tends to be unsatisfactory and it is exacerbated by the migratory situation. Thus, when a woman sues her husband he may decamp on receiving the news, leaving his place of employment and disappearing completely in order to avoid having to pay maintenance. The wife, then, must perforce earn her own living or, as explained above, 'take up' with another 'husband'. Thus, the vicious circle is started and one deserted woman becomes the cause of yet another broken home.

Desertion, in fact, is often far easier and cheaper than legal divorce, and in her discussion of marital instability in Johannes-burg, Longmore regards 'divorce – desertion – separation' as synonymous terms in the breakup of the relationship between a man and a woman, presumably a husband-wife relationship. She found that the occupational status of deserters seemed to be mainly unskilled labourers and those employed in domestic service. Indeed, marriage in the urban township had become such an economic burden that both men and women doubted the wisdom of contracting a legal marriage. It is far easier to indulge oneself by leaving the home to take up one's abode with another man or woman without marrying, especially since a deserted wife finds herself without much hope of redress. The responsibility of the children falls on her and so little is to be gained by marriage if she has in the end to depend on her own ability to support them and herself (Longmore, 1959, pp. 265–7).

That desertion is apparently more prevalent among the lower income groups may be partly due to men who are better off being restrained by economic factors. They may have a business that is locally established, or a job which it would be hazardous to re-linquish. This is another reason for the fact that in addition to those who have divorced or separated, many husbands and wives remain together but live in a state of unhappiness, in which the husband's inability or unwillingness to treat his wife as a partner may be to blame. In other words, the marital situation that develops fails to come up to the wife's expectations of a union based on mutual 'love' and affection.

A more basic reason – as already implied – is that at present many marriages apparently fall between two stools. On the one hand, kinship influence is strong enough to arouse a conflict of loyalties in the spouses.[22] On the other, kinsfolk have less say in what is going on and hence less responsibility for the way in which conjugal relationships are conducted. Formerly, any marital disputes quickly came to light and were settled 'in the house', both family groups having an interest in keeping the marriage intact. Today, marriage being largely an individual affair, it is not rare if the kinsfolk of the one party are strangers to the kinsfolk of the other party. It may no longer be a union of two lineages and families; and so, today, there is less pressure on the couple to maintain the marriage.

This is a further reason for the instability of many marriages; but there are also positive implications to the matter and these will be considered in the next chapter.

[22] Harrell-Bond (1971) has so much rich, illustrative material on this point that one hopes the study will soon be in print.

10 Matrimonial power, parity, and partnership

In the last chapter we stressed the increasing desire of women for monogamous marriage. Yet, many of these unions appear to be marred by disharmony and an important reason seems to be the influence of the traditional family system. Not only does this involve a conflict of aims and interests between kinsfolk and the conjugal relationship, but it has had in many cases an important pre-conditioning effect. This is the case because many of the young people concerned grew up in a domestic situation which was adapted to the general organization of the compound or homestead as the basis of agricultural, herding and other economic activities. Since it was to this extent a 'business' enterprise, the welfare and smooth working of the extended kinship grouping mattered more in people's minds than the relationship of man and wife. The fact that such a grouping was largely self-contained prevented outsiders meddling with its affairs, and so marital disputes were settled ordinarily by the lineage itself. On the whole, such a situation made husband and wife more susceptible to the opinions of relatives around them than concerned about their feelings for each other. It detracted from whatever tendency there might be to adjust more than minimally to each other's temperament and personality and supported instead the ingrained loyalties of both parties towards their respective kinsfolk. In other words, the conjugal relationship was encouraged to persist but not to develop into a deeper understanding between man and wife than was compatible with the kin group's corporate existence. If marital love and affection did grow and mature this was in spite of rather than through the familial environment surrounding the spouses.[1]

The result so far as the 'modern' ideal of marriage is concerned

[1] It is difficult satisfactorily to generalize about this intricate situation which has rarely been analysed in sufficient detail. Possibly, Mary F. Smith (1954) provides the most useful description available, but her study was made in a Moslem community.

166

is that numbers of the 'new' élite lack the requisite conjugal model. Nor are they ready or prepared for the idea that monogamy means more than the numerical reduction of spouses to one, and that it is, in fact, a marital system involving values of its own. This point has been expressed forcefully by Longmore on the basis of her Johannesburg study. She writes:

> The chief difficulty encountered by urban Africans is that they are striving after a culture of which they seldom have inside knowledge, practical experience or guidance. No doubt, the emerging middle class strives consciously for the values of the white group, but it is no easy task under existing conditions. It would seem that in adopting Western marriage the African has taken over some of the external trappings without the inner significance; the values and ideals of Western monogamy are lacking in their Bantu form, and the new and modified forms are not holding their own under urban conditions. They are inadequate and point to a disequilibrium in urban African domestic institutions. Western monogamy, without its accompanying values and ideals, is meaningless and ineffective . . .
>
> The white man's education without the white man's environment working on the African must have results different from those in a white community, and will be unable to make the African participate fully in Western culture unless the limits imposed upon African expansion and desire to better himself are withdrawn. (1959, pp. 15–16)

Some of Harrell-Bond's (1971) conclusions are not dissimilar. She found, in Freetown, that quite often the men have accepted many aspects of 'this idealized version of the husband's role', but most of them continue to behave in a more traditional way once they have married. They expect their leisure time to be spent away from the household and consider that, as in the traditional village, their chief concern is their position in the community. Although they hope that their marriages will enhance their prestige, the men do not apparently think it necessary for them to direct much of their energy into family relationships. Conflict between the expectations of husbands and wives leads to considerable tension within the conjugal relationship and is reflected in the nature of the disputes which occur. Acceptance of the importance of romantic love, with its emphasis upon the couple's own relationship during courtship, does not necessarily mean that there will be a similar emphasis after marriage.

It is also not uncommon to find a difference between the qualities allocated to wives in general and the qualities expected of a man's own wife. Thus, in his Kinshasa study (1968, p. 126 and *passim*) Bernard discovered that most young teachers agreed in principle to the equality of the sexes, and the model of the ideal woman seemed to be a smart radio speaker with straightened hair; an air hostess, or a school teacher. In addition, nearly all the young teachers considered *that in the future* (my italics) women would have political as well as social responsibilities, and mainly they agreed with the modern image of women as offered by *Eva*, the feminist newspaper in Kinshasa. Yet, even the most determined propagandist of feminine emancipation did not want his *own* wife to work and have responsibilities *outside*. Even when the wife had been trained as a teacher, the husband preferred her to stay at home; and, in fact, only one per cent had allowed their wives to carry on teaching. Thus, the dualistic attitude referred to earlier (Chapter 8) apparently applied because although most of the young teachers expected their wives to be able to wear Western clothes with ease and speak some French, this was only because it might help the husband himself up the social ladder. They saw their wives firstly as housekeepers, as obedient and respectful companions, as mothers and as sexual partners. The expectation was that educated women would be better house-keepers and mothers than uneducated women, but there was the familiar fear that the husband's authority would be questioned by an educated wife. Nor did husbands want their wives to know how much they (the husbands) earned (Bernard, 1968, pp. 93ff.).

The women themselves were often dissatisfied with this kind of marriage; but they, too, did not necessarily perceive that reality and wishful thinking are different things. They complained about their husbands going out, would like to know what they were doing, and felt a lack of communication between their spouses and themselves. Bernard formed the opinion, however, that less than 20 per cent of the wives were adulterous themselves and that in most cases a wife's infidelity was a reaction to her husband's misbehaviour. (There were also cases of men remaining faithful despite the infidelity of their wives.)

This somewhat ambivalent situation makes difficult the satis-factory interpretation of data concerning African spouses' respec-tive expectations of marriage. What does seem to emerge, however, is that the new marital norms are actually followed more closely when both husband and wife have in their childhood received a degree of preparation for partnership in marriage. This means, among other things, that the spouses concerned should be adept at handling situations involving the divergent interests of kinsfolk and of their own marriage. Thus, in Oppong's study of Ghanaian senior civil servants there were strong signs that the second and third generations of educated people, with spatially and socially mobile parents, were more apt to avoid such conflict-prone sets of relationships than were those with little parental experience of such new social situations. In addition, the second and third generations of educated people were apparently both more intent upon cutting down financial obligations outside the conjugal family and more successful in avoiding them. This was partly because expectations of help had diminished, as had feelings of obligation to matrikin, and so the percentage of men educating children of kin decreased with each successive generation of education and its consequent social and spatial mobility (Oppong, 1973a).[2]

What follows sociologically from this kind of development has considerable implications for the nuclear family. It signifies, in short, the gradual appearance of the latter institution in terms of being a primary group on its own rather than a mere cog in the kinship wheel. This much is clear despite the evidence often being more implicit than explicit. Thus, although only 4.5 per cent of the girls in Little's Sierra Leone sample positively declared that they would side with their husband in the event of a quarrel between him and their kinsfolk, 93 per cent said that they wanted to live in a house of their own (1966a, p. 152). This view was expressed almost as strongly by the young men, and Bernard, too, found that Zairean (Congolese) families apparently preferred to house themselves away from the family compound and tried to avoid kinsfolk interfering in their affairs. He was also told that when displeased by her husband, the wife refused either to speak to him or to cook,[3] but that rows between them were usually kept private.

The prototype of this type of household, sometimes called the 'Victorian' family (see Lloyd, 1967), was introduced largely by evangelism among a number of peoples in the West Coast

[2] Of course, in the men whom Oppong studied matrilineal ties were involved and the husbands concerned were seen to stand 'balanced between two sets of people, differentiating their roles according to their involvement'. Their divergent economic interests were purposefully separated to a more marked degree than among their non-matrilineal colleagues, especially when financial ties with kin were strong (cf. Oppong, 1973a; Little and Price, 1967, p. 422).

[3] The cooking of food has considerable symbolical significance in relationships between men and women in most African societies, including the urban as well as the rural situation. For a wife to refuse to cook for her husband is indicative of her extreme displeasure and tantamount almost to a sign that she is about to leave him. Similarly, for a husband to accept and eat food cooked for him by a woman other than his own wife or a relative is tantamount in her eyes to his committing adultery.

especially Liberated Africans in Sierra Leone. The members of these early families were among the first Christians of the town, and Selormey's *The Narrow Path* (1968) provides an interesting illustration of the kind of conjugal relationships that were involved. The *locale* of this novel is eastern Ghana in the earlier years of the present century and the husband, 'Nani', appears as a highly dominant figure whom his wife, 'Edzi', invariably obeys. She does rebel strongly, however, at 'Nani's' suggestion of the family taking up residence in his father's big family house, because 'Edzi' knows that she could not live a single day with these wives of her husband's senior relatives. 'Edzi' proposes, therefore, to stay instead with her own mother and refuses to entertain the idea of the children being looked after by her husband's people. She protests to her husband:

> No-one cares properly for the children but their own mother. You have often said that the husband, wife and children should live together as a family, and that parents should bring up their own children without interference from relatives. (pp. 164-5)

'Edzi's' expostulation is significant because it points to a familial situation in which, although domestic roles may remain segregated, stress is placed on the individual rather than on the corporate group. This is the essential consideration even though, as Bernard's further data show, the husband may continue to be authoritarian and the central figure. Thus, about 40 per cent of the teachers interrogated considered that a woman's first duty was to 'help' her husband; that is to say, she must give him moral support when he is in difficulty, comfort him, always be available and look after the house in ways that he likes. In fact, in this respect the major consideration was, apparently, the organization of a stable home where the man could rest; and, although the wife's ability to look after her husband's creature comforts was important, only about 7 per cent of the sample felt that she would be capable of advising him about his difficulties. Some 13 per cent, however, mentioned illness as an occasion when the wife was needed: and 'love' was frequently associated with 'help', but not in a passionate sense. Rather was 'love' expressed in terms of affection, devotion, care of the husband and pleasing him (see Chapter 6). However, it also appears that the Zairean (Congolese) wife was not always subservient. Quarrels sometimes broke out and the most frequent causes were the husband going out too often, refusing to buy his wife a dress she wanted, or failing to provide sufficient money for housekeeping. The wife also raised a storm if she suspected infidelity or if her husband drank too much. The husband, on the other hand, would not accept a rebuke, since this could be regarded as a threat to male authority. Also, when displeased with his wife he would remind her of her duty to be obedient, and some husbands shouted at and beat their wives. Generally, the wives did not contest their husband's authority and would accept a reprimand. Since, however, the wife had less control over the marital situation than her husband, occasions arose when she felt obliged to call her own kinsfolk in. This happened when the husband kept her too short of money. The matter would then be thrashed out by the two kin groups, and the husband was expected to accept their decision.

About 33 per cent of the Kinshasa teachers wanted their wife's obedience and in some 39 per cent of cases this was the quality that the men found first in their own wives.[4] It was clear that the husband's authority in this regard was reinforced by the wife's economic dependence and the importance of this factor as well as of others is demonstrated by Oppong's (1970) study of Ghanaian civil servants and their wives. As explained in the previous chapter, Oppong paid special attention to 'power relationships' among them. In addition to the *autonomic* type already mentioned, in which spouses each made their own decisions, she employed two other categories in her analysis. These were respectively the *syncratic*, in which man and wife share their main decision-making, and the *autocratic*, in which the husband makes the majority of decisions affecting himself and his wife. Oppong provides the following case-study of the *syncratic* type of power relationship:

> Mr and Mrs Ekow were both born in coastal towns and attended local schools. Mr Ekow was an early graduate of the University of Ghana and became a senior administrative officer, working for several years at provincial government station, before being transferred to Accra. His wife has a junior administrative post. (Her promotion to a higher grade has been hindered by her atypical reluctance to leave her

---

[4] In Stanleyville, Clément found that men thought highly of a wife who 'minds what her husband says', but they no longer demanded of her the same constant reserve, the same self-effacement and submissiveness. However, she should obey her husband's orders about the work falling to her lot. Similarly, it was most desirable that she should anticipate her husband's various wishes or hasten to satisfy them when expressed. Finally, she should look after him when he is sick and be his first 'doctor'. 'For us blacks', one man said, 'the wife should be like a mother to her husband' (1956, p. 435). (See also a reference to this sentiment in the closing paragraphs of Chapter 3. It has also been noted by Harrell-Bond, 1971.)

home and family for a year or two to do any further training.) They have each spent only a few weeks abroad at different times on courses connected with their jobs.

They were married ten years ago and have four children. Apart from occasional visits by educated kin, the husband says that he is cut off from most of his relatives on both his father's and mother's sides. He has not visited his home village since his father's mother died fifteen years ago. His father does not live there, as he is still teaching. Of his few educated kin, his own father's and father's brother's children, there are some he has not heard of for a year or more. Several of them are studying abroad. His own mother died thirty years ago and he has no financial or other claims from his mother's kin, in fact he seldom sees them. The question of matrilineal inheritance does not concern him. His wife sees relatively little of her kin too. Her elderly aunt, her mother's sister, comes to stay with her each time she has a baby and she goes home for a funeral occasionally. Most of her educated relatives are scattered about. She hears news of them through her mother's sister.

Both husband and wife report that they discuss everything they do together. They keep a monthly account of their expenditure in a book in which they write down everything they want. In the same way, when they bought their present house, they each put down half of the deposit out of the money they had earned prior to marriage. As regards chores, some are considered his, such as caring for the rose garden, the car and the general repairs and decorating in the house. The cooking is the wife's responsibility which she does with the help of a maid. Jobs such as bathing the children and helping them with homework they both do. He also helps with the laundry by washing and ironing his own shirts. They go to work together, drop the children at school and return home at lunch time to eat with the children and then they both go back to work together. Each praises the other highly for the part played in the home. (1970)

What Oppong discovered was that power distribution in the home is affected by the wife's use of her training, whether she works and, if she does, the use to which she puts her money. In fact, twice as great a proportion of husbands of housewives as of working wives asserted that they were dominant in the home. On the other hand, the tendency was for wives who are shouldering a larger share of the financial responsibility with their husbands, also to share more frequently in decision-making. There was *no* significant difference between the power relationship of couples in which wives do not work and those of couples in which wives work but make a relatively low contribution to domestic expenses. There was, however, a significant difference between couples in which the wife makes a nil or low contribution, on the one hand, and couples in which she makes a medium or high contribution, on the other. In other words, joint financial provision is associated with joint decision-making, and it is not merely a question of the wife's influence increasing with her experience in wage-earning.

Oppong also found that there was a statistically significant difference in mode of decision-making reported between those husbands and wives in the same and adjacent age groups and those that had a fairly wide age gap of six or more years. A primary condition, therefore, was the comparative ages of husband and wife, and the incidence of couples reported to be making joint decisions was distinctly higher among couples in which husbands and wives were in the same or adjacent age groups than among those in which the husband was considerably older. In other words, a narrowing gap in age tends to make joint consultation on domestic matters more likely and easier. If this is the case Oppong suggests that presumably the converse is also true and a widening gap in age tends to make joint consultations less likely and more difficult.

Oppong also discovered that it is those couples in which the wife's educational level most closely approximates that of her husband who are more likely to have a *syncratic* power relationship. This was apparently the case because 69 per cent of men with secondary education and college educated wives said that they made joint decisions with them, and only 42 per cent of the men with wives with elementary education reported joint decision-making, and 17 per cent claimed that they made the main decisions themselves.

Finally, the relation of decision-making to the husband's occupation within the civil service hierarchy was explored. In this case, two different categories of men at different social levels were seen to have fewer than average *syncratic* relationships and more than average *autocratic* relationships. They were the doctors and the non-graduate administrators. The doctors have wives with relatively high levels of education, but more of them are housewives than in the rest of the population. The non-graduate administrators have wives with comparatively low levels of education. In both cases, the wives' contributions to the households in educational and financial terms were relatively low in comparison with those of their husbands. On the other hand, teachers were remarkable for their joint decision-making and joint provision for household needs. In other words, according to Oppong, it is not merely the case that the higher the social status of the husband the greater his power. Comparison with that of his wife must be made, and it is only by examining the resources of both partners simultaneously that the meaningful differences between categories of couples emerge. Oppong concludes that –

> with regard to the domestic authority patterns of the cultures to which the couples belong, autonomy is still characteristic of the power relationship of a large minority of these educated spouses. It is particularly evident among the couples in which educational levels are comparatively low. Thus it is reported in 40 per cent of the cases in which the wife has only elementary education [5] . . . and is found in 46 per cent of the couples in which a husband is a non-graduate administrator. On the other hand, a trend towards egalitarianism is apparent among couples in which both spouses have received some higher education. (1970)

Thus, Oppong shows that important power-giving resources in conjugal families of Accra senior civil servants include education and an occupational status, relative age and income. Spouses derive their potential power position in the conjugal family from access to a deployment of those resources, and husbands and wives are more likely to share their major decision-making when their respective contributions of resources are more nearly equal. The more the husband's age, education, or occupational status exceeds the wife's, the less likely is decision-making to be shared and the more likely he is to be the dominant partner.

These findings are important because of the need, sociologically, to differentiate between egalitarianism in terms of Oppong's concept of 'decision-sharing', and egalitarianism as a mere sign and symbol of élite social behaviour. All that the latter means is that a husband may, in private, completely dominate his wife; but he cannot, with impunity, treat her in front of other people as an inferior (Jellicoe, 1955a). If he does he will run a grave risk of being stigmatized as 'bush' [6] and losing prestige. In other words,

---

[5] This point seems to be borne out also by the 'authoritarian' attitude displayed among Bernard's (1968) sample of school teachers whose educational level was generally higher than that of their wives.

[6] To be specific, the question – 'Do you beat your wife?' – has real meaning in this situation, because an answer in the affirmative would sociologically and socially mark the man concerned as a non-élite person.

Elaborating on this point Longmore says that despite the apparently

sometimes 'egalitarianism' is for *public* consumption alone and attempts to demonstrate it may, on occasion, backfire. This is illustrated, with obvious irony, in Ike's account of his hero, 'Amobi's' determination that his own wife-to-be shall receive the right amount of education. 'Amobi' recalls in this connection the experience of their Latin master at school who

> At the time he chose a wife . . . had no idea that he would one day travel to the United Kingdom for further studies. His ideal was a girl with a primary school leaving certificate, for he argued that such a girl would find it easier to accept a husband's authority than a girl with a higher level of education. He lived very happily with his wife before his departure . . . The headaches began after he got back with a degree in Classics. Shortly after his return, the Principal and some other members of the staff called at his house to welcome him home.
>
> 'Darling !' he called to his wife, in an attempt to be British.
>
> 'Sir !' she answered from the kitchen.
>
> The arrangements for Nwakaego's education would prevent such embarrassing episodes. A girl with a Higher Elementary Certificate would make a wife suitable for even the Vice-Chancellor of a University . . .   (1965, pp. 11–12)

In Mbale, Uganda, nevertheless, it is reported that most women not having secondary school education, are regarded by élite men as their social inferiors (Jacobson, 1970, p. 55). Observation of the Ibadan élite, on the other hand, suggests that where there is the same advanced degree of education, husbands and wives have more interests in common, including intellectual ones, than do married couples lower down the educational scale. Sharing domestic tasks is not often called for because most of the manual work is done by servants or by house-girls whom relatives have sent for training. Also, since these girls are members of the household they can be left to look after the younger children, thereby enabling the spouses to go out together (Lloyd, 1966, and Lloyd, 1967; see also Harrell-Bond, 1971 and Selormey, 1968). Facilitated by the family car, some amount of visiting therefore takes place,

high degree of promiscuity in Bantu urban society, it was generally agreed that educated men hardly, if ever, chastised their womenfolk. Many of the illiterate men, however, did; and wife-beating was still common among the Xhosa and, to some extent, among the Zulu. As in some 'working class circles of Western society, a woman expected to be beaten by a jealous husband as it indicated that he still loved her' (1959, pp. 116–17). (See also comment in Chapter 6 on this point.)

especially if the spouses work in the same place. In this event, they inevitably share more friends and, in Ibadan, Lloyd found that half of the best friends of élite men and women were well known to one another: a clergyman's wife cited as two of her best friends the wives of her husband's closest friends. Either spouse may gain new friends through the other; a third of the men Lloyd interviewed claimed between one and three friends gained through their wives and one half of the women had between one and four friends gained through their husbands. However, the extent to which husbands and wives share their leisure time is still fairly small; they may watch television together or go to cocktail parties to friends of either of them, but among one half of the Ibadan élite no shared friendship was found. In fact, most of the spare time of these Ibadan husbands and wives is spent in monosexual gatherings (Lloyd, 1967), although Peil was told in Kaduna that a married man was more restricted in his movements than a single one. She also found that in Ashaiman, a suburb of Tema, the married man is engaged with his wife and children and hence has less time for his friends and even for his relatives (Peil, 1973; also see Date-Bah, 1973).

There are, however, other bonds as well as mutual friends, and the most important of these is the children in whose upbringing both husband and wife frequently co-operate with zeal. The élite father plays ball with his children, reads to them and actively seeks a warm, friendly relationship. Parents take care to see that in their absence the servants never use physical punishment and they are told, instead, to report the children's misdeeds when the parents come back (Lloyd, 1966).[7] A child's subsequent career may bring prestige to its parents and both the latter want, as a rule, the same élite status for their sons and daughters. However, even élite families can rarely afford to provide more than one or two children with training up to the university or professional level that this involves, and so it is not perhaps surprising that élite wives desire fewer children than do less literate mothers. Thus, in a study carried out in Ibadan by F. O. Okediji, 80, 79·6 and 62·5 per cent of women with, respectively, university, technical/professional and secondary school education considered that the ideal number of children to have was four; while 65·3, 63·6 and 43·5 per cent of wives with, respectively, modern school, elementary school education and no education, felt that the ideal number

---

[7] Gamble (1963, pp. 214–22) makes a somewhat similar point. He shows that in up-country towns in Sierra Leone one of the practices which distinguishes educated families from families of men in unskilled work is the punishment of children. In the latter families it is often very severe.

was six. Of the wives with no education at all, 40·3 per cent put
the figure at 8. It is suggested that this trend among the professional
groups reflects these women's high aspirations for their children's
subsequent careers (1967, pp. 70–6).[8] In furtherance of these aims,
almost universally, one parent – usually the mother – checks each
child's homework daily (Lloyd, 1966).

Finally, in the opportunistic circumstances spoken of, it appears
to be fairly evident that for the educated class in general, physical
mobility and social mobility are closely linked.[9] In other words,
the individual young man or woman who is ready, at a moment's
notice, to pack up and move, stands a better chance of occupational promotion and of social betterment than those who are
unwilling or unable to dig up their roots. Thus, civil servants, for
instance, are frequently expected to transfer not only to a different
ministry but from one town to another; University lecturers find
a more senior job in another university; businessmen open new
branches; and some categories of the élite, such as diplomatists,
are posted from country to country. This means that not only are
members of the educated families as mobile as the illiterate
migrants, but they, too, are obliged to make many fresh adjust-
ments. Indeed, in the rapidly changing circumstances of contemporary urban life, a capacity to do so is essential.

If, therefore, Oppong's findings are correct, it is probably not an
accident that people with spatially and socially mobile parents
are more apt to avoid the pressure of kinsfolk. True, quite often
the husband makes the move on his own, leaving his wife and
the children behind, and a constant change of scene may create in
whole families a feeling of instability. On the other hand, it is
also arguable that, finding themselves in a different environment
from their home town with its kinship and other restraining
associations, the married couple concerned may learn out of sheer
necessity, if nothing more, to rely more positively upon each other
and upon their mutual resources. Such migratory families do not

[8] In line with this suggestion is the fact that nearly 87 per cent of
these Ibadan wives with a university, technical, or professional
education approved the use of contraceptives, compared with 25
per cent and 11·6 per cent in the case of wives with a secondary
or a modern school education respectively. Only 9·5 per cent of
wives with an elementary education approved. It is interesting,
therefore, that in terms of the actual number of children born alive,
the higher the education level of the women, the lower the average
number of children (Okediji, *ibid.*).

[9] Since the better jobs tend to go to people who have qualified overseas this lesson does not need to be learned. Its significance is already
expressed and understood by the young men and women concerned
in the term, ' been-to ' (see footnote 10, Chapter 7).

necessarily lack new neighbours and friends in their new abode, because as Jacobson has pointed out (1970, p. 58), the élite's very mobility keeps members of this category incapsulated in their own friendship network. Nor do they lose contact with or forget the lineage at home because, as has been repeatedly stressed, family sentiment invariably remains strong and through periodical visiting and in numerous indirect ways the network of kinship is preserved.

Nevertheless, since there is less face-to-face interaction, kinship norms are correspondingly less compulsive and man and wife have both greater incentive and greater opportunity to adjust to each other's personality. They may for this reason look towards one another for co-operation in the joint enterprise of making a home (see Bird, 1958; Crabtree, 1950) as in the Lagosian households Marris interviewed. Of them he reports:

> Many young husbands not only provided their wives with a means of livelihood, but gave or lent them additional capital, bought their clothes, added pocket money to their incomes. They helped with the housework, cleaning or washing, cooking or looking after the children when their wives were busy . . . The wives, in return, helped to meet the housekeeping bills, lent money to their husbands, or even maintained them altogether when their business was going badly.
>
> (1961, pp. 54–5)

In marriages of this kind, and as well as when the social effects of migration are cumulative, the husbands and wives are more than 'parties to a contract where each limits responsibilities for the affairs of the household'. In other words, in these situations, a new and more companionate pattern of conjugal relations may be established which, in turn, is nearer to the heart's desire of 'progressively' minded women and what they are aiming at.

11 Conclusions

As the foregoing chapters will have indicated, the position of the African urban woman is fraught with ambiguity. Attitudes towards her are frequently ambivalent and the impinging factors so complex that they cannot possibly be summed up in a single equation. Yet, there is one facet of the urban woman's behaviour about which it is possible to generalize and it is her empiricism. Unconventional some of her methods may be by Euro-North American standards, but the impression gained is that the 'city girl' is generally able to hold her own. She is frequently ready, whatever the circumstances, to 'chance her arm'; and related to these attributes is another which renders quite absurd much well-intentioned concern about the alleged treatment of African women as 'slaves' and 'chattels'.[1] This is the 'militancy' of which both urban and rural women are capable, however unpromising the circumstances. For example – even in South Africa – at St. Faith's, near Port Shepstone more than 1,200 African women, armed with sticks and clubs, demonstrated against the poll tax and influx regulations. They received the arrival of two armoured cars with derision, the demonstration being led by an African woman doctor wearing the colours of the African National Congress. This movement was remarkable for the dominant role of the traditionally subordinate Zulu women and, according to a newspaper report, by 21 August 1959, more than 10,000 women, excluding those in other demonstrations, had taken part in the disturbances (cf. Kuper, 1965, pp. 18–19).

Far, therefore, from their being down-trodden, spiritless creatures – *vendues comme les chèvres* – as a French writer (Binet, 1959, pp. 747–56) has remarked with conscious irony – the actual situation, more often, is precisely the opposite. Indeed, working women

---

[1] One such example was the enquiry conducted by a United Nations mission into the domestic conditions of a Bamenda household (former British Cameroons), mainly because the paramount chief concerned had reputedly more than 100 wives.

show, sometimes, a good deal more determination than their male counterparts. Also, not only do they frequently display complete self-confidence, but also a readiness, on occasion, to handle men as physically as women are handled by women.[2]

If we appear to stress these particular qualities it is because the dynamism generated provides this book with its most general conclusion. This is that, irrespective of how their traditional role is construed, African women are now on the march. They wish for themselves a significant place in the new society taking shape, and these aspirations have been fed by the spread of urban influences into the countryside. In fact, urbanization and the women's efforts to alter their position go hand in hand because the growth of urban economic and other institutions automatically holds out new and extra opportunities of achieving status. In seeking to take advantage of this situation the women are following the trend previously set politically and in other ways by the younger men. Whereas, however, many of the latter view urban migration and industrial employment as a makeshift, the women have often more to gain and less to lose by urban residence and experience. For them to move in a townward direction may be more than a temporary and expedient means to an end. It may be conceived of as an end in itself.

However, although urbanization encourages women to form new social alignments and relationships, women are by comparison with men educationally at a disadvantage in the urban economy. Moreover, the urban social structure involves conflicting norms and social values, the one system emphasizing individualism, the other a communalistic viewpoint. Since the latter traditional attitudes enjoin co-operation they facilitate the women's initiation of new forms of mutual aid suited to the urban environment, but, they are also employed by the men in defence of their accustomed authority as males. Numbers of men feel the need of this kind of moral support because, in contrast to the rigidly prescribed status of women in the countryside, the urban situation constitutes a relatively 'open' society in whose

[2] Examples of this have already been given and are supported by this writer's own experience during his field work. On one occasion, he entertained in his house a group of women recruited as singers as well as wives by a local 'big man' who took pride in having an expert 'choir' of his own. There were about a dozen of these ladies and, carried away by the songs they sang for my benefit and by draughts of a cheap but locally popular South African wine, they became distinctly playful. Seemingly only a large table, which blocked the way, prevented the kind of treatment that, according to Malinowski, Trobriander men sometimes undergo at the hands of the women !

economy sexual differences are instrumentally of much less importance than Western learning and technical know-how. The consequence is that the very criteria which serve to underpin male domination in a general sense act in an opposite way in the case of the well-educated woman. They place her potentially in a position to earn as much money as her husband and to occupy posts which give her authority over men.

It is not surprising that there is often on the part of the men a sharp psychological reaction to this reversal of roles. We explained that a few circles, mainly on the West Coast, are not unaccustomed to women being on the same level as their husbands, but we have also tried to make plain that many members of the 'new' educated class have conservative kinsmen to whom the idea of treating wives as 'equals' is anathema. The effect is to make a man feel that his personal prestige is at stake. Ready as he himself may be to raise his wife's standing to the same position as his own, this can only be done at the cost of losing face in the eyes of illiterate relatives already resentful of an educated woman's intrusion.

This situation explains a number of things already referred to, including some husbands' unwillingness for their wives to work and the equal determination of some wives to earn money for themselves. Thus, somewhat unlike the Ghanaian civil servants studied by Oppong, Harrell-Bond found (1971) in Freetown that a strict segregation of financial accounts was a general pattern among professional couples, the husband being responsible for the upkeep of the home, and the wives, if they earned, being free of this kind of financial obligation. This did not mean that wives necessarily made no contribution and had no responsibility for purchasing their own clothes and buying things for the home. Any such contributions, however, were made entirely of their own free will and no husband had a right to expect his wife to supplement their budget with her earnings. It was thought humiliating for a husband to have to borrow money from his wife or to ask her to assume some expenses. This meant that for the husband to be willing to take full responsibility for the expenses of the household, even when his wife did earn an income, was a means of protecting his authority.[3]

Thus, there are signs of a link between the preservation of male superiority and that of the kin group's integrity, with the two

[3] Some men take quite positive steps in the interests of this. Thus, instances are known of a husband seeking his wife's dismissal from a post, and in a particular case, the headmaster of a school forbade his wife accepting a job she was offered unless ways were found of increasing his own salary to the same level of pay.

attitudes reinforcing each other. This, in turn, may explain the apparent popularity of romantic love because to realize power and position in the new social structure needs a more individualistic effort than is compatible with the fulfilment of kinship obligations. There being no straightforward way of denying the latter an alternative sentiment to kinship has to be invoked which will justify a person concentrating economic and other resources upon his or her own interests and ambitions. Perhaps, therefore, it is for this reason that the importance of 'being in love' is so often referred to and why the notion of 'love' expressed in this particular context is difficult precisely to define.[4]

Possibly, too, the same set of complicated psychological factors are behind not only the ambivalent attitude towards wives, but towards the advance of women in general. This point is important because the right to vote now possessed by women in most African countries was sponsored, of course, by male politicians. As explained above, it appears to have been the women's reward, in some cases, for the part that women played as a revolutionary force in the nationalist struggle. Now, not only is this honeymoon period over[5] but the politicians concerned, having gained what they wanted in power, have seen the danger to themselves of carrying revolution too far. Stability is now what they most desire and, as events have shown, the women's mood is not always predictable. Also, although these leaders continue to require women's backing they are caught in a cross-fire between the latters' idealism and the conservatism of the male electorate. The strategic implication of this situation for women's position, is strikingly exemplified in the case of Kenya because of the militancy of the women's movements there.

What gave impetus to this was the politician's failure to fill the gap between the advances promised and what the women actually received on the coming of Independence in 1963. The Kenya African National Union (K.A.N.U.), for example, had been extolling a classless society where all individuals could fully develop their potential; the Government's sessional paper, too, stated that women's part in national building was equal to men's in every respect. In the event, however, government by Africans turned out to be no more, indeed even less, responsive to women's rights than had been the colonial administration. Apparently, it conceived of the women's sections of political parties merely as useful

---

[4] For a fuller exposition of this hypothesis see Little and Price, 1967, pp. 416–17.

[5] As a woman politician in the train of Achebe's ministerial character, 'Chief Nganga', remarks, 'I done say na only for election time. Women de get equality for dis our country' (1966, p. 21).

auxiliaries that would mobilize votes for selected male contestants. Not only was this very galling, but, in education, too, boys were still given preference over girls, and the National Youth Service was established to recruit boys only. Nor was there any readiness to change divorce and marriage legislation that favoured the men; instead, in June 1969 an all-male National Assembly abolished the one law that did give unmarried mothers and their offspring some protection. This must have been a particularly bitter pill because (as mentioned in Chapter 5) the women had fought with the men for Independence. Yet it was not until six years after its attainment that the first woman was elected to the National Assembly, and of the twelve special seats filled by appointment in 1965, not one was allocated to a woman. Consequently, it appeared that the traditional view of women's position was still held and that the Government was building and catering merely for men. Women, in short, were to be treated as an adjunct, rather than an integral part of the modernizing processes (Wipper, 1971a, *passim*).

Thus, it was from widely held feelings of disappointment that the equal-rights movement emerged with women's clubs as its backbone. The largest of these is 'Maendelo ya Wanawake', and its leaders are amongst the most outspoken within the movement as a whole. For example, it was 'Maendelo's' president who in 1964 warned that the women were impatient and wanted action –

> In the home, in public, in job valuation and even in day-to-day activities, men have always regarded women as inferior to them . . .
>
> It is time men started to change their thinking, for today's society can no longer be regarded as yesterday's. Women will no longer be subservient to men . . . May I remind you that all women need recognition, respect, privileges, participation, and their voices to be heard in all walks of life.[6]

To this complaint that the role allotted to women in the building of Kenya as a nation seemed indecisive, *Voice of Women* (Nairobi) added:

> According to the African man's view, a woman is only supposed to be in the house. Her role, educated though she might be, seemed to be only to look after the home and the entire nursing of the young ones. This view has been taken to such extremes that the men appear to neglect or completely underrate the part which our women folks [*sic*] can play in the nation.[7]

---

[6] *East African Standard* (Nairobi), 8 August 1964; quoted by Wipper (*ibid.* p. 433).

[7] June 1969, p. 1 (quoted by Wipper, *ibid.*).

'Maendelo' was the first association to be organized on a large-scale basis but other, more urban-based organizations include the Federation of University Women, the Kenya Women's Society, the Women's Seminar.[8] In addition, an overall co-ordinating body exists on the lines of women's national federations; this is the Kenya National Council of Women. Also, in the background of the women's movement there are – as in West Africa – church groups, welfare associations, auxiliaries to ethnic associations, and branches of the Y.W.C.A., the Red Cross, the Girl Guides, etc.

What precisely is the kind of situation that these movements seek to remedy? In West African countries, one of the problems creating a great deal of anxiety is the uncertainty of the literate woman's position once she has moved out of the traditional family system. In Kenya, the proportion of women involved in a similar transition from membership of wider kinship groupings to mono-gamous family units is probably, as yet, much smaller. Instead, therefore, it is the inferiority of their traditional role,[9] as the women in Kenya or as the militants define it, that has come under attack. There is criticism, in particular, of the rules of deference as well as the physical labour involved. In Kenya, women begin to carry loads when they are still young, and con-tinue into old age;[10] but interestingly enough, what evokes the greatest outcry is the norms of deference rather than the onus of physical labour. It is not on medical grounds but for its symbolic importance – women being treated as 'beasts of burden' – that there is objection to the arduous physical work required. In other words, women are developing a new conception of themselves, and particularly significant is the novel proposal that the Swahili term of respect for a European woman, *memsahib*, should be extended in its use to African women. 'We African women', a spokesman argued, 'can never expect to be respected by women of other races until our men change their attitude towards us'. In the colonial period, to address a European woman in this way made the status hierarchy quite clear : but, today (the argument runs)

[8] Actually, a committee convened every few years for the purpose of organizing conferences on woman's role.
[9] As was briefly pointed out in Chapter 1, in all African societies women informally exercise varying and sometimes extensive degrees of influence, and even the formal structure usually allocates con-siderable power to the senior wife. It has been argued, however, that studies of Kenyan peoples generally reveal male dominance in virtually every sphere.
[10] Possibly the presence of a relatively large European population in Kenya helped to inspire and propagate this particular criticism. European women had for years condemned the everyday drudgery of the African woman, as they saw it.

women have not only rejected the traditional rules of deference, they have reversed the status hierarchy – men, therefore, must show deference to women.

In the attack on male 'superiority', men are accused of not performing their roles adequately. The women complain that they are lazy, drunken, adulterous, and brutal. These accusations, including the assertion that women work harder than men, are – according to Wipper – generally acknowledged to be fairly accurate.[11] Through the mass media, the public platform, pamphlets, conferences, and debates, the militants spread their ideas; and the feminist campaign extends all the way from university class rooms to informal gatherings of a few tribesmen. Even members of the Masai, proudly disdainful of European civilization, and persevering in their traditional ways, have not escaped the women's ire. A group of them were given a stern warning by 'Maendelo's' leader. She told them:

> The time has come for you men to start taking better care of your wives. Just because we wear skirts, you tend to regard us as your slaves. But no more. Women are on the march.[12]

How does the Government respond to this protest? Since women are, after all, more than half the electorate, they are too important a group to offend. Radical women, on the other hand, represent only a small minority, and since they lack wide public support, the men know they can circumvent their promises to women with impunity. Second, highly generalized values, such as 'African Socialism', leave largely undefined the specific implications for action, and so, when the women protest that these edicts

---

[11] Assuming that male apathy and irresponsibility do, in fact, exist, Wipper suggests as a possible explanation that the man's traditional role has suffered far severer dislocations than the woman's. Jobless men have drifted into the pattern of sporadic work, drunkenness and broken marriages. The woman, left on her own to support her family, works hard to eke out a meagre living by cultivating the family shamba and trading at the local market. In caring for her family, she develops a toughness and an ability to cope often lacking in her male counterpart (1971a, p. 436).

[12] (*Reporter*, 22 December 1962. Quoted by Wipper, 1971a, p. 438.) The result, according to a newspaper, was that:
> A row of rather sheepish looking Masai tribesmen rattled their earnings and uttered confused 'aahs' and 'ees' . . . as Mrs. Ruth Habwe stood up before them . . . and gave them hell . . . Most of the Masai men who were hanging around went back to their *manyattas* (homes) with an air of having finally decided that this civilization is definitely something which is an affair of God and in which they should not interfere. (*Ibid.*)

are not being met, the men's rejoinder is that they are doing enough for women and everything cannot be achieved at once (Wipper, 1971*a*, pp. 463–82).

In fact, according to Wipper, the women are handled by a judicious employment of 'tokenism', especially on ceremonial occasions. 'Progressive' women are given assurances by the Government and are told that they can rely on its fullest support; women delegates are hospitably entertained, the women's leaders flattered and the meetings and conferences they organized are graced by the presence of high-ranking officials and ministers. The Government also demonstrates its apparent acceptance of women's equality by appointing a woman to an important position, such as a place in the United Nations delegation.[13] As mentioned, 'Maendelo' is the most militant as well as the largest of the women's organizations, and since its aim of raising the living standards of rural women coincides with official policy, the Government has let it be known that is expects 'big things' from 'Maendelo'. In effect, the Government's own largest contribution has been through officers of the Department of Community Development who have worked with the association at the community level. However, in order to manage 300 branches effectively, a good deal of money is needed and 'Maendelo' has never been able to depend upon the Government for this. When asked to provide personnel, training facilities, etc., its spokesmen have stalled and even countered with the rationalization that 'Maendelo' should stand on its own feet; otherwise it would be branded as an organization of the Government (1971*b*).

In West Africa, as mentioned, several women have held cabinet positions, but in Kenya the men argue that women are not yet qualified for political office. Women must prove themselves; they should behave like men; they are not aggressive enough. Yet when women showed these qualities they were said to be opportunistic. It was also suggested that women were naive, potentially unstable and weak-charactered; or, if women's present character was not faulted, it was predicted that involvement in politics would give them a character to fault. They would become 'big-headed' and 'power-hungry'. Instead of losing their full status as Africans, women lose their full status as adults. They are seen to need protection from the harsh realities of life.[14] A related strategy

---

[13] This appointment, Wipper points out, serves the double purpose of affirming the Government's belief in the norm and, if a militant woman is chosen, of assuring it relief from her presence.

[14] Note the close analogy with Victorian attitudes towards the middle-class wife. She was to be protected by the 'sterner sex', from danger, from vice and even from serious work.

consists of dismissing the women leaders as unrepresentative of rural women; it being claimed that they have lost touch with the ordinary woman in the street.[15] Indeed, a whole set of catastrophes was predicted if women entered public life. African customs would be lost, homes would break up, the divorce rate would soar, the population would decrease, illegitimacy would rise and mal-nutrition would spread; and, since women are 'gullible', the 'imperialists' could perpetuate neo-colonialism through them. Humour is also used, the implication being that the women's demands are too ridiculous to be taken seriously,[16] and closely linked to this tactic is the ploy that a woman already enjoys power in their homes as 'Minister for Home Affairs' (Wipper, 1971b, *passim*). In short, the complaint is that the men hardly encourage women in politics. As the president of the Union of African and Malagasy women has remarked in a quite different region of the continent, 'When you discuss it they give a little smirk'.[17]

The above does not mean that all Kenyan politicians deny the rightness of women's claims. Many of them appear to be genuinely proud of some women's accomplishments. 'There is evidence', Wipper mentions, 'that the humble, strong, hard-working mother is revered. Time and again, a leading political figure has paid homage to the selfless devotion of his own mother, who from a pittance provided his school fees, the beginning of his path to advancement.' In part, therefore, such men are in favour of the ideal of women's equality. They recognize the moral validity of their claims, but find themselves in a dilemma where political pressures push them to act otherwise.

These developments in Kenya are of special interest because of the relatively late date at which African women in East Africa as a whole took positions in governmental and other modern in-stitutions. Ganda women, to be sure, effectively exploited their

[15] This is true to the extent that having travelled and being innovators of new values in a society that is still largely traditional, the educated woman is not any more like the masses than the politicians.

It is interesting, however, that prior to Independence precisely the same kind of argument was used by colonialists to discredit the role of the African 'intelligentsia' as nationalist leaders.

[16] The analogy is again very close with the opposition to women having the vote in Britain. For example, it is said that although the first draft of the 'Charter of Rights and Liberties', compiled in 1838, included women's suffrage, it was removed in case it made the Chartists' agitation appear silly. John Stuart Mill, who risked his political career for the sake of the women's cause, was derisively referred to as the fellow who 'wants to get girls in Parliament'.

[17] Thérèse Kuoh Moukoury, quoted in *Africa Report*, July–August 1972, p. 16.

right to freehold land and carried on their private lives without regard to their kinsfolk's wishes. Also, having more education than others they were able to organize in the event of their rights being threatened as well as giving an increasing number of women 'respectable' economic independence through employment in offices and the professions (Parkin, 1969, pp. 92–3). But in most other tribes the women are under the men's control and, although there are now women lawyers and magistrates, in the East and Central African countries in general the number of women in professional and public life bears no comparison with West Africa. Thus, it was not until 1962 that the first African health visitor in the then Central Africa Federal Government was appointed; that Nyasaland's first African woman doctor qualified; and that Kenya's first African police woman completed a three-month training course. Nor, unlike West Africa, was there much alteration in women's position after the Second World War or around Independence. Instead, between 1950 and 1965 it was the men who took the initiative.

Today, however, East African women are on the move and, according to a report from Tanzania:

> there seems . . . to be a hunger in women for change, as though they had been left behind and are only now catching on to the many possibilities for improving their lot. There seems to be a terrific openness and sense of movement, of achievement, in women at this time. The self-image of women seems to be changing very rapidly, almost faster at this point than is evident in men.[18]   (Staub, 1971, pp. 8–10)

Also, observations recently made in Kampala, for example, suggest that women there are now engaged in economic pursuits to an unexpected extent. Not only are they very prominent in the local markets, but they are also behind counters in small *dukas* and in fashionable shops and boutiques. They are dressmakers and beauticians, they operate ranching schemes, breed and market chickens and eggs and engage in real estate. In addition, there is a growing number of women, mostly university graduates, who are in junior executive jobs (personal communication, Mrs Isis Southall).

Naturally, this apparent 'awakening' of the women in East

[18] In addition, a study group of the Tanzanian Christian Council has mentioned, in reference specifically to women, 'the sudden awareness of people's rights'; and it suggests that 'this awareness has produced a change in individuals both in speech and action'. People feel that they have not only 'the right to speak, but also the ability to act' (Beetham, 1967).

Africa is associated with urbanization because save for the 'Swahili coast', there were almost no towns in East Africa before the European colonialists arrived. Nor, indigenously speaking, did women take much part in public affairs except in a few societies, such as Buganda. Mostly they were agricultural workers while the men fought as warriors or herded cattle. Such markets as existed were local and small and it was unusual for women to travel far from their own homesteads and villages. In West Africa, by contrast, not only have substantial pockets of urbanism existed for centuries, but women were already active in commerce in some of the areas which were subsequently opened up to overseas trade by European pacification of the hinterland. These parts of the country were, in consequence, characterized by social systems which, although under male control, permitted women their own sphere of interaction with which the men did not interfere. This meant that while political authority remained a male prerogative, there was between the sexes a working relationship which fully recognized women's personal rights and interests. It meant, in effect, that men and women accommodated to each other as groups.[19]

Possibly this West African pattern of behaviour was 'rural' in the first place. One cannot say for certain; but what does appear to be clear from the solidarity of illiterate and semi-literate women today is that urban experience has consolidated and made it firmer among these classes. Educated women stand somewhat outside the system and although those who associate themselves with the uneducated women have prestige and are given a respectful hearing, their general position is, perhaps, rather different from that of Kenyan educated women. The latter, according to Wipper, are something more than leaders. In addition to organizing their less literate and rural sisters, they constitute an élite whose way of life and outlook are imitated and emulated down to the final detail. In contrast, the less literate class of West African women, being more self-sufficient and economically stronger, have less need to rely on the example of others. Certainly, they too desire to improve their position and to become even more independent, but when they move and take action as a group it is for a specific purpose. They have little or no interest in women's

---

[19] This point appears to be particularly marked in societies in which women organize girls' education, prepare them for marriage, etc. Among most of the peoples of Sierra Leone and Liberia, for example, the women's traditional associations are influential enough to protect women's rights *vis-à-vis* men and will brook no interference on the part of the male sex in 'women's business' (cf. among others Little, 1951).

rights in an abstract or philosophical sense. Full of self-confidence and well able to look after themselves, they are disposed to leave general questions alone but to seek, by individual bargaining with husbands and lovers, the specific benefits or concessions they desire. If these overtures fail, there is collective action to fall back on.

The implication of all this is that there is apparently lacking from Kenya (and perhaps from East Africa in general) the kind of 'gentlemen's agreement' that, it is suggested, exists between the sexes in some parts of West Africa. In the latter region there is, seemingly, a certain amount of give and take and a readiness on the part of both sexes, in the event of serious 'palaver', to talk matters over and to negotiate. In East Africa, on the other hand, women's own institutions being less highly developed and having less societal significance, it may be more difficult for the two sides to meet. Instead of having a complementary relationship, the sexes stand in opposition to each other and the absence of a West African type of *modus vivendi* leaves the women with direct confrontation as their only tactic.

The above formulations are bound to be somewhat conjectural, but are not necessarily invalid for purposes of prediction, especially if history should repeat itself. For, in terms of everyday life the strong domination of East African women by men seems – as briefly implied above – to bear a close resemblance to the position of Victorian women in England. Yet, in the Mau Mau insurrection the women's actions were as violent as the men's and when women in nineteenth-century Britain rebelled it became clear that women's apparent submissiveness was only a sham. Also, in the latter struggle educated and uneducated women made common cause and showed what could be achieved by dedication and determination and by a united attack on the myth of male superiority (see Fulford, 1957; Gregg, 1950; Hobsbawn, 1962; and Pearsall, 1969). This suggests that if the present trend reported from Kenya continues, a similar type of militant feminism could grow and become a formidable force throughout East Africa as a whole.

As implied, the situation in West Africa is more complicated. Previous paragraphs have already stressed the solidarity and strength of women's movements there and these, too, have the backing of educated women. Biographical particulars of a number of these leaders are provided in the appendix, including Mrs Adekogbe who founded the Nigerian Women's movement more than twenty years ago and gave up her career as a teacher in order to propagate the cause. Another Nigerian woman, Mrs Ekpo, headed the Eastern wing of the Nigerian Women's Union and was an equally tireless champion of women's rights. In Ghana, Mrs Hannah Kudjoe combined enthusiasm for nationalism with the women's cause and was the only woman present when it was decided to found Nkrumah's Convention People's Party. Another Ghanaian, Miss Mabel Dove, was the first woman in West Africa to be elected to Parliament by popular vote and became the main spokesman of her illiterate sisters. In Sierra Leone, Madam Ella Gulama brought the prestige of her office and knowledge of the traditional background of her people effectively to bear on women's problems.

On the other hand, in West Africa the structural factors just referred to do not necessarily favour feminism *per se*. Thus, not only does a larger proportion of the mass of women have less socially and economically to complain about than their counterparts in the other regions, but, paradoxically perhaps, the gap between different classes of women is sometimes broader than between the sexes themselves. Related to this is the greater economic development of much of West Africa which provides in the towns readier and wider opportunities for upward mobility. This applies even to illiterate women because it is by no means unusual for such a person to be paying her children's school fees, and this may result in her gaining prestige vicariously through a son's or a daughter's subsequent success in the professions (cf. Little, 1972*b*). In other words, there is less reason for sensitivity about sexual as well as social differentiation. True, women in West Africa, as well as other parts of the continent, may have to contend with male prejudice and opposition because as Mrs Olu-Williams has explained a 'double standard' is inevitable when they engage in identical activities with men. Mrs Olu-Williams was the first African woman to achieve the rank of permanent secretary in the civil service and she is reported as saying that 'a woman working in a man's world must do *more* than a man'. She considered that none of a woman's qualifications, skill, or ability will be taken for granted; she has to prove each ounce of her work.[20]

Nevertheless, the admission of West African women into the upper echelons of law and administration does seem to have gone quite steadily on, and the careers of Mrs Annie Jiagge, Miss Angie Brooks and Mrs Reeves Gorgla in particular, provide notable examples (see appendix). The effect, perhaps, is to 'cream off' some able women who otherwise might be active feminists because ardent as the attitude of such people may be, ascent to the top sometimes mellows it. For example, a woman to distinguish herself in the Congo-Kinshasa is Madame Sophie Lihau who be-

[20] From an interview given to *West Africa*. See appendix for particulars of Mrs Olu-Williams' interesting career.

came Minister of Social Welfare in the Government of President Mbotu (see appendix). Although personally concerned that girls should have as much opportunity of education as boys, Madame Lihau's official tone appears to have been diplomatic. She has stuck to what she said in an interview given to *Jeune Afrique* – ' I'm a woman minister, not a minister for women '.[21]

Let us summarize, therefore, by suggesting that there are two quite different systems in which women participate. There is the one in which the illiterate and semi-literate sections move more or less as a body in both work and leisure time, and in which even the wives of élite men take part when their educational and occupational position is much below that of their husbands.[22] This is a world on its own – a universe quite apart from that of the men – in which women not only interact mainly with women, but also vie exclusively with each other in terms of the conspicuous consumption of clothes and other material things and even in the acquisition of ' prestigious ' men as lovers. The other system is the one in which the more enterprising type of ' civilized ' woman aspires to make her mark. Though linked with the first by kinship and other ties this milieu naturally involves interaction and competition with men as well as women. Moreover, its being a milieu in which men have a near monopoly of the town's economy means that in the circumstances already described, the successful woman needs to be a somewhat exceptional person who, for preference, is well-to-do or highly educated. Failing these qualifications she may be virtually restricted to the role of prostitute, concubine or courtesan if, instead of marrying, she chooses to live on her own. Indeed, unless such a woman has a male protector it is possible that in some South African townships and doubtless elsewhere as well, she will be constantly in physical danger. On top of all this, not only is her position liable to be misinterpreted or misunderstood by people around her, but as a result of the latter's social pressures she may come herself to question it and to doubt her own motives. In a further book about urban life Ekwensi has summed up this psychological situation in a nutshell. In this novel, *Iska*, his character, ' Remi ' is ostensibly the sophisticated, hard-bitten ' city-girl ' but under this veneer she is insecure, uncertain of herself and feels ' out of place ' :

> Remi had a philosophy that any girl who lives alone in Lagos must have at least one serious illness a year. This is God's way of reminding single girls that they are not as independent as they think . . . Modern living may have enabled them to

[21] Reported in *West Africa*, 1967 (pp. 362–3).
[22] See Jacobson (1970) for a useful illustration of the latter point.

isolate themselves from father, mother, brother, sister, fiancé, husband and village community, but the umbilical cord has not been severed. (1966a, pp. 114–15)

A girl on her own has these feelings because, as Ekwensi implies, she is entirely unprepared for a type of existence in which she may not even have the company of girls who were her age-mates. Instead, the world she is now in is virtually dominated by men. They, through controlling the town's major institutions, create a peculiar atmosphere in which only a very strong-minded woman can survive without male reassurance and support. True, there are the ordinary economic difficulties which nearly everyone has to cope with and surmount, but a girl wishing to remain independent has an even greater problem. Where is she to find a man willing to befriend her without doing his utmost to draw her into an emotional and sexual relationship ?

Ekwensi explains this predicament as follows. When ' Remi ' first came to Lagos she had notions of romantic love. Lagos dis-illusioned her and she lived with one pick-up after another. Eventually, however, she met a boy who was honest with her and did not demand sexual services as the price of his friendship. As a result she gained a sense of security and self-confidence. ' A girl ', she says, ' must have a boy here in Lagos. A strong one. It helps a lot to have someone. When the men know you're some-body's girl they're not so keen and you know where you stand.' ' Remi ' emphasizes that a girl must be able to control herself and be capable of saying ' No '.[23]

Such questions of moral and psychological support bring us back, finally, to the position of women as both mothers and wives. This is bound up very much with the emergence of the urban household as a primary group, comprising man, wife and children alone. As we have stressed, in the traditional system each such elementary family is, functionally speaking, an integral part of the extended kinship grouping which usually provides most of its members' social, religious and economic needs. Such group-ings may comprise fifty or more people, but in the urban situation the size of the household frequently averages no more than four, five or six persons. It is as though, in other words, the original organization had been split up into a number of separate domestic units, representing a specialization of the wider kinship groupings' generalized function. This does *not* mean that the urban household in question necessarily takes the form of a nuclear family because, in fact, a large proportion of such domestic units include a wide

[23] *Ibid.* p. 117.

variety of relatives and dependants.[24] What it *does* imply is a substantial difference in the wife's role compared with her previous position as a contributor of food and children only. Now, the household being more of a primary unit on its own, the wife is invested with greater responsibility. Upon her largely devolves the care and rearing of her own children, and to the extent that she also controls the household's budget, she is in a pivotal position *vis-à-vis* the domestic group's other members. This means in other words, *that not only does the operation of the nuclear family largely depend upon the wife's own efforts and skill but that her own status and welfare are bound up with its successful functioning.*

Urbanization thus poses for women a dilemma. Through living in town they have, to a varying extent, readier access to opportunities of social and economic advancement and there are signs as well of their acceptance as ' citizens ' on the same basis as men. That women are making, as individuals, an increasing contribution to the general life of the nation is also evident; but the heart of the problem lies deeper. It consists in the fact that in its new urban form the family lacks a secure place in the framework of both society and state. It has gained a measure of autonomy but remains in a marginal situation partly because of the vicious circle in which the wife herself is frequently placed. Thus, on the one hand, there are the new familial circumstances which offer the wife a higher status provided she is able to play the requisite role of modern homemaker. On the other, are the traditional attitudes which tend to impede its successful performance and so to jeopardize both the nuclear family's *raison d'être* and her own. For unlike the developed countries, there are not available in Africa statutory or other public forms of social security and insurance. Consequently, if the urban family gets financially into low water, the cost of salvation may be the handing over of its affairs to the management of conservatively-minded kinsfolk.

Matrimonial conditions in Western Europe and North America, too, vary a great deal. We do not therefore suggest that the evolution, were it possible, of a more highly developed form of urban society on Euro-North American lines would produce in

---

[24] In fact, as implied earlier, there are numerous kinds of domestic arrangements and the situation also varies greatly from town to town. In Freetown, Banton found that only 6 households out of 268 contained more than one elementary family (1957, p. 202) and in Jinja the proportion in the Sofers' sample (1955) was 65·9 per cent. In Dakar and in Kinshasa, on the other hand, only 41 per cent and 10 per cent respectively of households were strictly elementary families (Comhaire-Sylvain, 1968, p. 150; Mercier, 1954. See also Acquah, 1958, and Fraenkel, 1964 in particular).

Africa a more truly egalitarian trend in marital relations. The question rather, is whether in existing urban circumstances the African woman, *as wife* (as distinct from mistress or concubine), has sufficient room in which to manoeuvre. Is this not perhaps the dilemma which fundamentally explains her desire for 'independence' and why she so often gives priority to earning money for herself? Moreover, not only does she evidently believe that an income of her own will enable her to face married life with more confidence, but her attitude may very well have some basis in fact. Thus, according at least to Oppong's findings, even among educated couples it was wives with money of their own who took more share in the running of the house than wives who lacked it. The evidence has also shown that, questions of state aid apart, there are ways at the 'grass-roots' whereby the urban household is 'buttressed' through voluntary associations. Such organizations, especially the regional type, have served widely and successfully as an adaptive mechanism when most of the migrants concerned moved to town as single individuals. Now, with permanent settlement replacing circular migration in some regions the influx is seen to be more in terms of whole families. This, in turn, may lead to a further development of the ethnic associations' function in terms of a still wider extension of membership to persons who are not directly connected with the particular clan, tribe, or district concerned.

There are analogous urban circumstances in which membership has been widened on these lines in, for example, Sumatra. There, in the rapidly growing city of Medan, Toba Batak migrants have formed urban clans which are simultaneously residence groups and voluntary associations. In order to join, a man must live in Medan and be a descendant of the clan ancestor. However, social affiliation is further extended as it is customary for each nuclear family to join both the clan and association of the husband *and* the clan association of the wife. The unnamed children become members of the two associations and may participate in the group. To put it another way, each urban clan association is open to both the male and the female members of the clan and their spouses (Bruner, 1961, *passim*). Not only does this double the membership and widen the scope of the relationships, but the family is affiliated as an entity to the associational structure, thereby gaining extra organizational support. In other words, if there were in Africa a similar kind of associational extension it might, by consolidating the urban family *per se*, reinforce the wife's position as well.

Such trends will be bound up in any case with the direction in which women in general are going. The women's right to a place in the highest circles of the nation has been widely and publicly acknowledged, but their fundamental status is, as yet, somewhat hypothetical. Its resolution hinges not on whether *individual* women are able to rise to fame, but on whether women *as a whole* are able to participate in the ' open ' as distinct from the traditional sectors of society. This is a matter about which the women's leaders themselves are somewhat undecided because, as indicated in Chapter 5, they are inclined to hedge. Though anxious to remove anomalies in women's position, they do not want to jettison what they regard as good in the older tradition. Thus, to be more specific, some leaders would like to get rid of polygyny but have no desire to undermine what they look upon as the special virtues of African womanhood; its focus on home life and on the care of husbands and children.

It is difficult, at times, to say whether the women who thus argue for the traditional values hold these ideas because they are genuinely opposed to radical change or because they are really motivated by other interests. Wipper, on the basis of her Kenyan experience, refers to women ' patrons ' who are recruited through the developing middle and professional classes. This type of women's leader takes part in the women's associations mainly for political and status reasons which involve her attending embassy affairs, presenting awards, sponsoring welfare projects and making speeches and officiating at annual prize-giving days. She is related through marriage to the political élite (Wipper, 1971*b*, pp. 472ff.), and this connection is instrumental in the patron's ' round of tea-pouring and handshaking, which fits in nicely with the Government's " do-nothingness " and propensity for ceremony rather than actions '. In other words, according to Wipper, there is to all intents and purposes a Government–patron alliance serving to block the militant women's efforts to force the Government's hand. It goes without saying that, as implied on previous pages, the *latter* category of women leaders are, by contrast, ardently and fervently opposed to any kind of compromise.

If, then, the above analysis is correct, it is tempting in con-clusion to assess the future of African women's status within the perspective of other apparently similar ' liberation ' movements. Of these the most analogous might seem to be nineteenth-century attempts to emancipate women in Britain. This feminist protest burgeoned and swelled despite the seemingly passive attitude of Victorian middle-class womanhood, and the impetus came largely from women of modest fame but possessed of considerable enthusiasm and personal attainments (cf. Fulford, 1957). Also, in the numerous petitions to Parliament, not only were the latter's signatures backed by women with experience of public affairs, but the most militant suffragettes included members of socially prominent families who, too, chained themselves to railings and went on hunger-strike. Yet the parallel, so far as it goes, ends there because, paradoxically as it may seem, African women are both by tradition and contemporaneously speaking better off in important respects than were their British Victorian counterparts. Thus, not only do most adult African females today already possess the vote, but even illiterate wives are often entitled by indigenous custom to own property of their own. The latter right did not come to married women in England until 1870, and it was not until 1928 that the franchise was gained on equality with men.

Since, therefore, African women already possess these important rights by law, possibly a more useful analogy is provided by the position of black Americans in relation to the United States Constitution. The Amendments to this guarantee the same liberties and rights to American citizens, irrespective of race, colour or creed; but until recent years the Deep South's social system was caste-like. State laws and customary sanctions separated black from white and prevented Negroes from improving their status except in terms of their own race's society. Only by moving north had black people any opportunity at all of achieving a place in the same social institutions as whites. Protest on the part of militant black leaders and groups backed by white liberal sentiment has had its effect on this racialism,[25] and since the 1950s some notable changes have been effected in the whole situation. Among these is the increasing tendency on the part of Negroes who win or are given public recognition to continue their identification with the black cause.[26]

American society is under the control of white people. Any analogy, therefore, between it and African women's position needs to be in parallel terms of their difficulties in a society dominated by men. Is it pertinent, in other words, to conjecture that African women's status will undergo further change in the same kind of manner as that of Negroes in the United States? Obviously, the relationships of persons of different race and the relationships of persons of different sex are not in themselves comparable phenomena. Nevertheless, if the interactions occurring are thought of in terms of group rather than individual behaviour,

[25] The influence of world opinion, especially at the United Nations, has also to be noted.

[26] Most readers will probably be familiar with these general facts concerning which there is, of course, a voluminous literature. Banton (1967, pp. 334–67) is one of several authors who provides a helpful summary of the situation referred to in the above paragraph and the succeeding one. See also, in particular, Pettigrew (1964).

certain features are common to both these situations. Firstly, one of the ways in which the American administration sought to deal with the Constitutional anomaly was by appointing individual Negroes to positions of national importance, usually in the international field. This is similar to the 'tokenism' reported by Wipper in the context of the Kenya Government's treatment of women's agitation.

Of more fundamental relevance, however, has been the exhibition of prejudice against a disadvantaged group and the latter's eventual development of notions of 'black power' – a phenomenon that arose largely out of the immigration of these same disadvantaged Negroes from the American south into the northern cities. It was, in other words, their ensuing urbanization which generated racial consciousness, just as in Africa it is urbanization which, by providing new social structures, brings women together, and facilitates their meeting and making common cause despite ethnic, tribal and other sectional differences.

It remains, therefore, to be seen, not only whether African women will, in increasing numbers, desire to break with tradition; but whether they are prepared for a species of 'sexual warfare'. In the latter event, since the outcome may be decided by the women's own strategy, much will obviously depend on the side taken by those educated women who, in particular, are socially to the fore. Will they fight for women's rights or will they, as Wipper puts it, 'be co-opted into the political élite, succumb to the role of patron, and lose any deep commitment to women's goals?'

But should it ever be mounted, such a campaign is unlikely to take the form colloquially known in Western Europe and North America as 'Women's Lib'. African women already have their own individual way of handling husbands and lovers and so there will be no comparable wielding of cudgels and no attempt at bludgeoning the men into compliance. Being forged out of inherited and age-old knowledge of their menfolk's virtues, foibles and frailties the weapons that African women possess are altogether sharper and more subtle. When combined with modern education these are likely to be the more effective kind of instrument if, through the female sex, Africa's own particular species of social revolution is to be effectively completed.

Some relevant 'portraits'

This appendix includes a short biography of African women who have made their mark, mainly since the Second World War, in social, political, educational, legal and business circles. Unavoidably, one of the principal criteria in assembling it was the actual availability of material and so, regrettably, there are important omissions simply because the information needed is lacking.

It will also be noted that very nearly all the women included are from West African countries. This is mainly due both to *West Africa's* excellent supply of such 'portraits' and to the more extensive part played by women in modern institutions in that area. Indeed, given racial discrimination in South Africa and the relative lag in educational development elsewhere it would be surprising if West African born women were not more to the fore in fields requiring an advanced education. After all, it was already quite common for girls from Sierra Leone to attend schools in Britain as well as Freetown at least half a century before a single school existed in other major regions of sub-Saharan Africa.

The latter consideration makes it, in fact, appropriate and historically relevant to begin with a member of one of the 'old' West African families mentioned in the text. This representative of the former social élite of the 'Coast' is *Mrs Jessica Otumba-Payne*. She was born in Accra in 1874, the year in which legislation was enacted for the abolition of the Gold Coast slave trade. During that year also, Lagos was removed from the 'West African Settlements', thus becoming a part of the Gold Coast Colony instead of being subject to a Governor-in-Chief in Sierra Leone.

Mrs Otumba-Payne's maiden name was Bruce and her father, the head of the family, was an extremely rich and progressive business man who sent his daughter, at the age of about seven, to school in England. The little girl spent some time in Scotland and later entered Tower Hill College, where another West African, Victoria Forbes-Davies, was a pupil, under the special protection of Queen Victoria, whose godchild she was. Jessica and Victoria were school 'chums' and in adult life devoted friends, for Miss Forbes-Davies married Dr Randall, one of the earliest and most important Nigerian nationalists, and went to live in Lagos. He also held the coveted honorary posts of chairman of the Lagos Race Club and Lagos Island Club.

Mrs Otumba-Payne was interviewed in 1956 for *West Africa* when she was in her 83rd year. She described as ' young boys ' such people as her nephew, Thomas Hutton Mills, a former Ghanaian Minister, and Mr Archie Caseley-Hayford, then Gold Coast Minister of the Interior. Lord Lugard, however, was a contemporary of hers and her face lit up at the mention of him :

> Fred Lugard ! Now there was a man after my own heart. He was so like his brother I used to enjoy teasing him. When I popped into Government House I would say, 'Tell me, is it Fred or is it Ned ? ' How he laughed at me.

Also, among Mrs Otumba-Payne's ' concert circle ' were Edmund Macaulay, who became Sir Akitoye Ajasa; Herbert Macauley ' who was a most accomplished musician and always fun '; Dr Henry Carr; Dr Adeniyi-Jones; and a few others. When asked gently about the public and political lives of these men, Mrs Payne looked vague and murmured, ' Oh, I was never interested in their politics. Those people were my *friends*.' She herself was musically gifted and she developed into an outstanding pianist and organist.

Perhaps because there were so few Africans in the United Kingdom, or because manners were more polished in those days, ' colour bar ' appears to have been unknown. Miss Jessie certainly never experienced any such discrimination, and was, seemingly, quite lacking in racial consciousness. In fact, it was at the great Colonial and Indian Exhibition of 1886 that she met her future husband. Mr. Payne, whose name is an anglicized version of the Yoruba, Adepeyin. He was a member of the Gbelegbuwa royal house of Ijebu-Ode, and became Registrar of the old Supreme Court in Lagos. The then Governor of the Gold Coast wanted to give Miss Bruce away in marriage, but she replied to his request, ' Thank you, dear Bradford, but not while my father is alive, if you please '. A member of her guard of honour was Mr Cecil Armitage, destined to become Governor of the Gambia. After a honeymoon in England where they were entertained like minor royalty, the newly weds returned to Lagos in 1894, where Orange House, Tinubu Square, was their residence.

In an era when young ladies allowed themselves to be feminine Jessie Bruce outdid her contemporaries in sauciness and gaiety and was a high favourite everywhere. In those days comparatively few Africans were thoroughly imbued with Western culture. Consequently, they and the representatives of the overseas mercantile firms, as well as British officials, mixed together with great cordiality, on the 'minority stick together' principle. In this society young Mrs Payne soon made a niche for herself. 'No party was considered complete without her diminutive presence, escorted by her stately bearded husband'. After his death in 1906, Mrs Payne's time was spent between Nigeria and the then Gold Coast (*West Africa*, 1956, pp. 29–30).

A much more recent member of Nigeria's women's élite, *Mrs Titilola Sodeinde*, has actively concerned herself with her country's social problems. She came from a middle-class Lagos family and was sent to Portway College, Reading, as a girl. After qualifying as a teacher, she joined the United Missionary Training College, Ibadan, the first of its kind for women, and for some years was the only Nigerian on the staff. In 1938 she joined the staff of Queen's College, Lagos, and, after serving there as the principal domestic science teacher, she was seconded by the Government to take charge of a new Domestic Science Centre. In 1942, after being appointed to Nigeria's first Cost of Living Commission, she served on a sub-committee to determine exactly what constituted a subsistence diet and what was ordinary Nigerian families' pattern of consumption. In 1953, however, she transferred to a somewhat different kind of position, being a Student's Adviser in the Federal Office in London until 1955.

In 1960, despite a full-time educational liaison job with the Shell Company of West Africa, Mrs Sodeinde's voluntary social work continued to grow. In addition to her work for the Girl Guides and Red Cross, she was on the National Council for Corona schools and was an active supporter of the Federation of Women's Clubs and Associations. Despite her busy public life Mrs Sodeinde found the time to marry, make a home and raise a family, her husband being Dr E. N. O. Sodeinde, M.B.E., sometime chief medical officer of the Nigerian Railway Corporation (*West Africa*, 1960a, p. 369).

It was stressed in Chapter 3 that individual African women have achieved considerable prosperity and economic success without possessing formal education. One of these, *Mrs Susannah Bardi*, was born in Ugbodu Town in Benin Province, the fourteenth child of her father who was a chief. He had considerable means, many wives – 50 in all, it was said – and many children, 50 male and 60 female. Each wife had her own house in their great compound and Susannah's job, since none of her elder brothers and sisters had survived, was to feed, bathe, and 'mother' the babies as they arrived – in between helping the women with the preparation of palm oil and kernels. She was her father's constant companion until she was twenty, and after his death she became a wardress in the Government prison. Many of the prisoners were pregnant women and it was part of a wardress's job to deliver the babies. When she was off duty she learnt bread-making – a skill that later was to pay Madam Bardi dividends.

It was about this time – the middle 1920s – that the historic city of Kano was gaining fresh renown as commercial centre for the ground-nut industry. A new township was springing up outside the walls of the sunbaked city into which poured people from the south to man commercial houses and Government offices and to construct a new railway line. Madam Bardi was by now thinking of going into business on her own and so she went north, took a room in ' *sabon gari* ', the ' strangers' district ' of Kano, and set up as a contractor to the railway. This involved journeying regularly to and from Minna for food to sell to workers on the railway line. She also started a piggery, and from six pigs and a butcher's stall in the ' *sabon gari* ' market, Madam Bardi had 200 by 1954 and was doing wholesale contracting to big concerns in Kano and Lagos. In the meantime she had also put her wardress training to good use and started a bakery. The hygienic condition of this and her proficiency came to the ears of the United States Army during the War and apprentice cooks were sent to her for training. In addition, she produced loaves for the R.W.A.F.F., and for the B.O.A.C. and Pan-American airlines. The Perseverance Hotel was a further venture which attracted a lively and colourful crowd of customers, it being so named because Madam Bardi believed that with plenty of perseverance anyone can get anywhere in life and to be a woman was no disadvantage. Certainly, she herself had reason to be confident for in a region where women can be kept in purdah and subordination she became in her own right a person of tremendous commercial and social consequence.

Susannah Bardi's English was ' individual '; but she talked loudly and was, undoubtedly, the ' Queen ' of ' *sabon gari* '. She was also respected as a woman who put charity before business, characteristically remaining ' mother ' to her 100 or so brothers and sisters and their children whose education and numerous wants she provides. A devout Catholic and President of the Women's League at the Roman Catholic Mission, Madam Bardi's house gave pride of place to her crucifix and a statue of the Virgin and the Christ-child. She was also President of the Ibo Women's Guild and helped Ibo wives in matrimonial and domestic problems (*West Africa*, 1954a, p. 437).

Few women in Central Africa have either the opportunity or

experience to build up a business on the almost gargantuan scale of Mrs Bardi. Yet, numbers of them show as much dogged determination and initiative even though the results are modest by comparison. One of these, *Mrs Anna Chilombo*, a Bemba woman, was born in 1929. After teaching for ten years she decided to go into business and work like a man. She resigned, therefore, from her school and became a saleswoman in order to gain business experience. After saving up enough money she bought a delivery van and operated as a fish-trader, selling fish on the Copperbelt and in a number of other places. This involved her travelling day and night to and from Lakes Mweru and Bang-wenlu and often sleeping on the road. Fish was not easily obtain-able; competition was keen and Anna had sometimes to wait a long time for her turn to buy. In the end it proved a paying business, but before that stage was reached she married and opened a grocery shop. Her husband was co-operative and Anna Chilombo became the first African woman to run a store in the Fort Rose-berry district, making about £10 per day from her sales (*African Women*, 1960).

Another Zambian woman owning a grocery store is *Anne Lengaleya* who was born in 1930, the eldest daughter of a pastor. She was educated at a mission school and after leaving she helped in teaching homecraft at a mission near Ndola in present-day Zambia. Teaching, however, was not Anne's ambition and so she tried nursing. Then, having saved £60, she heard that a shop was for sale. She bought it, opened her own grocery, and accepted the toil and drudgery of transporting goods from Lusaka twice a day on her bicycle – a distance of 18 miles – struggling with boxes of soap and some other bulky packages. By 1956, however, the days of carrying boxes were over because she had made enough money to buy herself a second-hand car. In 1957 she built a newer and larger shop, transferring her business there. It is a big, flat-roofed building with six rooms at the back. Her next ambition, she said at that time, was a double-storey house in ten years' time (*ibid.*).

In business on a much grander scale is a Yoruba woman, *Mrs Aduke Moore*, who, in 1957, was appointed a director of Mobil Oil (Nigeria) Ltd as well as being the legal adviser to and secretary of this company. Mrs Moore is the youngest child and only daughter of the late Sir Adeyemo Alakija's first marriage. She started her education in a 'dame's school' in Lagos and from there went to the United Kingdom, first to Penrhos College in Wales and later to the London School of Economics.

For some years after coming home Aduke worked in the Government Social Welfare Department where she initiated a flourishing chain of Girls' Clubs throughout Lagos and the then Colony. She also caused a much-needed Juvenile Court to be set up, being a probation officer of this court until her marriage. After the birth of her son she returned to the Juvenile Court as an assessor and worked there until she returned to England in 1949 to read law. Her 'class-mate' was Miss Gloria Rhodes, with whom she set up in practice after they had both been called to the Bar. There was considerable male prejudice against women lawyers, especially two such good-looking ones as Mrs Moore and Miss Rhodes. However, they regarded this attitude with good-natured contempt and Aduke was appointed a magistrate at the Juvenile Court, an appointment which she held until taking up her post with Mobil Oil.

The latter position made Mrs Moore one of the busiest and most successful salaried women in the country, but she continued to be deeply concerned with voluntary social work. As far back as 1945 she helped to form a branch of the British Leprosy Relief Association in Nigeria and she also became Chairman of the Discharged Prisoners' Aid Society, a member of the working committee of the Y.W.C.A. and with a keen interest as well in the Federal Nigerian Society for the Blind. Her voice has also been heard many times on the Nigerian Broadcasting Corporation programmes. In 1961, Mobil Exploration was granted off-shore licences by the Federal Government and in addition to being director of this concern Mrs Moore accepted the secretary-ship of the Lagos Chamber of Commerce. As she conceived the latter position, part of her main task was the training of a young professional Nigerian to take over from her (*West Africa*, 1967a, pp. 491–2). Despite this catalogue of 'good works' and business activities Mrs Aduke Moore has always been, as *West Africa* describes it, 'delightfully feminine'. She has generally taken a leading part in most of Lagos' social events and has been hostess, almost times without number, at local charities and dances (*African Women*, 1957, p. 133).

Continuing with African women in business, one who has established a reputation as a restaurateur and hotelier is *Miss Lucy Bishop*. She is the daughter of a Creole father and a Scotswoman and was born in the Gambia where, in infancy, she was stricken with poliomyelitis. The child was sent immediately to Britain for the treatment which was to continue sporadically throughout her school days in England and Scotland. After her father's death in 1929, Miss Bishop and her mother left their family house in Bathurst to live in a flat owned by the United African Company of whose Kingsway Store Miss Bishop was manageress. On moving to Freetown in 1953 she also managed Kingsway there, and finally retired from U.A.C. after 23 years' service. Her gratuity she used to start a boarding house. Its name was the Edna Guest House – yet people always spoke simply of 'going to Lucy Bishop's'.

Miss Bishop's aim was to provide a more homely atmosphere than can be found in hotels, and she was so successful that some of her boarders stayed with her for complete tours of over a year. Firms' representatives and junior diplomats, usually bachelors, were among her regular boarders. They, along with visitors from America, East Africa, Canada and the West Indies, enjoyed the cuisine and it was in order to allow Freetown people the benefit of her French-trained chef's cooking that Miss Bishop first started in 1961 to provide meals for non-residents. In 1963, however, she moved house again, put up a new sign and declared 'Lucy's Bar-Restaurant' open. Guests there could sit on the terrace over-looking Banana Water Bay, drink good wine and eat delicious food (often cooked in wine), excellently served by Sierra Leonean stewards. This new restaurant was frequented mainly by Europeans and Americans, and by bachelors, who could not entertain at home. The African clientele consisted mainly of higher civil servants, barristers and the élite in Freetown. People who know Miss Bishop personally say that her success in these enterprises was largely due to a talent for human relations as well as her *flair* for management and ability to provide high standard European cooking (*West Africa*, 1964, p. 965).

Turning now to public life, an outstanding personality among West African women is a member of the Mende people of Sierra Leone. She is *Madam Ella Koblo Gulama* and she stood success-fully nearly twenty years ago for election as paramount chief of the Kaiyamba chiefdom, despite there being fifteen other can-didates, all men. Madam Ella's father preceded her as paramount chief of the same chiefdom and her husband is also a paramount chief.

After leaving school Ella Gulama went to the Women's Training College in Freetown and subsequently became the first woman supervising teacher in the then Protectorate. Teaching, from which she retired when she married, gave Madam Ella special authority in the House of Representatives on educational matters. Also, she led Sierra Leone's delegation to the Conference of the Council of West African Women held in Conakry in July 1961, after selection as president of the Sierra Leone Women's Federation. Anxious always for women's educational rights and to see women take a greater part in public life, including senior posts in the Administration, Madam Ella herself pioneered the trail by becom-ing a Minister without Portfolio in the Margai Government, thus being the first West African woman to hold a Cabinet post. In addition to her parliamentary duties she has been a member of the Council of Fourah Bay College, now part of the University of Sierra Leone.

Madam Ella has also given a great deal of time to educational improvement among the 30,000 people of her chiefdom and it is said that as president of the Moyamba District Council, a local government organization, her work was tactfully as well as efficiently carried out. Also, as a member of the House of Representatives, Madam Ella had the unofficial task of representing Sierra Leone women's interests.

Madam Ella has travelled widely in Africa and in the United States, where she took the Sierra Leone dancing troupe for the New York World Fair in 1964. Despite, however, her activities on behalf of women and her having held high political office, there is no sign of either the grim-faced politician or the militant feminist. On the contrary, Madam Ella's smile is charming and relaxed, and in relation to her three children she is the typical mother. Also, she has put a real flair for clothes to showing how African dress can strikingly be worn to advantage (*African Women*, 1958 and *West Africa*, 1958b, p. 391).

Another West African woman who has achieved success in politics is *Madame Ouezzin Coulibaly*. She was appointed in 1958 as Minister of Social Welfare and Labour in the Government of Upper Volta, and was not any novice. As general secretary of the Women's section of the *Rassemblement Démocratique Africaine*, she had already organized women for political action, been a member of the policy committee of the Ivory Coast R.D.A., and a municipal councillor of Abidjan. These appointments followed an earlier experience of being sentenced to two months' imprisonment after visiting Moscow and Pekin.

Doubtless, being married to Ouezzin Coulibaly made a contribution to Madame Coulibaly's own career. He, in 1958, was Vice-President of Upper Volta. *Conseiller-Général* of the Territorial Assembly of Ivory Coast and Political Secretary of French-speaking Africa's major party. But Madame Ouezzin says that she became interested in politics, not because of her husband, 'but because when I saw how our people suffered in those days, I too had to do something about it'. Madame Ouezzin is indeed, as one official described her, '*une femme formidable dans la politique*', and her activities prior to Independence testify to this. When, for example, a woman member of the R.D.A. was imprisoned without trial on the complaint of an African hostile to the party, Madame Ouezzin organized all the army of R.D.A. women of Abidjan and descended on the prison in all the available taxis. Actually, the women

Some relevant 'portraits'

merely sat quietly outside the prison, maintaining perfect discipline throughout, but they were sufficient in number to obtain the prisoner's release.

But Madame Coulibaly's greatest triumph came when the Policy Committee of the R.D.A. were jailed *en bloc* and went, to a man, on hunger strike. She was in Paris at the time, but she flew back to Abidjan and led a small but formidable enough section of the women straight to the Governor's Palace. He refused to see them and so the next day Madame Ouezzin organized the general mobilization of Abidjan women. They, at three in the morning, descended on the prison for the second time, surprising the guards and invading the jail grounds. This certainly jolted the Government and two days later the R.D.A. leaders were released. In effect, the R.D.A. movement, despite the absence of its male leadership, was, thanks to Madame Ouezzin, kept very much alive. She had given it inspiration not only in Ivory Coast, but throughout Francophone Africa.

After these events Madame Ouezzin ceased her 'Pankhurstian' activities, but remained in control of the Abidjan women, organizing them to line the route for a welcome visitor and boycotting a visit she disapproved of. Like Madam Ella Gulama, Madame Ouezzin's obvious charm lies in her ability, at will, to forgo her role as a politician and be a woman and a mother (cf. *West Africa*, 1958*a*, pp. 319 and 1,013).

Also, in the field of administration is the remarkable career of yet another Sierra Leonean. She, *Mrs Murietta Olu-Williams*, was the daughter of a Freetown doctor and the first woman, not only in Sierra Leone, but in the whole of Africa, to achieve the rank of Permanent Secretary in the civil service. For decades, West Africa has produced women traders, teachers, doctors, and even lawyers who can more than hold their own with their male counterparts. The civil service, however, is another matter, and even in a highly developed country, like Britain, the appointment still occasions comment.

Without dismay, Mrs Olu-Williams recognizes the double standard, in Western society at least, when men and women engaged in identical activities are judged. To *West Africa* (1963, p. 857) she revealed her calm acceptance of this, saying that 'a woman working in a man's world must do *more* than a man'. Murietta considers that none of a woman's qualifications, skill, or ability will be taken for granted; she has to prove each ounce of her worth.

> This initial effort is necessary, partly to overcome the early mistrust of a woman by her male colleagues, but also to

ensure that as few as possible small mistakes are made. Such mistakes, for which a man might be excused in the early days of a new appointment, would, in a woman be blamed on her whole sex, excuse would be made on the grounds of her sex, rather than of her being a newcomer. This sort of thinking can quickly lead to ' what more can you expect of a woman '.

Murietta Olu-Williams' early work was with the Ministry of Education where she was concerned with the problems of students, having first joined the Civil Service in 1950 as a supervising teacher.[1] In 1962, however, she transferred from the professional to the administrative service, and in addition to Education she has served in a senior capacity in the Ministry of Lands, Mines and Labour, and the Ministry of Information. In both of the latter she says that she met with ' undreamt-of co-operation ', and she modestly asserts that it was the exodus of many older ex-patriate civil servants after Independence in 1961 that gave her and other younger people opportunities for promotion. In addition to study in Oxford, Mrs Olu-Williams has represented Sierra Leone at international conferences on education in Geneva and New Delhi.

Another woman appointed to ministerial office was *Madame Sophie Lihau*, who, as one of the first Congolese graduates, became Minister of Social Welfare in Congo-Kinshasa at the early age of twenty-six. Sophie Lihau received much of her primary and secondary education in Brazzaville, and actually finished her studies in a boys' school because in 1960 the girls' school closed down when teachers and most of the pupils withdrew at the time of the Belgian exodus. The next year she went to the University of Geneva, obtained a degree in Sociology and stayed on as an assistant lecturer while studying for a doctorate. Before, however, her thesis was completed she was in office and her present position, spending most of her first years, she has reported, studying her department's problems. Indeed, housing alone was a full-time job because with a population estimated by that time at one and a half million, Kinshasa was probably the biggest city in Black Africa.

As a member of the Congo-Kinshasa delegation to the 1967 O.A.U. (Organization of African Unity) summit in the capital, Sophie Lihau took over the leadership of the delegation to the Council of Ministers' meeting when the Congolese Foreign Minister was chosen Chairman. As explained earlier, Madame Lihau has interested herself in the advance of women, and she has been personally concerned that girls should have as much opportunity

[1] At school she had been a pupil of the late Mrs Benka-Coker, one of the first African pioneers of girls' higher education.

of education as boys. Not surprisingly, therefore, she has a good word for President Mobutu, who apart from bringing a woman into his government, gave women the vote in 1967 (*West Africa*, 1967b, pp. 362–3).

The first woman to become an M.P. in West Africa was *Mrs Remi Aiyedun*. She was given a seat in 1953 in the Nigerian Western House of Assembly as a Special Member in order to represent women's interests. To *Mrs Elizabeth Adeyemi Adekogbe*, however, this was but the beginning. The Nigerian woman, she considered, was entitled to being more than an 'appointed' member of a legislature. She was as fit for politics as the men who held her in bondage for generations. She need not only pay rates and taxes but ought also to contest and win elections – even if she did not hope to become Prime Minister. It was in this 'feminist' conviction that Mrs Adekogbe founded the Nigerian Women Movement at Ibadan in December 1952, 'to champion the cause of women' and to secure for them a place 'in the economic, educational, social and political set-up' of the country. At the same time, as a trained teacher and wife of a Co-operative Society official, she was not a mere dreamer or an indolent visionary. On the contrary, one day she would be found at Ibadan deeply involved in the ceremonial presentation of Thrift Society certificates to a group of women, and the next making a speech at Lagos, 120 miles away, to new members of her movement. Yet a third day finds her at Ijebu attending an Executive Committee Meeting of the local branch of the movement.

Better known later as Chief Iyalaje of Ikija, Elizabeth was educated at a Catholic Training College in Lagos; and, after her marriage to Mr L. A. G. Adekogbe in 1940, she became Assistant Inspector of Prices – a wartime post to check the spread of the black market. Although Chief Iyalaje prided herself on being a housewife there was so much to do that seldom did she cook Mr Adekogbe's dinner or eat it with him for more than a few days in the week. Indeed, as an African woman she was atypical, because not only did she give up teaching, but political obligations came first. So, whenever the choice was between the kitchen and a movement meeting she would readily jump into her seat on the Lagos-Ibadan bus or at the back of a produce lorry plying to the hinterland. 'There is need for this sacrifice now', the Chief would say, 'and somebody must make it'.

'And your husband ?'
'He is a civil servant, but he believes that I am entitled to serve the nation in a different way from him.'

(*West Africa*, 1953c, p. 917)

209

Another woman who has enthusiastically taken part in political campaigns is *Mrs Hannah Kudjoe* of Ghana. When Nkrumah moved acceptance of his Government's White Paper on Constitutional Reform, the approaches of the Assembly were clogged with C.P.P. supporters, including a gay sprinkling of women. Many of them were dressed in bold red and green, ' with scarlet turbans swathed after the manner of an eighteenth-century *grande dame*, but pinned in front by twentieth-century C.P.P. membership badges '. Mrs Kudjoe was one of the people most responsible for this mobilization of feminine enthusiasm. As a C.P.P. National Propaganda Secretary she habitually travelled 2,000 miles a month and was a forceful speaker. On one occasion, for example, having strayed accidentally over the frontier, she was arrested by a Dahomeyan policeman, but never reached the police station : on the way she talked him into joining the C.P.P. !

Mrs Kudjoe's entry into politics was, in fact, due largely to a chance meeting with Nkrumah himself when he was Secretary of the United Gold Coast Convention. Previously, she had not conceived of a political role for women. Once converted, however, she canvassed vigorously, visiting villages, enlisting the sympathy of the chiefs, and summoning people together to hear news of the campaign for self-government. She served the U.G.C.C. voluntarily for two years and followed Nkrumah when it split, being the only woman present at the memorable meeting at which it was decided to found the Convention People's Party. She devoted all her energy to the new party and at a Rally in December 1949 she not only took part in the discussion on Positive Action, but also cooked for 170 people. When Nkrumah and his colleagues inevitably required the assistance of counsel, she tirelessly collected money; and when her fellow politicians burned their copies of a Positive Action proclamation for fear of police search she kept her own copy and used it to considerable effect. She would send her taxi in one direction, and go off in another, so that the police were focussing attention on it while she was making a speech many miles away. She would often work under cover of darkness, and villages willingly broke curfew to listen to her.

Later, Hannah Kudjoe as a C.P.P. full-time organizer went to live in the North Territories. There, she transformed herself into a voluntary welfare worker, living in primitive buildings and eating unpalatable foods in order to gain an insight into living conditions. To persuade girls in remote villages that dress was both attractive and desirable, she wore clothing made from locally-woven material; and, as the women had no knowledge of hygiene, she would boil water and bath their children. The fact that Mrs

Kudjoe's achievements were in colonial times makes them the more significant and answers any complaint that African women lack political initiative. Also, according to *West Africa*, those who talk about unfeminine stridency in women politicians have their answer in Hannah Kudjoe's generous, unassuming and attractive personality (*West Africa*, 1953a, p. 725).

Women politicians in the northern part of Ghana are rare. Nevertheless, *Mrs Lydia Akanbodin-Po Kugblenu*, born in the Upper Region, was among the 140 newly elected members – in fact, the only woman among them – who swore their oaths of allegiance to the Second Republic on 5 September 1969. It was, however, only after teaching at several Accra schools that Mrs Kugblenu agreed to stand as her own people's candidate. The electoral campaign was hard; there are few roads and plenty of rain, but she pedalled around the villages on her bicycle, ruining more than one dress in the process. The result was victory – 4,107 votes out of 9,764 votes cast – despite protests from an opponent who, having taught Lydia at school, felt that a pupil had no right to do such a thing to her teacher. Mrs Kugblenu skilfully handled the combination of traditional customs and modern politics involved, and this may have been one of the reasons why she won. Since her electioneering was carried out in what is probably the most conservative area in Ghana, she avoided involvement in arguments about the sexes' equality. Also, when some of her constituents refused to discuss such things as votes and rural improvements with a woman, she quite happily bowed to custom and spoke through a man. The same tact applies in her private life because Mrs Kugblenu firmly believes that in the home her husband comes first. She continued, therefore, to cook, as she always had, convinced that she and her husband should work together as one rather than as two individuals going their own ways.

Nor was Mrs Kugblenu worried about being the only woman in Parliament. Unlike Nkrumah and his followers, she believed strongly in parliamentary democracy as opposed to the one party state. Moreover, she considered that, as the elected representative of her people, her mission was to improve their conditions and to speak for them as a part of Ghana. Yet, although very disturbed by the North's shortage of drinking water, roads and dispensaries, she was also conscious of national unity and concerned lest the provision of her own constituency's needs should detract from the rest of the country's welfare (*West Africa*, 1969b, p. 1,361).

As mentioned earlier, a particularly earnest champion of the women's cause is *Miss Mabel Dove*. Her father was a well-known Freetown lawyer, her mother a Ga woman, and like other daughters of the 'old' families of the West Coast, Miss Dove enjoyed all the advantages of long schooling in Britain. In 1954, however, she became a member of the Gold Coast Legislative Assembly, and the fact that she was the first woman in the whole of West Africa to be elected by popular vote may have been a triumph for herself but it was also a reflection on women's status. It meant, in fact, that inevitably she became the focal point of the large mass of illiterate womanhood with an obligation to voice the needs which they felt but could only express imperfectly. Moreover, although at middle age by this time, Mabel Dove herself was only an earnest beginner on the political ladder and had to sense instinctively when things were not right instead of arriving at the same conclusion by complicated mental processes. There was an example of this in 1951 when, on a visit to Freetown, she became involved in agitation over the high cost of living. *West Africa* (1954c, p. 67a) reported the incident as follows:

> 'The Gold Coast', says Mabel, 'was then very much in the news and people looked to me to do something.' The logic of what followed is not very clear, but Mabel certainly did not let the Gold Coast down. With two other women she went to the market place ringing a large hand-bell and when a crowd gathered exhorted the people to make a mass protest. Later, says Mabel, 20,000 women, with banners flying, marched through the streets of Freetown, and a petition protesting against living costs was presented to the Governor. Today, Mabel admits that she has no idea what caused the inflated prices, or what steps were taken to reduce them – all she knew was that rice, the staple diet, became cheaper.

Miss Dove has also been well-known as an author and journalist. When she returned from schooling in England she began writing in local newspapers under a variety of *noms de plume*. For example, as Marjorie Mensah, she wrote the women's columns in the *Times of West Africa*. Its editor was then Dr J. B. Danquah, whom Mabel Dove was later to marry and, many years later still, divorce. In addition, when Dr Azikiwe ran the *African Morning Post* in Accra, Mabel Dove as 'Dame Dumas' wrote a column for it, and as 'Ebun Alakija' she contributed to the Nigerian *Daily Times*. Also, she worked on the *Accra Evening News*, the C.P.P. newspaper, writing a political column and one of her short stories (1964) effectively satirizes the husband who jettisons his customary law wife for a 'frock lady'.

Another ardent exponent of women's cause has been *Mrs Margaret Ekpo*, who accompanied as an adviser the representatives of her country to the Nigerian Constitution Conference in 1953. Efik-born, Margaret Ekpo was the daughter of a Scottish mission minister in Calabar and a one-time school teacher. Despite opposition from her people, she married an Ibibio doctor, and since the Duke of Windsor's troubles seemed to form some parallel, the young people called their home 'Windsor House'. (When the bride started tuition for girls at her home it became known as the Windsor Sewing Institute.) Eight years later, at the instigation of Mrs Ransome-Kuti, Mrs Ekpo became head of the newly-formed Eastern wing of the Nigerian Women's Union; and later, with that forceful lady, Mrs Ekpo travelled through the East, forming branches of the union. It was the disturbances at the Enugu coal-mines and the shooting of Africans there that, Mrs Ekpo claims, brought her actively into politics. Her union pro-claimed a day of mourning and ordered shops to close. As a result, when rioting followed, suspicion fell on Mrs Ekpo; she had to report hourly to the police, and her home was searched. In the streets women union members gathered in support of their union's president, and these events apparently did more than anything else to confirm her position as a leader among the women.

Yet, although championing the women of eastern Nigeria, Margaret Ekpo had no unstinting praise for them. Strange as it might seem, it was the English woman whom she held up as the example for her own sisters. This attitude was gained from a visit to the United Kingdom. She had, of course, met English women in Nigeria, but the English women she saw in Britain were different. For when Mrs Ekpo went holidaying there with her husband in 1947, it was the hard-working, houseproud house-wife, the girl shop assistants, the factory workers whom she met. And so, on her return to Nigeria, Mrs Ekpo wrote about English women in the Press, in pamphlets, and published a book, *English-women in Their Homes*. She would continue to fight for the rights of the women of eastern Nigeria, but 'housewives in England work very hard', she said, 'in Nigeria they are very, very lazy. I keep telling them they will get nowhere unless they work as the women of England do'.

Indeed, much of Margaret Ekpo's life, it seems, was spent upbraiding her own sex. Writes *West Africa* (1953b, p. 773):

> Speak to her of her work among Nigerian women and pictures came floating out into space of Margaret Ekpo mounted on a table in the Ohoadi division, facing a crowd of angry women who were demanding that the district officer should release their husbands, imprisoned for non-payment of the

education rate. And what soothing words did Margaret use to
this crowd of threatening women ? 'Let the men pay the
education rate or stay in prison. Why should they avoid their
responsibilities by hiding behind you women ? ' was her
theme.

Another woman who holds strong views about the modern
situation of her own sex lives on the other side of the continent.
She is *Mrs Grace Ogot*, the wife of the former Deputy Vice-
Chancellor of the University of Nairobi. Possibly her husband's
position plays some part but the main reason for Mrs Ogot's influence among Kenyan women is probably her capacity for understanding and making clear the ambiguities of their contemporary
role. Thus, characteristically, she does not define herself as being
predominantly either a 'traditional' or a 'liberated' African
woman. 'I'm both', she says, and she argues that the inequality of
the sexes 'is purely a white man's idea'. Consequently, Mrs Ogot
denies that woman's place is solely in the home. When educated
women get married 'they must continue their work in nursing,
education or community development or the like' for the 'good
of the nation' (Mohr, 1972, pp. 21–2).

It is also of interest that Mrs Ogot's assessment of her female
compatriots' physical output is quite different from that of Mrs
Ekpo, the Nigerian leader. 'African women', Mrs Ogot declares,
'work three times as hard as white women in America or Europe '.
Possibly this opinion has been influenced by observation of a
European settler society which is very different from that of the
British working class whom Mrs Ekpo saw. However, there is no
doubt at all about Mrs Ogot's own energy because in addition
to her business interests and all the family responsibilities of an
African housewife and mother, she has the reputation as well of
being one of East Africa's leading women writers.

Then, in diplomatic circles, there is Liberia's *Mrs Myrtle Reeves
Gorgla* who represents the emancipated position of women on
the one hand and the informal, rather personal spirit pervading
government in Monrovia on the other. Her grandfather was an
American and both her parents came to Liberia when adolescents.
Miss Reeves herself grew up internationally-minded in general
and American-minded in particular. After graduation and a short
spell in education she became secretary to the U.S. Public Health
Service in Monrovia and soon went to the States. There, after
completing an economic course, she joined the Liberian Consulate-
General in New York, later transferring to the Embassy as Secre-
tary. Her next position was in Madrid as Second Secretary at the
Embassy and as Vice-Consul. Several times she served as Chargé

d'Affaires during the absence of the Ambassador at the United Nations and on returning home in 1956 was appointed Director of the Bureau of European Affairs of the Department of State. She remained in this position until her transfer in 1960 as Liberian Consul-General in London.

That Mrs Gorgla as a woman could rise to this position, she herself has spontaneously attributed to the nature of Liberian society and to President Tubman's own influence. Right from his first administration he opened the doors to women, and there have been women as Assistant Secretaries to the Ministers of Education, War, Public Works and the Attorney-General. Naturally, much of Mrs Gorgla's own job as Consul-General had to do with ships – that is, foreign-owned ships registered in Liberia where taxes are low and regulations liberal. When, however, not at work Mrs Gorgla's hobby was interior decoration (*West Africa*, 1960b, p. 1,217).

But Liberia's most experienced diplomat is *Miss Angie Brooks* who was appointed Assistant Secretary of State (Foreign Minister) in 1956. In the preceding two years, she regularly represented her country at the United Nations where she took the chair of the Fourth (Trusteeship) Committee and of the Ruanda-Urundi Commission (1962). Her speeches at the General Assembly and her uninhibited comments in the Trusteeship Committee and other international gatherings have made her famous throughout the world.

The daughter of a Liberian Baptist preacher, Miss Brooks is a lawyer by profession – counsellor-at-law at the Supreme Court of Liberia. She also served as Assistant Attorney-General of Liberia from August 1953 to March 1958, thus combining for two years important responsibilities for both foreign affairs and for law and order. In 1958, when both the President and the Secretary of State were absent from the country, she acted for a time as Chief Executive of Liberia.

Miss Brooks' impressive record includes a B.A. in Social Science, an M.Sc. in Political Science and International Relations, and she also has an LL.B. from the University of Wisconsin, U.S.A., an LL.D. from London University and a law degree from the University of Liberia. In addition, she has served as a vice-president of the International Federation of Women Lawyers (1956–60) and part-time professor of law at the University of Liberia (1954–8). She has been awarded decorations by the Governments of Liberia, China, Cameroun, Yugoslavia, West Germany and Burundi (*The New Africans*, 1967, p. 242).

Turning next to the legal profession itself, although numbers of African women have won fame at the Bar, the career of

215

Annie Baeta is unique in some respects. She was born in Lome, in about 1924, and was one of the five children of the Head of the Presbyterian Church in the then French Togoland. The family moved in 1928 to Keta, and in 1934 Annie went as a pupil to the Teacher Training College in Achimota where, thanks largely to some private coaching by Mr Fraser, she took her teaching diploma and the School Certificate at the same time. Then she went back to Keta to teach in the Presbyterian Girls' School and very soon replaced a man as Head – a post she held for six years.

But Annie Baeta was more interested in becoming a barrister and so, to cut a long story short, she successfully undertook the necessary amount of study in England. Being called to the English Bar was one thing, getting into Chambers was another, especially as none of the other women had succeeded. Once again, however, she was lucky and was accepted by Mr Ogilvy Jones. Then, when the Colonial Office wanted someone to study social welfare and local government, Miss Baeta took on the assignment. She wrote her report, and also became closely associated with the activities of the Y.W.C.A., spending all her holidays in Europe: Switzerland, France, Germany, Belgium, Norway, Sweden and Italy. Later on, she was the Y.W.C.A. delegate representing the Gold Coast at various important world conferences in Geneva, in Italy and in Syria.

In 1953, Annie Baeta married a childhood friend, Mr Fred Jiagge, and was by this time fully established as a barrister in Accra. Mr Bossman, a well-known advocate, welcomed her into his Chambers, generously entrusting to her his junior cases worthy of the experience of a senior. She never failed him, or Mr Justice Ollennu, for whom she also worked. Then, having won fame at the Bar of the High Court, Mrs Jiagge was made a judge, thus becoming the first woman magistrate in the Gold Coast.

In an appreciative ' portrait' of her in its number of June 12 1954, *West Africa* referred to Mrs Jiagge having a 'first class brain . . . allied to the most delightful femininity and genuine unpretentious modesty'. It also remarked that 'she stands for everything sane and straight and good in Africa'. Perhaps, therefore, it was on account of her well-known probity that after the Nkrumah regime had been overturned it was Mrs Jiagge who was asked to hear the Commission of enquiry into the financial affairs of the ex-Ministers, District Commissioners, and the functionaries of the Convention People's Party (*West Africa*, 1954b, p. 533; and 1966, p. 1,141).

Finally, an unusual event in Africa was the appointment by the Nkrumah Government of a woman as a District Commissioner. She, aged only twenty-seven at the time, was *Miss Ramatu Baba*.

the daughter of the Chief Butcher of Yendi. Ramatu Baba was at Achimota,[2] and after schools in her home district she took a post in the Department of Social Welfare at Tamale, capital of the then Northern Region. Northern girls with such an education were still few, and soon she had left the civil service for the more exciting job of regional woman organizer for the United Ghana Farmers' Council (U.G.F.C.), a C.P.P. body. Then for three years Miss Baba toured throughout the region in the U.G.F.C.'s one vehicle and her work extended to teaching the men as well as the women. This was, therefore an excellent introduction to the job of District Commissioner there, particularly since so much emphasis was on the increase of food production, and since Yendi is a centre for yam exports to southern Ghana.

Obviously, not everybody in Yendi, a district of some 40,000 people and the biggest in area in the Upper Region, readily accepted such a young woman as the local representative of government. Her slightly Chinese features marked Miss Baba out in any gathering; and, although as respectful to her elders as any illiterate girl, she made no concession to rural fashion. But to be a woman as well as young, to be conscious of the need to assert oneself, and to be the choice of an authority seemingly very far away were great handicaps in an area where authority tended to be both male and elderly. It was therefore a sign of President Nkrumah's confidence in Ramatu Baba that he still appointed her as D.C. in Yendi because the success or failure of a woman in such a position could be significant for women's role nearly everywhere.

Perhaps it was Miss Baba's enthusiasm for the Party as well as her determination to make political administration a career that decided the President in her favour (*West Africa*, 1963c, p. 1,177) because soon afterwards Ashantiland, too, got its first woman District Commissioner. She, *Miss Mary Asantewao Osei*, was a foundation member of the C.P.P. and a stalwart who 'stood firm for my Party in the hectic days of the Ashanti Crisis because, though an Ashanti, I loved my nation more'. After working as a compositor and bookbinder at a time when the place of the Ghana woman was mainly the kitchen, Miss Osei was put in charge of some 500 men and women in the Builders' Brigade and took over within 18 short months as Superintendent at the Brigade Camp just outside Kumasi.

Mary Osei was quite at her ease with people from all walks of life, including foreign dignitaries, and she had energy in abundance. Rising at 5 in the morning, it was her habit first to take a swift

[2] For many years the then Gold Coast's best-known school.

look at the newspapers 'to inform myself of the political situation not only in Ghana, but throughout the world'. Then there were interviews and more interviews when she talked to a hundred people, perhaps, and yet found the right word for them all, tackling delicate matrimonial problems as well as the involved manoeuvrings of chiefly disputes. Indeed, Mary Osei's unchanging subject, along with the philosophy of Nkrumahism, was the role of women. In her own words, Mrs Osei could not 'subscribe to the view that politics is, or should be, the preserve of men . . . [She] would like to be privileged to be among the forefront of the new stage of the African Revolution – the struggle for a united Africa'. Such fighting language comes appropriately from a woman descended from the great Warrior Queen, Yaa Asantewaa (after whom Mary Osei is named), who led the famed Ashanti warriors on to the field of battle (*West Africa*, 1963b, p. 1,027).

These, then, are some of the African women who, in recent years, have won fame and renown in their own country and in a number of instances have achieved international recognition. Had they been citizens of Western countries most of them would certainly be found in the pages of *Who's Who*. Is it because these people are women not men that, as pointed out in the introductory lines to this book, so little is publicly recorded of their contribution to 'emergent Africa'?

References cited

Achebe, Chinua (1966). *A Man of the People.* London: Heinemann.
Acquah, Ione (1958). *Accra Survey.* London: University of London Press.
Addae, Gloria (1954). The retailing of imported textiles in the Accra markets. *Proceedings of Third Annual Conference.* West African Institute of Social and Economic Research.
Africa Report (1972). Vol. 17, No. 7.
Africa South of the Sahara (1971–2). London: Europa Publications.
African Women (1958). Vol. III, No. 1.
 (1960). Vol. III, No. 4.
 (1962). Vol. IV, No. 4.
Aidoo, Ama Ata (1970). *No Sweetness Here.* London: Longmans, Green.
Aluko, T. M. (1970). *Chief the Honourable Minister.* London: Heinemann.
Ardener, E. W. (1961). Social and demographic problems of the Southern Cameroons plantation area. In Aidan Southall (ed.), *Social Change in Modern Africa.* London: Oxford University Press for International African Institute.
 (1962). *Divorce and Fertility.* Nigerian Institute of Social and Economic Research.
Austin, Dennis (1961). Elections in an African rural area. *Africa,* Vol. XXIX, No. 1.

Baker, Tanya (n.d.). Women's Elites in Western Nigeria. Unpublished MS. Department of Social Anthropology, Edinburgh University.
Balandier, Georges (1955). *Sociologie des Brazzavilles Noires.* Paris: Colin
 (1956). Urbanism in West and Central Africa. In *Social Implications of Industrialization and Urbanization in Africa South of the Sahara.* Paris: UNESCO.
 (1969). *Ambiguous Africa. Cultures in Collision.* New York: World Publishing.
Bandoh, A. A. (n.d.). Unpublished MS.
Banton, M. P. (1957). *West African City.* London: Oxford University Press.
 (1965). Social Alignment and Identity in an African City. In Hilda Kuper (ed.), *Urbanization and Migration in West Africa.* Berkeley: University of California Press.
 (1967). *Race Relations.* London: Tavistock Publications.
Bascom, William R. (1955). Urbanization among the Yoruba. *American Journal of Sociology.* Vol. LXI, No. 5.
 (1959). Urbanism as a traditional African pattern. *Urbanism in West Africa, Sociological Review,* 7 (N.S.), 1.
 (1963–4). The urban African and his world. *Cahiers d'Etudes Africaines,* Vol. 4.
Bauer, Peter (1954). *West African Trade.* Cambridge: Cambridge University Press.
Beard, Mary R. (1962). *Women as a Force in History.* New York: Collier.
Beetham, T. A. (1967). *Christianity and the New African.* London: Pall Mall.

References cited

Bell, Jane (1962). Further Education for the Women of Uganda. *African Women*, Vol. 4, No. 4.

Bernard, Guy (1968). *Ville Africaine: Famille Urbaine: Les Enseignants de Kinshasa.* Paris: Mouton.

Bettison, D. G. (1959). *Numerical Data on African Dwellers in Lusaka, Northern Rhodesia.* Communication Sixteen, Lusaka, Rhodes-Livingstone Institute.

Binet, J. (1959). La femme et l'évolution de l'Afrique. *Revue de l'action populaire*, No. 139.

Bird, Mary (1958). Social change in kinship and marriage among the Yoruba of Western Nigeria. Unpublished Ph.D. Thesis, University of Edinburgh.

(1963). Urbanization, family and marriage in Western Nigeria. In *Urbanization in African Social Change.* Centre of African Studies, Edinburgh University.

Bird, Mary and Baker, Tanya (1959). Urbanization and the position of women. *Urbanism in West Africa, Sociological Review* 7 (N.S.) 1.

Birmingham, W., Neustadt, I. and Amaboe, E. N. (1967). *A Study of Contemporary Ghana*, Vol. 2. Evanston Ill.: Northwestern University Press.

Boetie, Dugmore and Barney, Simon (1969). *Familiarity is the Kingdom of the Lost.* London: Cresset.

Boserup, Ester (1970). *Women's Role in Economic Development.* London: Allen and Unwin.

Bosman, W. (1705). *A New and Accurate Description of the Coast of Guinea, divided into the Gold, the Slave and the Ivory Coasts.* London.

Bott, Elizabeth (1957). *Family and Social Network.* London: Tavistock Publications.

Breese, Gerald (1966). *Urbanization in Newly Developing Countries.* Englewood Cliffs, New Jersey: Prentice-Hall.

Brokensha, W. (1966). *Social Change at Larteh.* London: Oxford University Press.

Bruner, E. (1961). Urbanization and Ethnic Identity in North Sumatra. *American Anthropologist*, Vol. 68.

Burnley, Gwen E. (1964). Women's Work in the West Cameroons. *Women Today*, Vol. VI, No. 1.

Busia, K. A. (1950). *Social Survey of Sekondi-Takoradi.* Accra: Government Printer.

(1957). 'Africa in transition'. Project Papers No. 10, World Council of Churches.

Butcher, D. A. P. (1964). The role of the Fulbe in the urban life and economy of Lunsar: Sierra Leone. Unpublished Ph.D. Thesis, Department of Social Anthropology, Edinburgh University.

Caldwell, John C. (1968). *Population Growth and Family Change in Africa.* Canberra: Australian National University Press.

(1969). *African Rural Migration.* Canberra: Australian National University Press.

Capelle, M. (1959). The industrial employment of women in the Belgian Congo. *Inter-African Labour Institute Bulletin*, March.

Carey, A. T. (n.d.). Unpublished study of Keta, Gold Coast (Ghana). Department of Social Anthropology, Edinburgh University.

Carrière, M. (1916). Barroque. In A. Von Gleichen-Russwurm (ed.), *Kultur und Sittengeschiste allen Zelton unter Voelker*, Vol. II, Vienna: Gutenberg-Verlag.

Celina, Oloo and Virginia (1965). *Kenya Women Look Ahead*. Nairobi: East African Literature Bureau.

Clément, Pierre (1956). Social effects of urbanization in Stanleyville, Belgian Congo. In *Social Implications of Industrialization and Urbanization in Africa South of the Sahara*. Paris: UNESCO.

Coleman, J. S. (1958). *Nigeria: Background to Nationalism*. Berkeley: University of California Press.

Collins, Rosemary (1972). The second sex. *The Daily Telegraph*, 26 November.

Colony and Protectorate of Kenya. (1954). *Report of the Committee on African Wages*. Nairobi: Government Printer.

Comhaire-Sylvain, S. (1950). Associations on the basis of origin in Lagos, Nigeria. *American Catholic Sociological Review*, Vol. II.

—— (1951). Le Travail des femmes à Lagos. *Zaire*, Vol. 5, Nos. 2 and 5.

—— (1968). *Femmes de Kinshasa*. Paris: Mouton.

Crabtree, A. I. (1950). Marriage and family life among the educated Africans in the urban areas of the Gold Coast. Unpublished M.Sc. Thesis, University of London.

Date-Bah, Eugenia (1973). Some features of marriage patterns among the members of one elite group in Ghana. In. C. Oppong (ed.), *Legon Family Research Papers*. Institute of African Studies, University of Ghana.

Davis, Kingsley (1968). The urbanization of the human population. In Sylvia Fleis Fava (ed.), *Urbanism in World Perspective*. New York: Crowell.

Defoe, Daniel (1924). *Moll Flanders*. London: Simpkin, Marshall, Hamilton and Kent.

Dipoko, Mbella Sonne (1968). *Because of Women*. London: Heinemann.

East African Standard (1964). Nairobi.

Economic Commission for Africa (E.C.A.) (1962). *Introduction to the Problems of Urbanization in Tropical Africa*, Part 1. Workshop on Africa, SEM/URB/AF/17 March.

Ejiogu, C. N. (1968). African rural-urban migrants in the main migrant areas of the Lagos Federal Territory. In J. C. Caldwell and C. Okongo (eds.), *The Population of Tropical Africa*. London: Australian National University Press.

Ekwensi, Cyprian (1954). *People of the City*. London: Dakers.

—— (1961). *Jagua Nana*. London: Hutchinson.

—— (1966a). *Iska*. London: Hutchinson.

—— (1966b). *Lokotown and Other Stories*. London: Heinemann.

—— (1967). *Beautiful Feathers*. London: Heinemann.

Elkan, W. (1956). *An African Labour Force*. East African Studies No. 7. Kampala: East African Institute of Social Research.

—— (1960). *Migrants and Proletarians*. London: East African Institute of Social Research.

Evans-Pritchard, E. E. (1965). *The Position of Women in Primitive Societies*. London: Faber.

Firth, Raymond (1954). Social organization and social change. *Journal of Royal Anthropological Institute*, Vol. 84, Pts 1 and 2.

Forde, Daryll (1941). *Marriage and Family among the Yakö in South Eastern Nigeria*. Monographs on Social Anthropology, No. 5. London: London School of Economics.

References cited

Fortes, Meyer (1949). *The Web of Kinship among the Tallensi*. London: Oxford University Press.
  (1962). Kinship and Marriage among the Ashantis. In A. R. Radcliffe-Brown and Daryll Forde (eds.), *African Systems of Kinship and Marriage*. London: Oxford University Press.
Foster, P. J. (1965). *Education and Social Change in Ghana*. London: Routledge and Kegan Paul.
Fraenkel, Merran (1964). *Tribe and Class in Monrovia*. London: Oxford University Press for International African Institute.
Fulford, Roger (1957). *Votes for Women*. London: Faber.

Gailey, Harry A. (1970). *The Road to Aba*. New York: New York University Press.
Galleti, R., Baldwin, K. D. S. and Dina, O. (1956). *Nigerian Cocoa Farmers*. London: Oxford University Press.
Gamble, David (1963). The Temne family in a modern town (Lunsar) in Sierra Leone. *Africa*, Vol. 33, No. 3.
Garbett, K. and Kapferer, B. (1970). Theoretical orientations in the study of labour migration. *New Atlantis*, Vol. 2, No. 1.
Garlick, Peter C. (1971). *African Traders and Economic Development in Ghana*. Oxford: Clarendon Press.
Geertz, C. (1962). The rotating credit association: a 'middle rung' in development. *Economic Development and Cultural Change*, Vol. 10, No. 3.
Ghana 1960 Census (1964). Vol. IV. Accra: Census Office.
  Special Report 'A'. Accra: Census Office.
  Special Report 'E'. Accra: Census Office.
Ghana 1970 Population Census (1972). Vol. II. Accra: Census Office.
Gist, N. P. and Fleis Fava, Sylvia (1964). *Urban Society*. New York: Crowell.
Golding, P. T. F. (1962). An enquiry into household expenditure and consumption and sale of household produce in Ghana. *Economic Bulletin*, 6.
Goody, Esther (1963). Conjugal separation and divorce among the Gonja of Northern Ghana. In Meyer Fortes (ed.), *Marriage in Tribal Society*. Cambridge: Cambridge University Press.
Gregg, Pauline (1950). *A Social and Economic History of Britain 1760–1963*. London: Harrap.
Gregory, Joel (1971). Migration in Upper Volta. *African Urban Notes*, Vol. 6, No. 1.
Guardian (1971). 6 August.
Gugler, Josef (1969). Urbanization in East Africa. In R. J. Apthorpe and Peter Rigby (eds.), *Society and Social Change in East Africa*. Kampala, Nkanga Editions, 4, Makerere Institute of Social Research.
Gutkind, P. C. W. (1962–3). African urban family life: comment on and analysis of some rural-urban differences. *Cahiers d'Etudes Africaines*, Vol. 3 (2), 10.
  (1968). The poor in urban Africa. In G. W. Bloomberg and H. J. Schmandt (eds.), *Power, Poverty and Urban Policy*. Beverley Hills: Sage.

Hance, W. A. (1970). *Population, Migration and Urbanization in Africa*. New York: Columbia University Press.
Hanna, William John and Judith Lynne (1972). *Urban Dynamics of Black Africa*. Chicago and New York: Aldine.

References cited

Harrell-Bond, Barbara (1971). Study of marriage among the professional group in Sierra Leone. Unpublished Report to the Department of Social Anthropology, Edinburgh University.
Heisler, Helmuth (1971). The African work force in Zambia. Civilisations, Vol. XXI, No. 4.
(1973). Urbanization and Government of Migration. London: C. Hurst.
Hennin, R. (1965). Les structures familiales en milieu urbain (Elizabethville, Villes Congolaises). Problèmes Sociaux Congolaises, 68.
Henriques, Fernando (1962). Prostitution and Society, Vol. 1. London: MacGibbon and Kee.
Herskovits, M. J. (1938). Dahomey. New York: Augustin.
Hobsbawm, E. J. (1962). The Age of Revolution. London: Weidenfeld and Nicolson.
Hodden, B. W. and Ukwu, V. I. (1969). Markets in West Africa. Ibadan: Ibadan University Press.
Hodgkin, Thomas (1956). Nationalism in Colonial Africa. London: Muller.
(1961). African Political Parties. London: Penguin.
Holas, B. (1953). La Goumbé, an association of Muslim youth in the lower Ivory Coast. Kongo-Overzee, Vol. 19.
Houghton, D. H. (1960). Men of two worlds. Some aspects of migratory labour. South African Journal of Economics, Vol. XXVIII, No. 3.
Hunt, Morton (1969). The Affair: A Portrait of Extra-Marital Love in Contemporary America. New York: World Publishing Company.

Ike, Vincent Chukwuemeka (1965). Toads for Supper. London: Harvill.
(1970). The Naked Gods. London: Harvill.
Institut de Science Economique Appliquée (1963). La Femme Africaine et les marchées Dakarois. Dakar: processed.
International Labour Office (1961). The employment and conditions of work of African women. Geneva: processed.
(1964). The employment and conditions of work of African women. Report II, Second African Regional Conference at Addis Ababa. Geneva: processed.
Izzett, A. (1961). Family life among the Yoruba. In Aidan Southall (ed.), Social Change in Modern Africa. London: Oxford University Press for International African Institute.

Jacobson, David (1970). Friendship and mobility in the development of an urban elite African social system. In J. Gugler (ed.), Urban Growth in Sub-Saharan Africa. Nkanga Editions, No. 6. Makerere Institute of Social Research.
Jahoda, Gustav (1955). The social background of a West African student population. British Journal of Sociology, Vol. 5, No. 4 and Vol. 6, No. 1.
(1958). Boys' images of marriage partners and girls' self-images in Ghana. Sociologus, Vol. 8.
(1959). Love, marriage and social change. Letters to the advice column of a West African newspaper. Africa, Vol. 29, No. 2.
Jellicoe, Marguerite (1955a). Family life among Freetown Creoles. Unpublished London University Thesis for Diploma in Social Studies in Tropical Territories.
(1955b). Women's groups in Sierra Leone. African Women, London University, Institute of Education. Vol. 1, No. 2.
Junod, Violaine (ed.) (1963). Handbook of Africa. New York: New York University Press.

References cited

Kenya 1962 Census (1964). Vol. III. Nairobi. Statistics Division, Ministry of Finance and Economic Planning.

Kenya 1969 Census (1971). Vol. II. Nairobi Statistics Division, Ministry of Finance and Economic Planning.

Kinney, Esei Sylvia (1970). Urban West African music and dance. *African Urban Notes*, Vol. 5, No. 4.

Koroma, M. S. and Proudfoot, L. (1960). Freetown morning. *African Affairs*, Vol. 59, No. 234.

Krapf-Askari, Eva (1969). *Yoruba Towns and Cities*. Oxford: Clarendon Press.

Kuper, Leo (1965). *An African Bourgeoisie*. New Haven and London: Yale University Press.

La Fontaine, J. S. (1970). *City Politics: A Study of Léopoldville, 1962–1963*. Cambridge: Cambridge University Press.

Lander, R. and J. (1832). *Journal of an Expedition to Explore the Course and Termination of the Niger*, Vol. 1.

Le Cour Grandmaison, Colette (1969). Activités économiques des femmes dakaroisses. *Africa*, Vol. 39, No. 2.

Lefancheux, Marie-Helene (1962). The contribution of women to the economic and social development of African countries. *Int. Lab. Rev.*, Vol. II.

Leith-Ross, S. (1939). *African Women*. London: Faber.

(1956). The rise of a new elite amongst the women of Nigeria. *Int. Soc. Sci. Bull.* Vol. 8.

Leslie, J. A. K. (1963). *A Social Survey of Dar es Salaam*. London: Oxford University Press.

Little, Kenneth (1948). A Mende musician sings of his adventures. *Man*, Vol. 48, No. 26.

(1950). The significance of the West African Creole for Afro-American studies. *African Affairs*, Vol. 49, No. 194.

(1951). *The Mende of Sierra Leone: an African People in Transition*. London: Routledge and Kegan Paul.

(1965). *West African Urbanization: a Study of Voluntary Associations in Social Change*. Cambridge: Cambridge University Press.

(1966a). Attitudes towards marriage and the family among educated young Sierra Leoneans. In P. C. Lloyd (ed.), *New Elites of Tropical Africa*. London: Oxford University Press for International African Institute.

(1966b). The strange case of romantic love. *The Listener*, No. 714.

(1972a). Some aspects of African urbanization south of the Sahara. In *Current Topics in Anthropology*. Reading, Mass.: Addison-Wesley.

(1972b). Voluntary associations and social mobility among West African women. *Canadian Journal of African Studies*, Vol. 6, No. 2.

(1973a). *Urbanization as a Social Process: An African Case-Study*. London: Routledge and Kegan Paul.

(1973b). Methodological perspective and approach in African urban studies. In C. Oppong (ed.), *Legon Family Research Papers*, Institute of African Studies, University of Ghana.

Little, Kenneth and Price, Anne (1967). Some trends in modern marriage among West Africans. *Africa*, Vol. 37, No. 4.

Littlejohn, J. (1963). *Westrigg: The Sociology of a Cheviot Parish*. London: Routledge and Kegan Paul.

References cited

Lloyd, B. B. (1966). Education and family life in the development of class identification among the Yoruba. In P. C. Lloyd (ed.), *New Elites of Tropical Africa*. London: Oxford University Press for International African Institute.

Lloyd, P. C. (1967). The elite. In P. C. Lloyd, A. L. Mabogunje and B. Awe (eds.), *The City of Ibadan*. Cambridge: Cambridge University Press, in association with Institute of African Studies, Ibadan University.

Lombard, J. (1954). Cotonou: ville africaine. *Bulletin de l'Institut Français d'Afrique Noire*, Vol. 16, Nos. 3 and 4.

Longmore, Laura (1959). *The Dispossessed*. London: Cape.

Lytton, David (1960). *The Goddam White Man*. London: MacGibbon and Kee.

Mabogunje, A. L. (1959). Yoruba market women. *Ibadan*, No. 9.

— (1962). The growth of residential districts in Ibadan. *Geographical Review*, Vol. 52.

— (1968). *Urbanization in Nigeria*. London: University of London Press.

McCall, D. F. (1961). Trade and the role of the wife in a modern West African town. In Aidan Southall (ed.), *Social Change in Modern Africa*. London: Oxford University Press for International African Institute.

McHardy, Cécile (1968). Love in Africa. *Présence Africaine*, Vol. 68.

Mair, Lucy (1969). *African Marriage and Social Change*. London: Cass.

— (1971). *Marriage*. London: Pelican.

Mandeville, Elizabeth (n.d.). Unpublished study of Kampala.

Marris, Peter (1961). *Family and Social Change in an African City*. Evanston: Northwestern University Press.

Marshall, Gloria (1962). The Marketing of Farm Produce: Some Patterns of Trade among Women in Western Nigeria. *Conference Proceedings*. Nigerian Institute of Social and Economic Research, Ibadan.

Martin, V. (1968). Mariage et famille dans les groupes christianisés ou en voie de christianisation de Dakar. In C. G. Baëta (ed.), *Christianity in Tropical Africa*. London: Oxford University Press for International African Institute.

Mayer, Philip (1961). *Townsmen or Tribesmen: Conservation and the Process of Urbanization in a South African City*. London: Oxford University Press.

Mayhew, Henry (1861–2). *London Labour and the London Poor*. London: Griffin Bohn.

Meillassoux, Claude (1968). *Urbanization of an African Community*. Seattle and London: University of Washington Press.

Mercier, P. (1954). Aspects de la société africaine dans l'agglomération dakaroise: groupes familiaux et unites de voisinage. *Etudes Sénégalaises*, No. 5.

— (1960). Etude du mariage et enquête urbaine. *Cahiers d'Etudes Africaines*, Vol. 1, No. 1.

Miner, Horace (ed.) (1967). *The City in Modern Africa*. London: Pall Mall.

Mitchell, J. Clyde (1954). *African Urbanization in Ndola and Luanshya*. Rhodes-Livingstone Communication No. 6.

— (1956). Urbanization, detribalization and stabilization in Southern Africa. In, *Social Implications of Industralization and Urbanization in Africa South of the Sahara*. Paris: UNESCO.

— (1959). The woman's place in African advancement. *Optima*, September.

Mohr, Norma (1972). In *Africa Report*, July–August.

Morgenthau, Ruth Schacter (1964). *Political Parties in French-Speaking West Africa*. Oxford: Clarendon Press.

225

References cited

Nadel, S. F. (1942). *A Black Byzantium.* London: Oxford University Press for International African Institute.

Negri, Pola de (1962). Yoruba Women's Costume. *Nigeria,* No. 72.

Newbury, G. E. and C. W. (1969). *Bibliography of Commonwealth Migrations I: Africa.* (Roneoed).

New Society (1963). 21 November.

Nicol, Abioseh (1965). *The Truly Married Woman.* London: Oxford University Press.

Nypan, Astrid (1960). *Market Trade. A Sample Study of Market Traders in Accra.* Research Division, University College of Ghana.

Nzekwu, Onuora (1961). *Wand of Noble Wood.* London: Hutchinson.

Okediji. Francis Olu (1967). Some social psychological aspects of fertility among married women in an African city. *Nigerian Journal of Econ. and Soci. Stud.* Vol. 9, No. 1.

Okediji, Francis Olu, and Oladejo O. (1966). Marital stability and social structure in an African city. *Nigerian Journal of Econ. and Soci. Stud.* Vol. 8, No. 1.

Okpewho, Isidore (1970). *The Victims.* London: Longmans, Green.

Omari, T. Peter (1960). Changing attitudes of students in West African society towards marriage and family relationships. *Brit. Jour. Soc.* Vol. II, No. 3.

(1962). *Marriage Guidance for Young Ghanaians.* Edinburgh: Nelson.

Ominde, P. (1952). *The Luo Girl.* London: Macmillan.

Opadike, Patrick O. (1971). Aspects of domesticity and family relationships. *Journal of Asian and African Studies,* Vol. VI, Nos. 3–4.

Oppong, Christine (1970). Conjugal power and resources: an urban African example. *Jour. of Marr. and the Fam.* November.

(1973a). *Marriage among a Matrilineal Elite.* Cambridge: Cambridge University Press.

(1973b). Norms and Variations: A Study of Ghanaian Students' Attitudes to Marriage and Family Living. In C. Oppong (ed.), *Legon Family Research Papers.* Institute of African Studies, University of Ghana.

Ottenberg, Phoebe (1959). The changing economic position of women among the Afikpo Ibo. In W. R. Bascom and M. J. Herskovits (eds.), *Continuity and Change in African Cultures.* Chicago: University of Chicago Press.

Parkin, David (1966). Voluntary associations as institutions of adaptation. *Man,* Vol. 1 (N.S.), No. 1.

(1969). *Neighbours and Nationals in an African City.* London: Routledge and Kegan Paul.

Paulme, Denise (ed.) (1963). *Women of Tropical Africa.* Trans. H. M. Wright. London: Routledge and Kegan Paul.

Pearsall, Ronald (1969). *The Worm in the Bud.* London: Weidenfeld and Nicolson.

Peil, Margaret (1965). Ghanaian university students: the broadening base. *Brit. Jour. Soc.,* Vol. 16.

(1972). *The Ghanaian Factory Worker: Industrial Man in Africa.* Cambridge: Cambridge University Press.

(1973). Men's Lib ? The Effects of Marriage on the Social Life of Men in Ashaiman. In C. Oppong (ed.), *Legon Family Research Papers.* Institute of African Studies, University of Ghana.

Peristiany, J. (1939). *The Social Institutions of the Kipsigis*. London: G. Routledge.

Pettigrew, T. F. (1964). *A Profile of the Negro American*. New York: Van Nostrand.

Phillips, A. (ed.) (1953). *Survey of African Marriage and Family Life*. London: Oxford University Press for International African Institute.

Phillips, Arthur, and Morris, Henry F. (1971). *Marriage Laws in Africa*. London: Oxford University Press, for International African Institute.

Plotnicov, Leonard (1967). *Strangers to the City*. Pittsburg: University of Pittsburg Press.

Pons, Valdo (1969). *Stanleyville: an African Urban Community under Belgian Administration*. London: Oxford University Press.

Porter, A. T. (1963). *Creoledom*. Cambridge: Cambridge University Press.

Rado, E. R. (1956). Social and economic survey of Bentsir Quarter, Cape Coast. *Proceedings of Third Annual Conference*. West African Institute of Social and Economic Research.

Richards, Audrey I. (1960). Economic and social factors affecting the education of African girls in territories under British influence. UNESCO/ED/Cotonou/4.

Rivière, C. (1968). La promotion de la femme guinéene. *Cahiers d'Etudes Africaines*, Vol. 8 (3).

Rosberg, Carl G. and Nottingham, John (1966). *The Myth of the Mau-Mau*. London: Praeger.

Rouch, Jean (1954). *Migrations in the Gold Coast*. (English translation). Accra: Mimeographed.

Rouch, Jean and Bernus, E. (1959). Note sur les prostituées 'toutou' de Treichville et d'Adjamé. *Etudes éburnéennes*, Vol. 6.

Rubadiri, David (1967). *No Bride Price*. Nairobi: East African Publishing House.

Ruel, Malcolm J. (1964). The modern adaptation of associations among the Banyang of the West Cameroon. *Southwest Journal of Anthropology*, Vol. 20, No. 1.

(n.d.). Tribe and Class in Ikeja. Unpublished MS.

Segal, Ronald (ed.) (1961). *Political Africa, A Who's Who of Personalities and Parties*. London: Stevens.

Selormey, Francis (1968). *The Narrow Path*. London: Heinemann.

Servais, J. J. and Laurence, J. P. (1965). *Histoire et Dossier de la Prostitution*. Paris: Planete.

Shrubsole, A. C. (1965). Some problems of teacher education in a rapidly changing African society. In *African Women*, Vol. VI, No. 5.

Skertchly, J. A. (1874). *Dahomey as it is*. London: Chapman.

Skinner, Elliott P. (1965). Labor migration among the Mossi of the Upper Volta. In Hilda Kuper (ed.), *Urbanization and Migration in West Africa*. Berkeley: University of California Press.

Smith, Mary F. (1954). *Baba of Karo*. London: Faber.

Smith, M. G. (1957). The social functions and meaning of Hausa praise-singing. *Africa*, Vol. XXVII, 1.

(1959). The Hausa system of social status. *Africa*, Vol. 29, No. 3.

Smythe, Hugh H., and Mabel (1960). *The New Nigerian Elite*. Stanford: Stanford University Press.

Sofer, Cyril and Rhona (1955). *Jinja transformed: a social survey of a multiracial township*. Kampala: East African Institute of Social Research.

References cited

Sofoluwe, G. O. (1965). A study of divorce cases at Igbo-Ora. *Nigerian Jour. of Econ. and Soc. Stud.*, Vol. 7.

Southall, A. W. (1961). Introduction. In A. W. Southall (ed.), *Social Change in Modern Africa*. London: Oxford University Press for International African Institute.

(1966). The Growth of Urban Society. In Stanley Diamond and Fred G. Burke (eds.), *The Transformation of East Africa*. London: Basic Books.

(1968). The pattern of migration in Madagascar and its theoretical implications. *African Urban Notes*, Vol. III, No. 1.

Southall, A. W., and Gutkind, P. C. W. (1957). *Townsmen in the Making*. Kampala: East African Institute of Social Research.

Staub, H. (1971). The changing role of women in Tanzania. *Rural Life*, Vol. 16, No. 2. Institute of Rural Life at Home and Overseas.

Steel, R. W. (1961). The Towns of Tropical Africa. In K. M. Barbour and R. M. Prothero (eds.), *Essays on African Population*. London: Routledge and Kegan Paul.

Sturtevant, E. (ed.) (1917). Monumenta Germaniae. In *Vom guten Ton in Wondel der Jahrhunderte*. Berlin: Bong.

Tanzania Census (1968). Recorded Population Changes, 1948–1967. Dar es Salaam. Central Statistical Bureau, Ministry of Economic Affairs and Development Planning.

Tardits, Claude (1958). *Porto Novo*. Paris: Mouton.

Temple, P. H. (1968/9). Kampala markets. University of East Africa Social Sciences Council Conference, 1968/9 Geography Papers. Makerere Institute of Social Research.

The New Africans (1967). Ed. Sidney Taylor. London: Hamlyn.

Thomson, Moffatt (1933). The Native Affairs Conference held at Victoria Falls. Mimeographed.

Trutenau, H. M. J. (1958). Some moral paradoxes concerning Europeans and Ghanaian women. *Ghana Jour. of Soc.* Vol. 4, No. 2.

Tucker, Martin (1967). *Africa in Modern Literature*. New York: Ungar.

UNESCO (1960). The education of girls in tropical Africa. UNESCO/ED/ Cotonou/2. Paris: processed.

Van den Berghe, Pierre (1969). Some social characteristics of University of Ibadan students. *Nig. Jour. of Econ. and Soc. Stud.* Vol. II, No. 3.

Van der Horst, Sheila (1964). *African Workers in Town*. Capetown:

Van Velsen, J. (1961). Labour migration as a positive factor in the continuity of Tonga tribal society. In A. W. Southall (ed.), *Social Change in Modern Africa*. London: Oxford University Press for International African Institute.

Voice of Women (1969). June, Nairobi.

Warmington, W. A. (1956). Some aspects of industrial relations in the Cameroons plantation. *Conference Proceedings*, West African Institute of Social and Economic Research.

Wells, F. A. and Warmington, W. A. (1962). *Studies in Industrialization: Nigeria and the Cameroons*. London: Oxford University Press, for Nigerian Institute of Social and Economic Research.

References cited

West Africa (1953a). No. 1902.
  (1953b). No. 1904.
  (1953c). No. 1910.
  (1954a). No. 1942.
  (1954b). No. 1946.
  (1954c). No. 1952.
  (1956). No. 2029.
  (1957). No. 2120.
  (1958a). No. 2138.
  (1958b). No. 2141.
  (1958c). No. 2167.
  (1960a). No. 2235.
  (1960b). No. 2265.
  1963a). No. 2409.
  (1963b). No. 2415.
  (1963c). No. 2420.
  (1964). No. 2465.
  (1966). No. 2575.
  (1967a). No. 2602.
  (1967b). No. 2629.
  (1969a). No. 2733.
  (1969b). No. 2737.
Wilson, G. (1941–2). *An Essay on the Economics of Detribalization in Northern Rhodesia*. Livingstone: Rhodes-Livingstone Institute, Papers 5 and 6.
Wipper, Audrey (1971a). Equal rights for women in Kenya. *Jour. Mod. Afr. Stud*. Vol. 9, No. 3.
  (1971b). The politics of sex: some strategies employed by the Kenyan power-elite to handle a normative-existential discrepancy. *African Studies Review*, Vol. XIV, No. 3.
  (ed.) (1972). *The roles of African women: past, present and future. Canadian Journal of African Studies*, Vol. 6, No. 2.
Wirth, Louis (1938). Urbanism as a Way of Life. *American Journal of Sociology*, Vol. XLIV, No. 1.
Women Today (1964). Vol. VI, No. 2.

Xydias, Nelly (1956). Labour: conditions, aptitude, training. In *Social Implications of Industrialization and Urbanization in Africa South of the Sahara*. Paris: UNESCO.

Zalinger, Alvin D. (1960). A study of African students in the United States. Working Paper in George H. T. Kimble (ed.), *Tropical Africa*. New York: Twentieth Century Fund.

Index

Abeokuta, 51
Abidjan
    demographic data, 8
    prostitution, 88, 89–90, 98
Accra
    demographic data, 8, 9, 10, 10n
    female traders, 45
    growth rate, 12
    marriage survey, 147
    migrants' associations, 55–6
    prostitution, 83, 88, 89–90
    rise of, 8
    sex ratio, 10
    wage employment, 11
    women in professions, 31
    women's clubs, 141
Achebe, Chinua, 4, 34n, 77, 128n
Adekogbe, Mrs Elizabeth Adeyemi,
    190, 209–10
adultery
    divorce and, 153, 154, 155
    female view, 78, 107
    male view, 151–2
    with *femmes libres*, 152–3
    see also extra-marital relations
African élite, defined, 5
Africanization
    advancement in status and, 19
    female employment and, 17
African Socialism, 185
age
    at marriage, 158–9
    difference in, of married couples,
        157–8
    differences and decision-making,
        173, 174
    migration and, 18–19
    of women in employment, 33–4
    political opportunity and, 19
    preponderance of young over old
        in modern city, 10, 13
agriculture, 7
Aiyedun, Mrs Remi, 209
Aluko, T. M., 4, 152–3
l'Ambiance, 71

American racial problem, analogies
    with, 3, 33n, 197–8
Asante
    pre-marital relations, 135
    Queen Mother, 6
aspirations, female
    education and, 54
    means of achieving, 35
    money and, 34–5, 41–2
    political, 180
    urbanization and, 180
    'Western', 5
    see also clothes, independence,
        marriage, status
attitudes to women
    ambivalence of, 179, 182
    attacks on male, 184–6
    Kenyan, 182–90
    male, 179, 180–1
    male superiority and, 181–2, 185
    of other women, 108–9, 127–8, 192
    women as adjuncts, 182–3

Baba, Miss Ramatu, 216–17
'bad' and 'good' women, 151
Baeta, Annie, 216
Bailor-Caulker, Madam Honoria, 74
Bakweri women, 86–7
Bamako associations, 56–8
Banyang prostitution, 83
bara, 56–7
Bardi, Mrs Susannah, 201–3
bar-tending, 42
beer and spirits
    attitudes to, 42, 44
    drinking of, 39
    prostitution and sale of, 91
    women selling, 39, 42–3, 45
Bishop, Miss Lucy, 204–5
black power, 198
Brazzaville societies, 99
bridewealth
    as a social transaction, 84
    free marriage and, 125
    function of, 145, 146–7
    in 'civilized' marriage, 138

231

Index